GUERNSEY COASTAL WALKS AND SCRAMBLES

Written and illustrated by Alan Hill

A Guernsey Press Publication

While every effort has been made to ensure the content of this book is accurate, the author and The Guernsey Press Company Limited accept no responsibility for any accident or misadventure that may be associated with its use.

GUERNSEY COASTAL WALKS AND SCRAMBLES

ISBN 0 902550 44 6

First published in Great Britain 1991

Published by The Guernsey Press Company Ltd.,
Braye Road, Vale, Guernsey, Channel Islands.

Made and printed by The Guernsey Press Company Ltd.,
Guernsey, Channel islands.

Dedicated to my Parents

ACKNOWLEDGEMENTS

Firstly my thanks go to Linda Broad for both her encouragement and tolerance. I must also acknowledge the help of Gregory Stevens-Cox, who was a fund of knowledge, and Eric Grimsley who gave much information about Guernsey's fortifications. Thanks also go to Brian Anthony and Peter Hancock: without their help I'd still be using a typewriter. I must also thank John Nicolle, Mick de Pomerai, Mike Sebire and John Geering for their invaluable snippets of information, and Dr Harry Tomlinson for help with place names. Several reference books have been particularly useful, especially the work of James Marr, Marie de Garis and C. J. Howlett.

Lastly I would like to thank the members of Guernsey Mountaineering Club for their help with this project, and for being such good companions over the past seven years.

Comments, criticisms and advice can be sent to the author, c/o Bream Bay College, Ruakaka, Near Whangerei, New Zealand.

Front Cover: The Pea Stacks from Moulin Huet
Back Cover: The Cliffs at Les Ecrilleurs

BIBLIOGRAPHY

Dictiounnaire Angllais-Guernesais: Marie de Garis. Phillimore. 1982

Guernsey Bailiwick Harbours and Landing Places: James Marr. Toucan. 1987

Prehistoric Monuments of Guernsey and Associated Folklore: J. Stevens-Cox. Toucan. 1976

Railways in Guernsey: Frank E. Wilson. Paramount-Lithoprint

The Historical Development of the Martello Towers in the Channel Islands: Eric J. Grimsley. Sarnian Publications. 1988

Les Fouaillages and the Megalithic Monuments of Guernsey: Ian Kinnes and J. A. Grant. Ampersand Press. 1983

The Channel Islands, a New Study: Victor Coysh (Editor). David and Charles. 1977

Review of the Guernsey Society Volume XLVI No. 2. Summer 1990

Runaway Rig: Dave Prigent. Guernsey Press. 1978

A Brief Guide to Lihou Island: Robin Borwick. Guernsey Press. 1986

A Visitor's Guide to Guernsey: Victor Coysh. Moorland Publishing. 1983

Customs, Ceremonies and Traditions of the Channel Islands: Raoul Lempriére. Robert Hale. 1976

Wrecked on the Channel Islands: David Couling. Stanford Maritime. 1983

Guernsey Legends: Freda Wolley. Guernsey Press. 1986

Guernsey Street and Road Names. History of the Parishes and Their Folklore: C. J. Howlett. Guernsey Herald. 1983

The War in the Channel Islands Then and Now: Winston G. Ramsey

Battle of Britain Prints International. 1981

Landscapes of the Channel Islands: Nigel Jee. Phillimore. 1982

Guernsey's Natural History: Nigel Jee. Guernsey Press. 1972

The Story of the Channel Islands: John Uttley. Faber and Faber. 1966

Folklore of Guernsey: Marie de Garis. 1986

Bailiwick Bastions; the Fortifications of the Bailiwick of Guernsey: James Marr. Guernsey Press. 1985

Wild Flowers of the Channel Islands, Books 1 and 2: Jarrald Nature Series

Outline and Guide to the Geology of Guernsey: R. A. Roach

The National Trust of Guernsey, Official Handbook

Lihou. The Holy Island. Patrick Wootton

Guernsey Bailiwick Harbours and Landing Places c. 2000 BC to 1987: James Marr, Toucan Press. 1987

Guernsey Evening Press and Star 'Weekender' Number 326. 'Wreck of the Briseis' by Peter Girard.

Rock Marks of the Bailiwick of Guernsey: R. Cave

The German Occupation of the Channel Islands: Charles Cruickshank, Guernsey Press, 1975

CONTENTS

LIST OF MAPS

MAP KEY

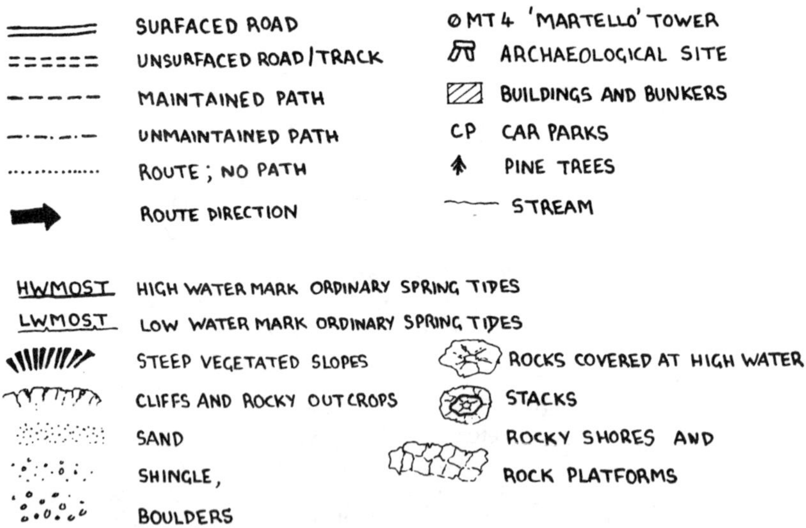

SURFACED ROAD
UNSURFACED ROAD / TRACK
MAINTAINED PATH
UNMAINTAINED PATH
ROUTE ; NO PATH
ROUTE DIRECTION
MT 4 'MARTELLO' TOWER
ARCHAEOLOGICAL SITE
BUILDINGS AND BUNKERS
CP CAR PARKS
PINE TREES
STREAM
HWMOST HIGH WATER MARK ORDINARY SPRING TIDES
LWMOST LOW WATER MARK ORDINARY SPRING TIDES
STEEP VEGETATED SLOPES
CLIFFS AND ROCKY OUTCROPS
SAND
SHINGLE,
BOULDERS
ROCKS COVERED AT HIGH WATER
STACKS
ROCKY SHORES AND ROCK PLATFORMS

INTRODUCTION

THE walks and scrambles in this guide lead the reader around much of Guernsey's coastline. We start on the south-western tip and head in an easterly direction along the rugged south coast. Here the cliffs feel the force of the elements, and though the seascapes are magnificent, the landscape is harsh and treeless. As we approach the south-eastern point of the island the cliffs are dissected by deep wooded valleys and sandy bays, and take on a more friendly aspect. Turning onto the east coast the cliffs lose their stature and the slopes are densely covered in trees and shrubs, thriving in the sheltered environment. Here the views across to the neighbouring islands are superb. After reaching the built-up areas of St Peter Port and St Sampson, we leap frog to Bordeaux Bay and head around the north coast. Here the walking is much less strenuous, never more than a few metres above sea level. The west coast is indented by several large bays, and here we perhaps see the worst side of Guernsey's economic growth: housing estates and hotels crowd into the few remaining open spaces, and ancient marshes are drained to become neat golf courses. Our walks here take us around the headlands where the rocks have been sculpted by the waves into fantastic shapes, and are the scene of many shipwrecks.

Postscript: While reading the proofs of this book, I heard that Cuet Tower, or Krahenest, had toppled into Ronez Quarry. I have left references and drawings of this landmark in the text, in its memory. The text is marked (†). But please don't go looking for it!

"When I think what has happened to our island, I could sit on the ground and cry."

From *The Book of Ebenezer Le Page* by Gerald Edwards

THE WALKS

Where possible, the walking routes in this guide are "loop walks", taking a separate route back to the starting point. In many cases the return legs involve walking along the island's network of narrow lanes. These can make pleasant walks in their own right, for the steep banks are havens for wild flowers. Those with an aversion to tarmac can avoid the roads by retracing their steps along the coastline, catching a bus or arranging other transport at the halfway point.

Guernsey has a fascinating history, and I have tried to point out sites that may be of interest. Each section is treated independently of the others, and this has led to some repetition of information. Hopefully this will not prove tedious, and cross references are used at times so that the interested reader can refer to other sections for information.

The routes vary in length, and there should be enough to suit all tastes. They can be easily joined together or shortened as required. Distances in the text are for the full loop.

THE SCRAMBLES

HIDDEN below the well-trodden cliff path are some of the least-frequented spots on Guernsey. On an island that is becoming increasingly congested and urbanised, it is becoming difficult to escape the crowds. The Guernsey cliffs offer one such escape: apart from the occasional angler, the even rarer climber, and the passing fishermen, one is unlikely to meet anyone else. We can leave the multitudes on the beach and enter a world of soaring rock walls, screaming gulls and crashing waves. The scrambles in this guide are aimed at opening up this environment to people who perhaps wouldn't normally consider venturing into these wild areas. It is with mixed feelings that I write this guide, though I doubt whether the scrambles will ever be so popular as to remove the peace and seclusion which is their attraction. No doubt I will be criticised for encouraging people into such potentially dangerous grounds, and there is no doubt that it would be very easy to have an accident in these inaccessible places. For this reason I have included lots of detail on each traverse: tides, grades, maps, access routes and escape routes as well as points of interest. Armed with this information, it should be possible for inexperienced scramblers to choose a route that is within their capabilities.

For the more experienced scrambler and climber the detail may prove tiresome, or take away some of the adventure. For them I hope the guide will merely be a pointer, so that they can choose the most suitable route for their ability and the day's tide, leave the book at home and have the fun of pioneering their own way along the cliff foot.

All but three of the scrambles in this guide are affected by the tide: its importance cannot be over stressed. The majority of the routes must be attempted near low water, and several require an extra-low spring tide. A poor choice of tide, or a late departure, can turn a relatively easy scramble into an epic.

Each route is given a recommended tide, e.g. the scramble from Petit Bôt to Le Jaonnet Bay requires a minimum of an 8.2 metre tide. This refers to the height of the tide at high water, and the route should be attempted towards low water on such a tide. Locals tend to refer to a very low tide in terms of its high water level, and hopefully this won't be confusing.

Where can tidal information be found? The Guernsey Press gives details for the coming week, and tide tables are available from many of the boat chandlers, usually free. Tide times are also broadcast on the radio, and on the pre-recorded weather forecast (telephone 64033). When using the tide tables don't forget to add one hour during British Summer Time.

DATE	HIGH WATER A.M. TIME	HIGH WATER A.M. HEIGHT METRES	HIGH WATER P.M. TIME	HIGH WATER P.M. HEIGHT METRES	LOW WATER A.M. TIME	LOW WATER A.M. HEIGHT METRES	LOW WATER P.M. TIME	LOW WATER P.M. HEIGHT METRES
6 FRI.	05.59	7.74	18.19	8.07	00.03	2.26	12.19	2.23
7 SAT.	06.43	8.00	18.59	8.30	00.45	1.87	13.00	1.92
8 SUN.	07.24	8.10	19.38	8.45	01.23	1.58	13.37	1.72
9 MON.	08.02	8.26	20.16	8.50	02.01	1.41	14.14	1.63
10 TUE.	08.38	8.27	20.52	8.48	02.35	1.36	14.48	1.65
11 WED.	09.13	8.20	21.27	8.38	03.10	1.41	15.22	1.75
12 THU.	09.50	8.08	22.04	8.20	03.44	1.56	15.58	1.93
13 FRI.	10.28	7.89	22.45	7.94	04.22	1.78	16.39	2.18

From the table we can see that the Petit Bôt to Le Jaonnet Bay scramble would be feasible between the afternoon of Sunday 8th and up to and including Wednesday 11th, when the tides are above the recommended 8.2 metres. The best time to set off would be around one hour before low water e.g. at 12.37 p.m. on the 8th, 1.14 p.m. on the 9th, etc. Beyond the 11th the tide range becomes too narrow as they fall towards neap tides.

The tide range varies with the waxing and waning of the moon. Spring tides occur on or around the full moon and the new moon, while neap tides are on the first quarter and last quarter of the moon. During a month the tides will therefore change from springs — neap — springs — neaps, and in an average fortnight it should be possible to attempt most of the scrambles.

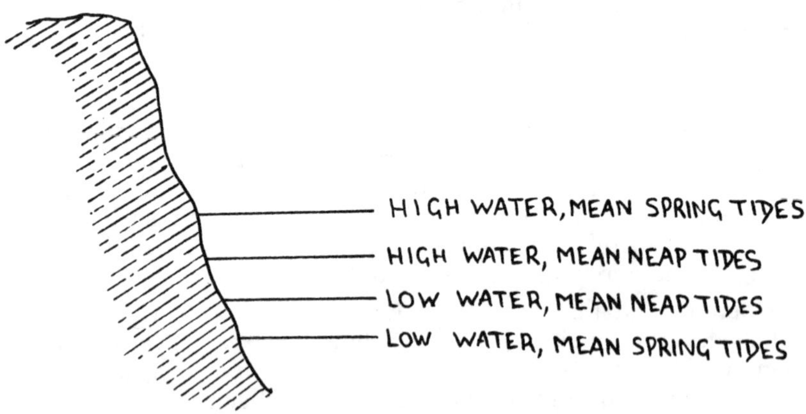

Several sections require a large spring tide. These tides have the largest range and occur when the sun and moon combine to exert the maximum gravitational pull on the oceans. The largest spring tides have a range of nearly 10 metres and occur in the spring and autumn. Tides in excess of 9 metres do not occur every month, which means that some scrambles can only be attempted on a few occasions each year.

In the Channel Islands there is a never-failing rule which can be used to determine whether the tide is a spring or a neap. If low water is between 12 and four o'clock it is a spring tide, and if low water is between 6 and 10 o'clock then it is a neap tide. This means that any routes needing low water on a spring tide must be attempted in the afternoon.

A further complication to tide levels is the effect of weather conditions, which will distort published tide levels. A high pressure system can push the low water level below the forecast level, and this will improve matters. However a low pressure system can mean low water is as much as half a metre higher than forecast, and this could be enough to make a traverse impassable. The wind direction and strength is also a factor, and a strong south-westerly builds up water in this part of the Channel, again preventing tides falling to published levels. A strong swell is also an important consideration, as this can again make a sea level traverse impractical (though the swell tends to die away as the tide falls).

Guernsey has one of the largest tide ranges in Britain, and because the tide is diurnal i.e. two high and two low waters per day, this means the rise and fall of sea level is very rapid. It takes approximately six hours for the tide to rise from low to high water, but the rate at which it changes varies. This is reflected in the "Rule of Twelfths', which is worth bearing in mind.

1st hour of tide rise/fall, height change $^{1}/_{12}$th of total
2nd hour of tide rise/fall, height change $^{2}/_{12}$ths of total
3rd hour of tide rise/fall, height change $^{3}/_{12}$ths of total
4th hour of tide rise/fall, height change $^{3}/_{12}$ths of total
5th hour of tide rise/fall, height change $^{2}/_{12}$ths of total
6th hour of tide rise/fall, height change $^{1}/_{12}$th of total

Thus the tide is falling/rising fastest around the half tide mark, and changing relatively little near high and low water. This may be important if one is waiting for a crucial section to dry e.g. one hour before low water on an 8 metre tide the level will only drop a further half metre. Remember that the larger the tide the faster will be the rise/fall, perhaps as much as 4 cm per minute on the largest spring tides. It is always best to set off when the tide is still falling, usually an hour before low water for most routes.

Don't be put off by all this gloom and doom! Choose your tide carefully, and consider the following guide lines:

1. Choose a route within your capabilities.
2. Avoid linking sections without checking if this is feasible.
3. Use the recommended escape routes.
4. Don't go alone or in very large groups: 3 is ideal.
5. Check the tides.
6. Check the weather forecast.
7. Set off before low water, not when the tide is rising.
8. Leave a note of your route and your expected time of arrival with someone.

Most of the traverses are along the foot of the south coast cliffs, out of sight of the main cliff path, and with few escape routes: they must not be undertaken lightly. The routes have been kept deliberately short to reduce the chances of becoming stranded, but competent and experienced scramblers will be able to link several sections together, and suggestions are given in the text. The distances in the text are for the scramble only, and do not include the access and return walk along the cliff path.

The grading system attempts to evaluate the seriousness and technical difficulty of each route:

Grade I/I+ Easy walking/Rough walking.

Grade II Easy scrambling, possibly exposed. Possibly some awkward moves but these will be in a non-serious situation.

Grade III Quite difficult scrambling, sometimes in an exposed position.

Grade IV Difficult scrambling, should only be attempted by those with experience of rock climbing.

Grade V Hard scrambling, with technical moves in an exposed situation.

Grade VI Very hard moves in an exposed situation: experienced rock climbers only!

If in doubt, start on a I+ and work upwards! The grades given are for the recommended tide. Some traverses are possible on other tides, but usually at a much higher grade.

Straying from the recommended route will also lead to much greater difficulty.

Escape routes are outlined to provide a way out in the event of injury or stranding. It is advisable to keep to these recommended routes: an easy-looking escape often proves to be much steeper and looser than it appears from the cliff foot. Take care; people have to be rescued from innocuous-looking slopes every year. Several escape routes are serious propositions in themselves and should only be used as a last resort: it is usually more advisable to retrace one's steps. The grades for escape routes are I to III with the refinement of + and – signs.

Grade I/I+ Easy walk-off/easy scramble.

Grade II Steeper ground, may be quite exposed.

Grade III May involve technical moves on steep ground and should only be used as a last resort unless the party is very experienced.

EQUIPMENT

I recommend that scramblers carry a small rucsack containing a first aid kit, waterproofs, spare clothes, exposure bag, food, drink and emergency rations. I have found the best footwear to be soft-soled training shoes. On all but the easiest routes a helmet is advisable and on the hardest routes climbers should carry a rope and a small selection of nuts.

ACCIDENT PROCEDURE

In the event of an accident, firstly ensure the safety of yourself and the rest of the group, then apply first aid. If the injuries are too serious for self-evacuation, try and attract help. If this is not forthcoming, then the fittest member(s) of the group should seek help, leaving at least one person with the injured person. Dial 999 and ask for Cliff Rescue. Information which would be useful to St John Ambulance would include: (a) The exact location of the accident; (b) Number of injured persons; (c) Nature of the injuries; (d) The time of the accident; (e) The number in the party.

FLORA AND FAUNA

WHATEVER the time of year there are always flowers in bloom on Guernsey, but it is perhaps in the spring that the cliffs really come to life. Sea campion, with its white flowers, are scattered over the cliff slopes like snow, especially around Le Bigard. Thrift grows into pink cushions on the south coast, while Rock Samphire, (locally Perche Pierre) with its yellow flowers and fleshy leaves which release a pungent smell when crushed, grow from many crevices. The coastline is a colourful rockery, with tiny flowers, particularly the English stonecrop with its white flowers and red fruits, in every soil-filled crack. In the sheltered valleys primroses, foxgloves, bluebells and daffodils create a palette of colour. The gorse bush, with its yellow flowers which give a nutty smell to the air, can be found along much of the coast and flowers in most months. The island's mild climate allow several continental species to thrive here. Mesembryanthemums, or Kaffir Fig, originally a South African plant, was introduced from the Mediterranean. It has thick fleshy leaves, and in the spring has large pink or yellow flowers. The plant forms long hanging carpets on many of the south coast cliffs, but is badly hit by frosts.

The island is rich in bird life, but space permits just a few to be mentioned here. The routes in this guide cover a wide variety of habitats including woodland, heath, cliff, and sandy beaches. The commonest bird of prey is the kestrel, and many pairs nest on the cliffs. Look out for cuckoos in the spring, particularly around Pleinmont and Le Bigard. The Dartford warbler is a very rare, shy bird, but can sometimes be seen amongst the dense gorse at Le Bigard and Le Gouffre. Ravens nest on the cliffs at Les Sommeilleuses, and can be spotted soaring along much of the south coast.

Many species of gull are represented, from the black headed and not-so-common common gulls, to that huge pirate, the great black-backed gull. Fulmars have recently colonised the cliffs, where these masters of the air can be seen skimming the rocks. A common sight are large black birds, hanging their wings out to dry. These are usually shag, and occasionally cormorants, creatures which had a price of 6d. on their heads in the 1920s. Look out for the common terns as they swoop and dive for small fish. A colony nests on Le Brehon Tower in the Little Russel, and they are numerous on the east coast. On the heathland to the north of the island stonechats and wheatears can be seen, and gannets often fly overhead towards their nesting grounds near Alderney. Possibly the most frequently seen shore bird is the oystercatcher, easily recognised by its striking black and white plumage, orange bill, and its noisy yelping alarm call. A flash of bright blue is often all that is seen of the kingfisher as it hunts the rock pools.

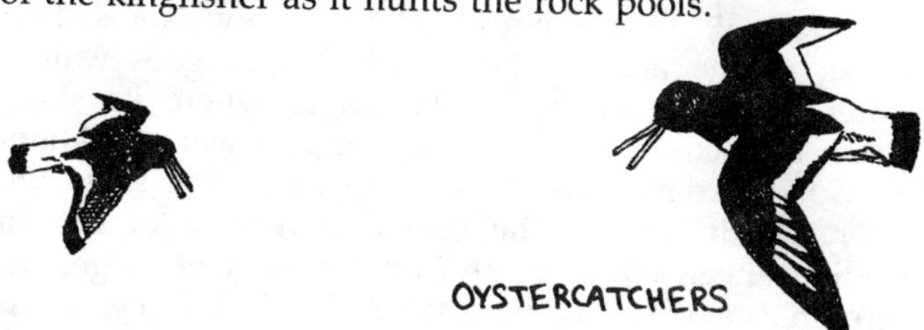

Many of the mainland mammals, such as squirrels, badgers and foxes, do not inhabit Guernsey. The mammal we are most likely to see, apart from man, is the rabbit. Originally introduced in the twelfth century, it has made a successful comeback from myxomatosis, and is numerous on the cliffs and common. Guernsey's voles and shrews are slightly different from their mainland cousins, and although rarely seen they must be quite numerous judging by the number of kestrels. One remarkable absence is the mole, which is numerous on Alderney and Jersey, but unknown on Guernsey, Herm and Sark.

Guernsey also has few reptiles. There are no snakes, and the nearest one will see is the slow worm, which can be spotted on the warm south coast slopes. The island's only lizard is a Continental species, the green lizard, which inhabits the cliffs near Fermain Bay.

The tide range on Guernsey is very large, sometimes in excess of nine metres. Consequently a large area of shore is exposed as the tide ebbs, and a wide variety of species can be studied. The rock pools are beautiful miniature worlds, and where the water cannot escape they almost invariably have a pink lining. This is lithophyllum, a seaweed. Numerous fish dive for cover as we pass, and the most common species is the blenney. Translucent shrimps can be found in the pools nearest sea level, and they are sometimes netted for food on the large "shrimping tides". Sea anenomes are very common, particularly the beadlet which is dark red and appears as a lump of jelly when exposed to the air. Less common is the snakelocks anenome which has long green tentacles.

There are several species of crab, which can be found under rocks, in crevices and hiding in the seaweed. The common shore crab has a dark green back, while the chancre, or edible crab, has a more orange hue. The lady, or velvet crab as it is known on the mainland, has blue-black markings and fine hairs. Watch out for its pincers: it is more dextrous than the chancre and can reach behind its head to nip the unwary.

There are many species of winkle, topshell and whelk, some of which are not found on mainland Britain. Limpets, or fflie in Guernesiase, are numerous on the rocky shores. Look closely for tracks in the algae, where each limpet goes walkabout at high water before returning to its home, where its shell has ground down perfectly to fit the rock. Limpets were traditionally collected on Good Friday, cooked on dried furze and eaten with cakes and cider. Much rarer is the ormer, a relative of the limpet. It is a Mediterranean creature, and on the limit of its geographical range here in the Channel Islands. A local delicacy, it is vigourously beaten until soft, then cooked slowly in a casserole. They were once quite common, but can now only be gathered on certain low tides each year, and it is illegal to use scuba diving equipment. The name ormer derives from oreille de mer, ear of the sea. The shell is ear-shaped, with a row of holes along the edge, and a muscular foot. The lining is mother-of-pearl, and the ormer is used as a decorative shell on many walls and houses.

ROUTE 1 A cliff and woodland loop walk

MAP 1

PORTELET TO L'ANGLE
DISTANCE — 3 miles

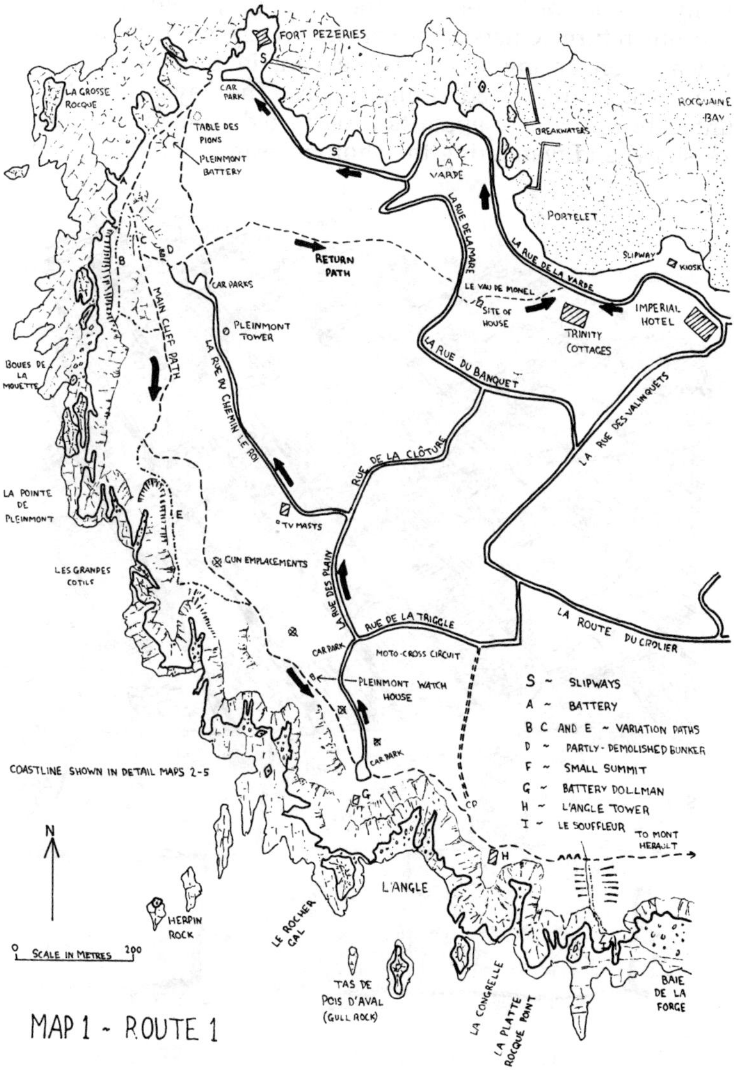

A FINE introduction to the cliff walks of Guernsey, taking us around the south-western tip of Guernsey and across the plateau above Pleinmont Point to the craggy fastness of L'Angle. There are numerous pathways which allow for a circular walk, and many variations are possible.

We start near the Imperial Hotel, which is above the southern shore of Rocquaine Bay. Beyond the kiosk a slipway leads down to the tiny harbour of Portelet ("Little Harbour"), a good place to cool off on our return. Offshore are anchored cages which are visible at low water on spring tides. These contain ormers, mussels and oysters which are reared commercially. The bay is reputed to be haunted by the lonely apparition of an old woman, wrapped in a black shawl and wandering the shore in search of her lost son.

VRAIC SLIPWAY, LA POINTE DES PEZERIES

La Rue de la Varde is presently closed due to subsidence, and is likely to remain so, thus providing a peaceful stroll to the point. Despite the tarmac underfoot this is a delightful walk, and so much the better for the lack of cars. The road takes us past the white Trinity Cottages, home to the lighthousemen of Les Hanois, and we emerge from a stand of pines into an open area where there are fine views across to Lihou Island and Fort Saumarez. As the road curves around to the left Fort Grey can be seen, and a German bunker explored. During the Occupation the road here was blocked with a tank trap. The rocky ridge up on our left is La Varde (The Heights, or Watch-post). Before the lighthouse had a radio link the keepers' wives would communicate with their husbands from here, using semaphore.

Continuing along the road Fort Pezeries comes into view across a small bay. The road cuts around a slope of bracken and blackthorn, and past a plantation of small pines to reach La Pointe des Pezeries.

The point has much of interest and a short diversion is worthwhile. Fort Pezeries was constructed in 1680, and guarded the southern part of Rocquaine Bay against attack. It was strengthened in the troubled times of the Napoleonic Wars, and the powder magazine was built in its centre. Barracks were constructed on what is now the car park. The slopes below the fort are clothed in Mesembryanthemum, or Kaffir Fig, a species which was introduced from the Mediterranean and suffers in even the mildest of frosts. It has thick fleshy leaves and large yellow or pink flowers in the spring.

Several finely-constructed slipways emerge from the small bay at this point. Seaweed, or vraic (pronounced as in rack), was once the main source of fertilizer, and large quantities were used on the land. Not only was drift weed used, but living weed was harvested from the rocks and ploughed in either fresh, or dried and burnt to provide an ash rich in minerals. The slipways were built to allow the horses to pull up cartloads from the shore. Dried weed was also important as a fuel and was burnt by the poorer folk.

The area was also used for fish-drying until the turn-of-the-century, and Pezeries comes from the word eperquerie which means "a place for drying fish".

At the very end of the road are more slipways, and views across to Grosse Rock and Les Hanois lighthouse. Beyond the granite pillars is a circle of stones surrounded by a trench. This construction is known as The Fairy Ring, or La Table des Pions ("The Footmen's Table"). The first name refers to the fairies which are said to meet here, while the second to an ancient custom called La Chevauchée de St Michel. This was held once every three years to check that the roads were clear for the procession of the Blessed Sacrament on the Feast of Corpus Christi. Officials rode on horseback, and included the Porte-lance, whose eleven and a quarter feet wand was not allowed to meet any obstruction on the road. Any walls, trees or other objects which it touched had to be cleared away, and the owner fined. The officials were attended by the footmen who were fed at La Table des Pions while the cavaliers were feasted in Fort Pezeries. The custom was banned in 1837, when a footman abused the privilege of kissing the maidens en route, by embracing the Governor's wife too passionately!

LE TABLE DES PIONS

We have a choice of paths beyond The Fairy Ring. The main path takes us up a slope on the left, towards the German bunker visible on the skyline.

A more challenging variation path (B) takes us directly through the gap in the rocks ahead of us. This cleft in the rocks is known as Les Portes (The Doors), and at times the wind furiously funnels its way through here. The buttress on the left is capped by a man-made wall which forms Pleinmont Battery, and an 18-pounder cannon was mounted here during the French Revolutionary Wars. Descending steps beyond the gap we reach a grassy bowl surrounded by small crags. More fortifications have been constructed here, and on old maps this is called Mouette Castle. There is a low earth wall above the shoreline, and at its far end a stone wall and platform of granite flags are the remains of a small cannon mounting (A). At this point we have another choice of routes. A rocky ridge (C) leads up from here to join the main cliff path. Alternatively we can scramble down some well-worn rocks to gain a path which takes us along the cliff edge and gives us good views of the stack on La Pointe de Pleinmont. A flat rock with the painted letters FRR marks a split in the path: the right-hand fork takes us down to the sea, where the offshore rocks are called Les Boues de la Mouette ("Kittiwake Reef"), while the less distinct left-hand path meanders up the slope to join the main cliff path.

Those of us who take the main path from the Fairy Ring pass to the left of Pleinmont Battery and through the bracken to a path junction. If we follow the path signed to Le Creux Mahie ("Mahie's Cave", which is some four miles away) we pass a partly-demolished bunker (D) to a viewpoint with a bench. From here we can look over a grassy bowl to Pleinmont Battery, and across Rocquaine Bay to Lihou Island (which looks like part of the mainland at low water), and the Germanised Martello Tower of Fort Saumarez. The plateau is a bleak area: few trees survive on its windswept slopes,

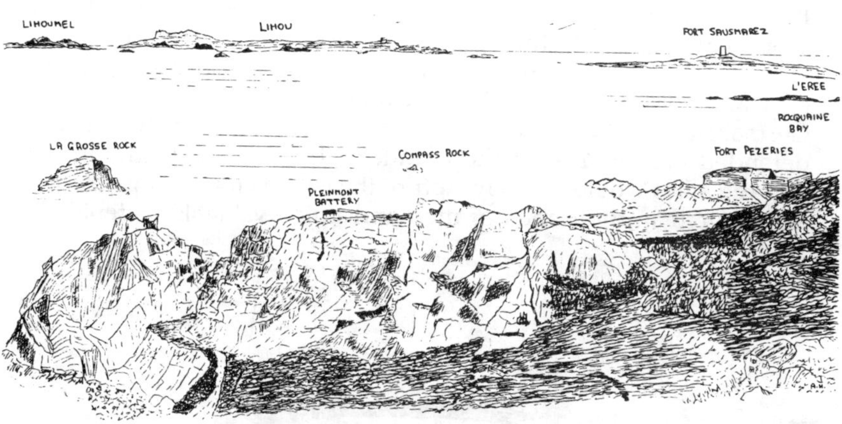

VIEW NORTH FROM PLEINMONT PLATEAU

and with its numerous man-made intrusions it is not an attractive place. Pleinmont means The Folded Heights.

There are also excellent views across to Les Hanois lighthouse, and the saw-tooth reefs which surround it. Scores of ships and many hundreds of lives were lost in this area, but the many representations to Trinity House fell on deaf ears until work finally began in 1860. The massive construction of Cornish granite rises up nearly 120 feet from Le Bisseau rock, and its diameter is 32 feet at the base. A familiar sight is the Trinity House helicopter carrying a

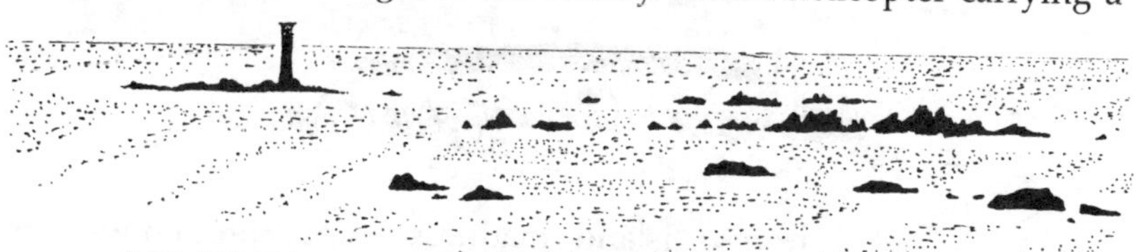

LES HANOIS

huge bag of supplies to the landing pad which has been built on the top. Plans are afoot to automate the lighthouse in the near future. On a clear day the French lighthouse of Les Roches Douvres can be spotted on the horizon to the south south-west.

A prominent feature of the plateau is the 55 feet high circular German tower. Similar structures can be found at L'Angle, La Prevôté, Chouet and Fort Saumarez, and they were known as Marinepeilstaende und Messtellungen to the Germans. They are unique to the Channel Islands (perhaps inspired by the Martello Towers!) and were used for observation, range-finding and signalling. The Pleinmont tower was built in 1942 by the forced labour of the Organisation Todt. The tower was cast entirely by hand, with barrows of concrete pushed up a spiral ramp leading around the wooden shuttering to the top. There were some 7,000 slave workers in Guernsey, consisting of many Russian prisoners of war and labour from the occupied countries. Pleinmont was Germanised to "Westburg" during the occupation, and was heavily defended like the rest of the island. Hitler was obsessed with fear that the allies would try to recapture the islands for prestige reasons, and poured in thousands of men and much valuable material. His

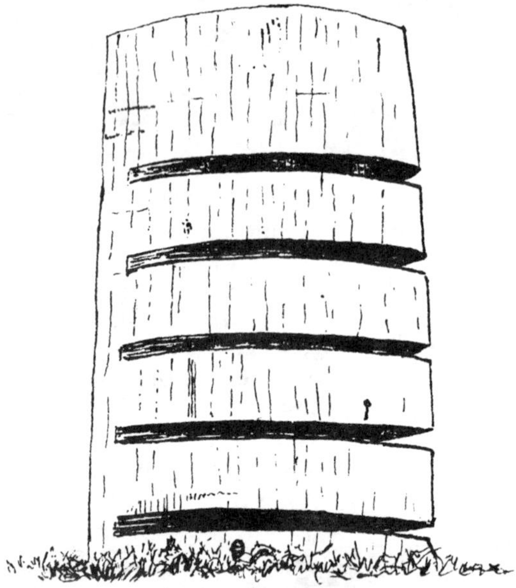

PLEINMONT TOWER

opponents called it his "island madness", and throughout our walks we meet numerous relics of the Occupation. The Channel Islands Occupation Society have renovated the tower and it is open to the public on occasions in the summer.

As we approach La Pointe de Pleinmont the path again splits, with the main path heading leftwards, while a fainter track (E) leads to a spoil tip with three metal barbed wire stakes. Cutting down at this point we have good views of the steep grey walls of the point, which is joined to the mainland by a narrow isthmus (known locally as a coupée). This has suffered much rockfall in recent years and should be avoided. A second rocky headland is visible to the south-east, and we can follow a faint track around the backwall of a gully and up the slope opposite towards this headland, which is called Les Grandes Côtils (The Big Cliffs). A noticeable feature is a low raised earth and stone wall which has been constructed below the path on the cliff edge. At one time these south-facing slopes were intensively cultivated, and potatoes grown here. Sheep were also grazed on the common ground. It is possible to escape to the main cliff path at any point. Our variation leads us to a grassy saddle below the headland, and it is worthwhile making the short climb to its summit (F) and enjoy the views of Herpin Rock ("Harpoon Rock"), La Pointe de Pleinmont and Les Hanois. Several scree slopes are visible on the cliffs in this area. These are not natural, but are spoil from the excavations of the numerous German bunkers which riddle the plateau. An obvious path takes us from the saddle back to the main cliff path.

For those who stay on the main path we can look across to the impressive headland of Les Grandes Côtils. La Pointe de Pleinmont itself is hidden from view until we reach the top of the next slope, where we can look back to the steep peninsula. The large scar to the right of the promontory was caused by a major rockfall, and the coupée is being rapidly eroded. Looking ahead we can see the outline of a German bunker, the Battery Dollmann (G), on the western headland of L'Angle, our destination. Keep a lookout on the left of the path for several circular gun placements.

A short distance further on we reach the remains of Pleinmont Watch House, which was constructed during the American War of Independence around 1780, when the French became allies of the American Colonists. There were a series of these buildings along the coast, and a chain of beacons which would have been lit as a warning signal. The ruin is now more often called "Victor Hugo's haunted house", as it featured in the Frenchman's famous book, *Toilers of the Sea,* written during his 15-year exile on Guernsey from 1855. The building was destroyed during the Occupation, partly because it interfered with Battery Dollmann's line of fire.

We soon literally reach the end of the road at L'Angle, where there are inspiring views of this sheer-walled bay. The black mass of Le Tas de Pois d'Aval ("The South-westerly Pea Stack") or Gull Rock as it is more commonly known, rears from the always-moving waters beyond the centre of the bay. It is a memorable sight when waves are crashing over its summit during the rough seas. In calmer weather large black birds are often visible on the rock. These are shag, a common seabird of Guernsey's coast. The view is dominated by the severe outline of L'Angle Tower (H), which despite its harsh intrusion almost enhances the scene. In the distance we can pick out, from left to right, Torteval Church, Mont Herault Watch House and the circular German tower at La Prevôté.

The energetic will want to continue to Mont Herault, and should turn to Route 5. We have several options to reach our starting point. We can retrace our steps or take the lanes past Pleinmont Tower to the edge of the plateau. From here we can either descend to The Fairy Ring or take the path on the right to Le Vau de Monel. At the Portelet-Creux Mahie path junction we continue straight on along the top of a wooded slope. There are good views across Rocquaine Bay to Lihou and Fort Saumarez, and the rocky ridge of La Varde in the foreground. At the next path junction we turn right then left on to National Trust land where there is a tiny pill-box emplacement (contortionists will have fun getting inside). We then descend through pines to a road. A left turn here takes us to La Rue de la Varde, but a more attractive alternative is through Le Vau de Monel. Le Vau means a little valley bounded by hedges, while Monel was probably a former owner. To reach it we head right and then left on to an idyllic green lane. This takes us past the foundations of an old house, now graced by a polished granite picnic table, and down through the trees and overgrown garden to the road near Trinity Cottages.

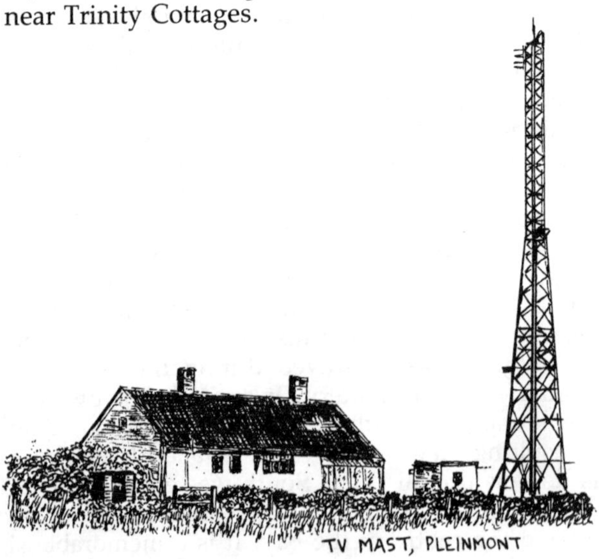

TV MAST, PLEINMONT

ROUTE 2 A sea level scramble

MAP 2

PORTELET TO LES GRANDES COTILS

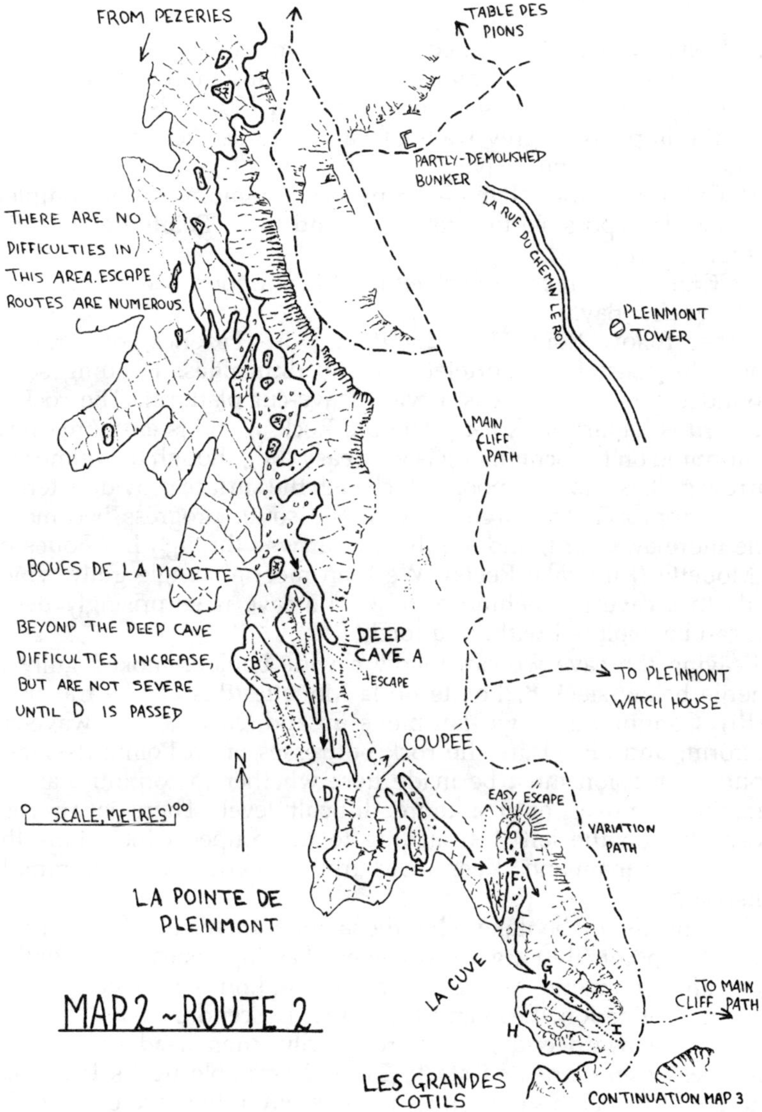

DISTANCE —	Portelet to La Pointe des Pezeries	0.5 miles
	Pezeries to La Pointe de Pleinmont	0.6 miles
	Pleinmont to Les Grandes Cotils	0.4 miles
GRADE —	Portelet to La Pointe des Pezeries	I+
	Pezeries to La Pointe de Pleinmont	II
	Pleinmont to Les Grandes Cotils	III

AN UNCOMMITTING expedition with many easy escape routes. Most of the traverse is at an easy standard and gradually increasing in difficulty to the crux section in the final 100 yards. En route we pass the impressive grey walls of La Pointe de Pleinmont and one of the island's deepest caves.

RECOMMENDED TIDE — 7.6 metres minimum for the complete traverse. It is possible to scramble round to La Pointe des Pezeries at high water.

ACCESS — Start from Portelet ("Little Harbour"), which is south of Rocquaine Bay.

Either follow Route 1 to La Pointe des Pezeries, or scramble along the coast from Portelet with no difficulties. Heading south around the point we cross a wide wave-cut platform. The rock to seaward is La Grosse Rock ("The Big Rock"), and is easily reached. Continuing on the scrambling is very easy (I+), though the numerous narrow gullies and rock pools which etch the surface provide interest. As we approach the large stack to the south progress becomes a little more awkward, and we thread our way through Les Boues de la Mouette (Kittiwake Reefs). We then meet a shingle gully which leads to a cave (A) behind a pool. The cave is surprisingly deep, but can be explored without a torch.

Leaving the cave we can follow a wide boulder-choked gully to emerge below stack B, Pointe de la Mouette (this can be traversed at III). Continuing on we can move up and left to a high wave-cut platform, and ahead are the rock buttresses of La Pointe de Pleinmont. A decision must be made here whether to continue, as the scrambling moves onto a more difficult level. There is an easy escape (C) on the left (I+) leading to the coupee which joins the point to the mainland. Keep away from the edge which is rapidly collapsing.

Care needs to be taken by those who traverse on: the rocks below the point (II+) are always slimy. Passing beneath the sombre grey cliffs we emerge before a small bay and on the far side we can see our destination, Les Grandes Cotils. Descending a few feet we cross the seaward end of a narrow gully, then head up a wider gully below an elongated stack (E), and scramble up its landward end (II−) to reach a gully on its far side. From here we can see the tottering remains of the coupee. Climbing higher we can make more rapid progress for 60 yards until we meet a deep smooth-sided gully (F), La Cuve. This can be gained by descending a groove (II–) some 30 yards from its landward end, and exited by following a rift which bisects the far wall (II–).

We are now well above high water level, and about to embark on the most difficult section. Descending some 20 feet, a ledge system can be followed past two awkward steps (III) to a large ledge underneath a short steep cliff (G). At the far end of the ledge a short wall is descended (III) to a large jammed boulder in the gully floor. Those who wish to prolongue the pleasure can head rightwards over the slabs to traverse around the point (H) to seaward. Alternatively head leftwards to emerge above a small bay which is beneath the walls of Les Crandes Cotils ("The Big Cliffs").

Our exit route is up the slabby rocks (I) to the left of the cliffs, to gain a grassy col. A track leads rightwards to the main cliff path. Alternatively a faint lower level track leads back above the clifftop to Pleinmont Point. From the western edge of the plateau there are several paths back to Portelet, and details are in Route 1.

POINT DE LA MOUETTE, PLEINMONT

ROUTE 3 A sea level scramble

MAP 3

LES GRANDES COTILS TO L'ANGLE

DISTANCE — 0.5 miles
GRADE — IV–

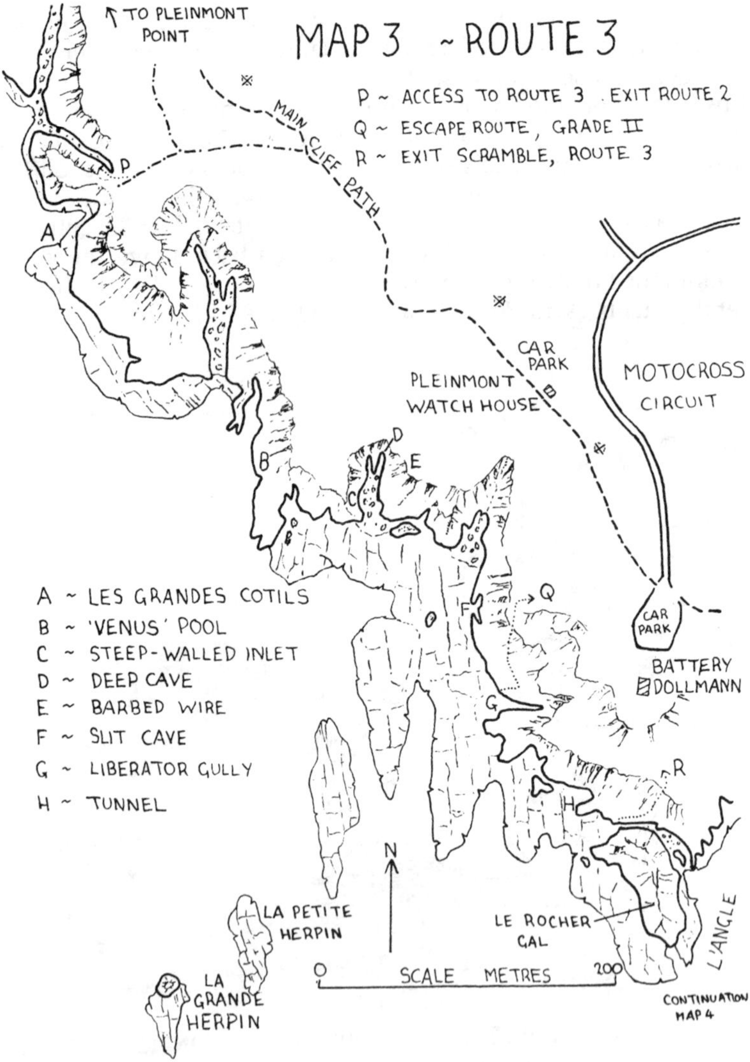

AN ENJOYABLE excursion with many interesting features. There are some difficult but avoidable sections, and many escapes in the initial section. In the last half of the traverse there are fewer and more difficult escape routes which add to the commitment. Overall a not-too-serious expedition, which can be easily split into shorter sections.

RECOMMENDED TIDE — 9 metres for the complete section. 7.6 metres with two short diversions.

LA POINTE DE PLEINMONT FROM LES GRANDES CÔTILS

ACCESS — Park by the ruin of Pleinmont Watch House. Follow the cliff path west past a small point with benches, skirt around the small valley and take a path on the left which leads to a saddle below a rocky knoll. Descend the far (west) side of the saddle and the cliffs appear on our left.

THE TRAVERSE — This west face of Les Grandes Cotils (A) has cliffs some 120 feet high, with a very smooth wave-sculptured base. Here we can drop down to sea level and traverse under the cliffs at grade IV−. This is worth a try on a hot day and calm seas: the water is deep and the penalty for falling off is only a dampened spirit! Alternatively it is possible to take a ramp up the cliff (demands care II−), or a safer option is to return over the saddle and descend to the east side of the point.

Beyond this is a large inlet with a cave on its eastern side. Exiting from this needs care: a right to left rising line up a slab seems the best option (II+). Traversing more easily round to the next point we pass a deep Venus Pool (B) and the jagged teeth of Herpin ("Harpoon") Rock appear. We soon reach an awkward inlet (C), with a steep wall below our feet. On a 9 metre tide the cliff can be easily avoided by descending near its seaward end. If this is flooded a difficult 25ft downclimb (IV−) can be made via a sloping ledge some 30 feet in from the seaward end. An easier alternative is to escape up the hillside and rejoin the traverse below the wall.

Two sets of jammed truck wheels can be found in the inlet. These probably date from the occupation, and could have been used to empty the spoil from the numerous bunker excavations over the cliff edge. A large patch of dumped stone can be seen near the cliff top. There is also an excellent cave, Le Creux de Jou (D), at this point. It is long, narrow and floored with coarse sand.

Emerging from the gully we pass a car engine, and below this is a squeeze tunnel. Up on the left is a mass of barbed wire (E) dumped over the cliff after liberation in 1945. Scrambling on we reach a platform with large boulders below a 100 ft cliff — a favourite playground of local climbers and known as Gaul Wall.

There are many interesting rock pools in the vicinity. After crossing the bay we exit up a rising ramp below the smaller Hanois Cliff, which is seamed with thin bands of quartz. At its base is a narrow horizontal cave (F): have a nice crawl! Beyond this the cliff starts to diminish in height, and we meet a short awkward rock step which can be avoided near sea level, or climbed on the left (II+).

VIEW OF LATTER HALF OF ROUTE 3, HERPIN ROCQUE

The cliff then degenerates into a 10ft step and it is possible to escape (II) up the righthand end of this to a ledge with a huge block. A vague path traverses west above the cliff from here, then up towards the watch house.

Those of us who continue must head down towards sea level and into another inlet, Liberator Gully (G). Just beyond this a massive wedged boulder has formed a tunnel, and then a deep gully cuts into our path. This is most easily avoided by a high route on the left, and we arrive at a cliff with an impressive right-angled corner. This is the line of Excalibur, an extremely severe rock climb. Near the corner is a tunnel (H), and we can slide through this to another right-angle in the cliff. Our escape is at the righthand (seaward) end of this right-angle, where we step off a boulder, then scramble off with care (II–).

BATTERY DOLLMANN

At low water it is possible to traverse around Le Rocher Gal, the stack on our right to reappear at the escape point via the gully which isolates the rock. The stack is awkward to gain (III), and the descent into the gully is tricky (IV−).

Scrambling up the vegetated slope to the cliff top we reach the Dollmann Battery which dominates the western headland of L'Angle. This steep-walled bay looks impregnable, but there are hidden ways down the precipices and the next scramble leads us through this rarely-visited part of the coast.

LE TAS DE POIS D'AVAL

ROUTE 4 A sea level scramble

MAP 4

L'ANGLE

DISTANCE — 0.4 miles

GRADE — II+

"THE CORNER", a somewhat prosaic name for this bastion of rock and sea. Surrounded on all sides by vertical cliffs spattered with yellow lichen and guano, no descents to its floor are apparent. The precipitous walls are a haven for birds and in the spring there are a multitude of nesting fulmars, gulls and shag. In fact the walls are referred to as "Gull Cliff" on some maps. The bay seems to have a calming effect on the sea and even in the most severe of gales the waters of L'Angle are comparatively tranquil. It is possible that L'Angle is a misnomer, and that the true name is L'Ancre ("The Anchorage"). No coastline is complete without its Lover's Leap, and L'Angle is said to be Guernsey's.

L'ANGLE

Beyond the centre of the bay is the large mass of Le Tas de Pois d'Aval (The South-westerly Pea Stack) or Gull Rock. It is a memorable sight when waves are crashing over its crest. Above L'Angle's eastern walls is a stark German observation tower which, despite its intrusion, adds to the grandeur of the scene. Against the horizon can be picked out Mont Herault Watch-house, and in the far distance the round Germanised tower at La Prevote.

The squat Battery Dollmann is the silent sentinal on the western headland of L'Angle, and its narrow slits lend it an evil appearance. Faced with this impressive spectacle one's heart sinks! However nature has created a ledge system which allows us into the bay without too many hairy moments!

ACCESS — Park at the end of the road above the west side of the bay. Scramble down the easy-angled cliffs beyond the battery to a rocky ridge above the seaward end of the steep west wall. Follow the ridge past a notch, until some 30ft above sea level a ledge system leads down to the boulders in the bay (II+).

RECOMMENDED TIDE — 9.2 metres for the complete traverse which includes reaching Gull Zawn. An 8.2 metre tide allows a full exploration of the bay, and coupled with an escape up La Col de Lambille, the long ridge which bisects the bay, makes a very worthwhile trip. However it should be stressed that this ridge is quite a serious proposition, and a much easier escape (II−) can be made up the gully on the western side of the ridge.

THE TRAVERSE — Purists who wish to traverse the entire south coast will not want to miss the short section between the descent ridge and the exit route from Herpin Rock. The easiest option is to descend the Herpin Rock exit (B), jump onto the stack and scramble around this in an anticlockwise direction to the gully floor below the ridge (III).

On reaching the floor of the bay we immediately encounter a cave (C) carved from a seam of brown rock (this layer cuts right through the headland and was encountered on the previous section). Heading east we scramble into La Petite Ancre ("The Little Anchorage"), where large blocks have fallen to create the overhangs above our heads and tunnels beneath our feet. An elongated ridge, La Col de Lambille, extends into the centre of the bay, and there is a useful exit route (D) up this (III−). It is not technically hard, but is very airy and surprisingly exposed: the nearest feature in Guernsey to an alpine ridge. To the west of the ridge is an unlikely-looking escape gully (II−).

Skirting the end of the ridge we follow a gully and beyond this the bay opens out into La Grande Ancre (The Big Anchorage). Here some narrow caves form "chimney" features through the cliffs. Our exit from the bay is achieved by boulder-hopping on a 9.2 metre tide (dries out completely on a 9.5 metre tide) out of the bay and around to Craque Tas, a deep chasm. The quickest escape (E) to the cliff top is up the left hand side of the zawn (II−), though the traverse across Craque Tas is a logical continuation (but significantly harder).

We reach the cliff top by the large tower on the east side of L'Angle, and it is a short walk back to the western headland.

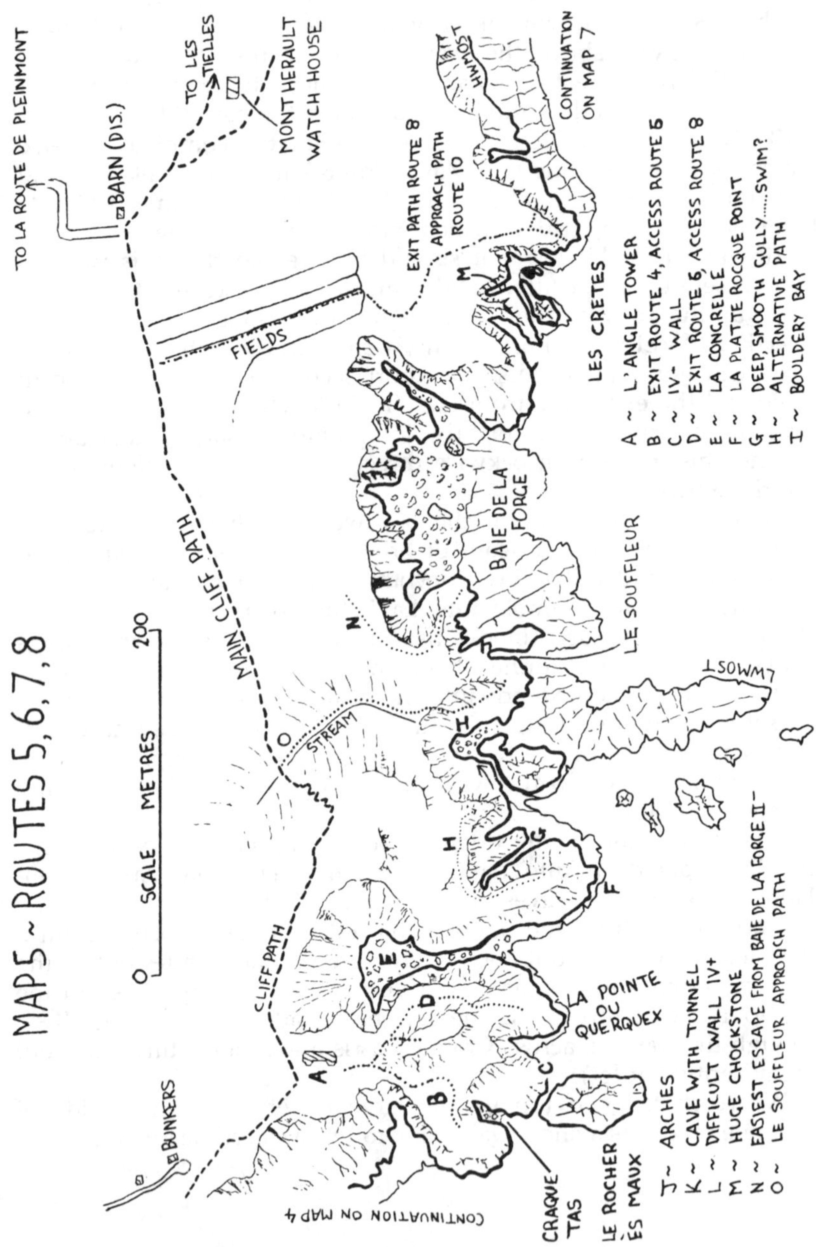
MAP 5 ~ ROUTES 5, 6, 7, 8
SCALE METRES
0
200
TO LA ROUTE DE PLEINMONT
BARN (DIS.)
TO LES TIELLES
MONT HERAULT WATCH HOUSE
FIELDS
EXIT PATH ROUTE 8
APPROACH PATH ROUTE 10
CONTINUATION ON MAP 7
HWMOST
LWMOST
MAIN CLIFF PATH
CLIFF PATH
STREAM
BAIE DE LA FORGE
LE SOUFFLEUR
LA POINTE OU QUERQUEX
CRAQUE TAS
LE ROCHER ÈS MAUX
BUNKERS
CONTINUATION ON MAP 4
LES CRETES
A ~ L'ANGLE TOWER
B ~ EXIT ROUTE 4, ACCESS ROUTE 5
C ~ IV- WALL
D ~ EXIT ROUTE 5, ACCESS ROUTE 8
E ~ LA CONCRELLE
F ~ LA PLATTE ROCQUE POINT
G ~ DEEP, SMOOTH GULLY.....SWIM?
H ~ ALTERNATIVE PATH
I ~ BOULDERY BAY
J ~ ARCHES
K ~ CAVE WITH TUNNEL
L ~ DIFFICULT WALL IV+
M ~ HUGE CHOCKSTONE
N ~ EASIEST ESCAPE FROM BAIE DE LA FORGE II-
O ~ LE SOUFFLEUR APPROACH PATH

ROUTE 5 A short cliff walk

MAPS 1 and 5

L'ANGLE TO MONT HERAULT

DISTANCE — 1.2 miles

A SHORT but interesting walk, passing impressive rock walls and chasms, German fortifications and a marvellous blow-hole to reach the Napoleonic watch house at Mont Herault.

Start from the end of the road on the west side of L'Angle. Here Battery Dollmann maintains its vigil over the Atlantic Ocean. L'Angle is Guernesiase for "The Corner": surely this fearsome, precipitous place deserved a more awe-inspiring name! It has been suggested that the bay's true name is L'Ancre (The Anchorage), and its waters can be surprisingly tranquil in a south-westerly gale. A large mass of rock rears out of the sea beyond the middle of the bay. This is Le Tas de Pois d'Aval, or Gull Rock, though it is favoured by the dark-coloured shag which are often on its summit, than the eponymous gull. On the far side of L'Angle is a German range-finding tower, a massive intrusion which despite its severe geometry, enhances the scene. Mont Herault watch-house is visible against the horizon, and the German tower at La Prevôté is on the headland in the far distance.

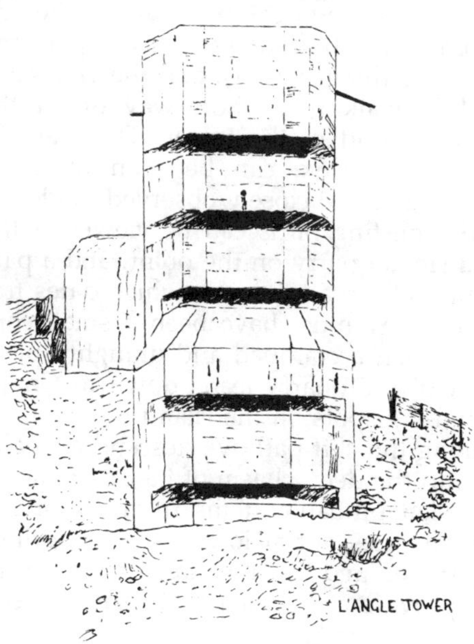

WEST HEADLAND OF L'ANGLE

Heading east along the cliff path we skirt L'Angle, and as we approach the German tower we pass above Gull Cliff, an inaccessible haven for seabirds. To our left is an area of rough ground which is used as a motocross circuit in the winter months. The tower is well worth exploring, and concrete steps lead up to the final stair well which unfortunately is now devoid of rungs. The adventurous will have fun climbing the shaft to the very top (sometimes a rope hangs down to make things easier), and the views are rewarding.

It is worthwhile walking a short way down the promontory beyond the seaward end of the tower. There are fine views into L'Angle, and a large cave can be seen on its far side. The two-tiered Gull Cliff can be closely observed, and in the spring and early summer the nesting birds can be viewed without disturbing them. There is a small quarry on the point, and a path to the left of this leads to a tiny observation niche which dates from Napoleonic tines. The superb view must have been a small compensation for keeping watch in such a cramped and draughty place! The narrow path to the right of the quarry leads down to Craque Tas, one of the best rock climbing spots on the island.

Continuing along the cliff path we descend a small dip where we can look down into the deep chasm of La Congrelle or "The Conger Eel", a name which probably stems from its long narrow shape. The bed of the rift dries out at low water on spring tides, so it is unlikely to be frequented by the conger. On a rough day the crashing waves provide a spectacular display, especially near high water when they surge through the narrow gap, and the air is full of swirling foam. When conditions are more amiable rock climbers can be observed scaling the steep walls which provide some exhilarating routes. Please don't be tempted to throw stones over the cliffs! Several local climbers had a lucky escape in La Congrelle in 1988 when a group on the cliff path trundled a large boulder over the edge, unaware that there were people below them . . .

It is hard to believe that some local deputies wish to see this ravine filled with the island's refuse.

LA CONGRELLE

Beyond La Congrelle we descend to a narrow valley which has a small stream and a dry stone wall. A path can be followed down to Le Souffleur, the most impressive blow-hole on the island (see Route 7). The path then takes us out of the valley through gorse, bracken and thorn to emerge on open fields. A diversion down to our right takes us to the cliff edge where we can look down into Baie de la Forge ("Smithy's Bay"). Continuing on, the cliff path coincides with a farm track leading to La Rue de Mont Herault, and a rough lane which can be followed to Mont Herault Watch House, a building which dates from 1804, a time when Guernsey was fearful of attack by Napoleon's forces. A number of these stations were constructed along the south coast and a chain of beacons would have been lit in an emergency. The watch house is in a good state of repair, but unfortunately it is almost invariably locked. Through the bars we can pick out murals on the wall depicting Medusa and Lucifer. A night spent in here can be a spine-chilling experience, and many locals refer to the building as the "haunted house"!

The quickest way back to L'Angle is to reverse our steps. Those who want a different route could join the track near L'Angle tower and follow the lanes around the far side of the motorcross circuit, and so to L'Angle's western headland.

L'ANGLE TOWER

ROUTE 6 A Sea level Scramble

MAP 5

L'ANGLE TO LA CONGRELLE

DISTANCE — 0.2 miles

GRADE — V or IV− depending on route

THIS short but technical section is a logical continuation to the traverse of L'Angle, but is included separately here as the complete L'Angle traverse is possible on such few occasions. Much of the traverse is taken up by a deep fissure known as Craque Tas.

RECOMMENDED TIDE — 8 metres minimum

ACCESS — Park at the end of the unsurfaced road near the two-tiered German observation tower on the east side of L'Angle. Follow a track seaward along the point beyond the tower, pass to the right of a small quarry (care needed here) and down to the head of a deep gully. Scramble through a gap on the right, then down the slabby right-hand side of the gully to sea level (II−). On a 9.2 metre tide it is possible to boulder-hop around into L'Angle.

THE TRAVERSE — Heading left we reach the mouth of Craque Tas, or Gull Zawn. The zawn is an impressive place and its steep walls contain the largest concentration of difficult rock climbs on the island. The rigours of the routes are reflected in their daunting names which include Hades, Styx Trip and Valediction. At the rear of the zawn is a narrow cave.

The narrow mouth of the gully is most easily crossed by a short jump and we meet a steep section of rock above the narrow barnacle-encrusted gully which separates Le Rocher ès Maux from the mainland. It is possible to traverse this wall at a sustained V; the prospects of sliding into the narrow gully are not encouraging. An alternative is to make a 30ft climb (II+) on the left, and descend to the far end of the gully. The stack itself can be reached by a short jump. On a calm day a large shoal of mullet can often be seen cruising up and down the gully.

From the far end of the gully we traverse round an arete and cross the base of a wall (C, IV−) until it is possible to gain the large fallen blocks. The cliff behind these is known as Mole Wall and it has a distinctive black spot, an intrusion of dolerite. The continuation from here is taken up in Route 8. An easy (I) escape is up La Pointe du Querqueux, along the left-hand side of La Congrelle (D) and so back to the German observation tower.

LE SOUFFLEUR

ROUTE 7 A walk with a short scramble

MAP 5

LE SOUFFLEUR

DISTANCE — 0.5 miles for round trip

GRADE — I+

FROM the moment they are born, blow-holes are doomed to die. The immense power of the breakers inexorably widens the source hole of the spout, until the pressure created by the swell is lost. Several retired blow-holes are evident along the cliffs, the largest being found between Fermain Bay and Le Bec du Nez. Le Souffleur has the distinction of being the largest working blow-hole in the Channel Islands, and provides a spectacular display when the tide and swell are at suitable levels.

ACCESS — Park near the large two-tiered observation tower on the east side of L'Angle, Pleinmont.

Follow the cliff path east past the deep rift of La Congrelle (E), and down a set of steps to a small valley. A track leads towards the sea, along a drystone wall. Twenty feet beyond the end of the wall scramble down to a ledge on the left, and follow this beneath a jutting rock to a grey slab overlooking arches and pools.

This really is a delightful spot at low water. The sea has carved out smooth bath tubs (ideal for cooling off on a hot day!), and there are two splendid arches. Near low water on a spring tide it is possible to scramble underneath the lower arch and along to the edge of Baie de la Forge (see Route 8).

Le Souffleur itself has its origins in the series of small holes which have been cut into the rock below the slab. At low water these holes often groan and roar, and warm compressed air is forced out in a powerful jet. Gradually this becomes mixed with spray, until some two hours after low water, given a good swell, a spout of water nearly forty feet high will be ferociously forced out. The roaring, spray and occasional rainbow combine to create a memorable display!

ROUTE 8 A Sea level Scramble

MAP 5

LA CONGRELLE TO LES CRETES

DISTANCE — 0.5 miles

GRADE — V–

THIS is an exciting trip. It takes us from the impressive chasm of La Congrelle and through the steep-sided Baie de la Forge to finish on Les Crêtes. A very large tide is needed to traverse the entire section, though with a short diversion the section can be tackled on more frequent tides. Some difficult climbing is necessary, but apart from the confines of Baie de la Forge, there are numerous escapes. We will encounter several impressive arches and caves, and pass the source of the biggest blow-hole in the Channel Islands.

RECOMMENDED TIDE — 8.6 metres with a short diversion on La Platte Rocque Point. It is worth looking into La Congrelle from the cliff path to check if the rocks at its seaward end are exposed enough to allow a crossing.

ACCESS — Park at the end of the unsurfaced road near the observation tower on the east side of L'Angle, Pleinmont. Walk on to the point to the seaward side of L'Angle Tower, then descend the grassy slope on the left (D).

After gaining the rocks near sea level we skirt under small cliffs until it is possible to cross over the seaward end of La Congrelle via the exposed boulders. La Congrelle is translated to "the conger eel", a name which must refer to its elongated shape as it dries out too frequently to be a habitat of this fish.

We then scramble round La Platte Rocque Point (F), which is always entertaining but nowhere desperate. On a calm hot day the sea looks inviting, with its deep pools and clear water. Indeed the snorkelling in this area is excellent. Tunnels have been formed by large blocks which have fallen from the cliff, and congers, wrasse and a shoal of mullet can frequently be seen.

As we round the point the large cliff on the far side of Baie de la Forge comes into view, and in the far distance is La Prevôté Watch-tower. We soon meet a smooth-sided gully (G), which I have never found dry enough to cross (a 9.6 metre tide and high pressure may be enough). Other alternatives are a horrendous leap, a short swim, or an escape up the groove on the left (III: easier escapes can be made from La Congrelle side of the point). After skirting the cliff behind the flooded gully (H), we can descend a grassy slope to rejoin the traverse by the bouldery bay (I).

If we are lucky enough to cross at this point, we continue over the seaward end of a dry gully with a Venus Pool. Escaping from this (several options) we arrive at a stack cut off by a narrow gully. We can traverse the ledges above this, then descend to a small bouldery bay (I). On a rough windy day this fills with thick foam which swirls around the cliff top in the turbulence. After exiting by a small stream, we scramble easily for 50 yards and reach Le Souffleur.

This is an atmospheric place, and has the most impressive blow-hole in the Channel Islands. A series of small holes just beyond the lobster pot anchors provide a wonderful spectacle when the tide and swell are at the right level. However we should be arriving here just after low water, so the blow-hole will not be working. But if there is even a small swell we should be able to hear a throaty gurgle from the darkness beneath the holes. These sounds emanate from a small cave, and at low water it is possible to dive under its lip to emerge in an eerie airspace. At the back of one's mind is the thought of a freak wave appearing, and of being extruded through the blow-hole like a mincemeat!

EAST TO LES CRÊTES FROM LE SOUFFLEUR

Continuing on we meet smooth "bath tub" rock pools, a perfect place to cool off. Passing through the lower of the two large arches (J), we traverse along the edge of a deep hole which was a permanent rock pool until the sea broke through in 1989 and destroyed the delicate microcosm. We then drop down to a large boulder (take a look at the narrow flooded cave behind it), then climb a short slab. Baie de la Forge is then before us (possible escape on the left, II–). As we scramble into this, a large grey slab becomes visible on the left and just beyond this is a marvellous little cave complete with arch (K). Near high water the waves crash into this and explode outwards in a ferocious exhibition. One wonders how the anemones which stud the cave manage to survive this bombardment!

The bay is covered with slippery rounded boulders, and on its far side we reach an impressive wall of rock, home to some very scary rock climbs and favoured by several pairs of nesting shags in the spring. Our exit from the bay is up the right-hand side of the cliff where it diminishes in height (L). Here we gain a ledge and climb up and rightwards from its seaward end. This is quite difficult (IV+), though on the biggest tides of the year it may be dry enough to traverse out below the ledge (unconfirmed) and so avoid the difficulties.

If the wall proves insurmountable, then it is best to reverse our steps across the bay, and escape up the ridge on the left-hand side of the grey slab (II−). An escape has been made up the second ridge west of the large gully, but this is very serious and cannot be recommended.

A little further on from our difficult exit we meet a short steep wall which should be avoided on the left (escapes of I+ in this area). We then drop down to a gully and cross its seaward end to arrive at the rocky bay below Les Cretes (The Folded Heights). We can cross to a stack and then work our way along this to a gully below a huge chockstone (M) jammed into a rift. Behind the chockstone is a long dry cave which is worth exploring. The gully below the chockstone is crossable about one hour either side of low water on an 8.6 metre tide. The exit up the far side proves a difficult V−.

From the far side of the gully we cross rock platforms, and soon reach a long shallow pool on the far side of the cliffs. Many tiny fish inhabit the crevices in this aquarium, and they can be tempted out by pieces of bread. A few yards past the pool is a short wall (II−), and we leave the sea at this point. A faint track leads back to the cliff path.

Once on the cliff path we head west and within a few minutes arrive back at our starting point. A short diversion can be made to Mont Herault Watch House, which is described in Route 5.

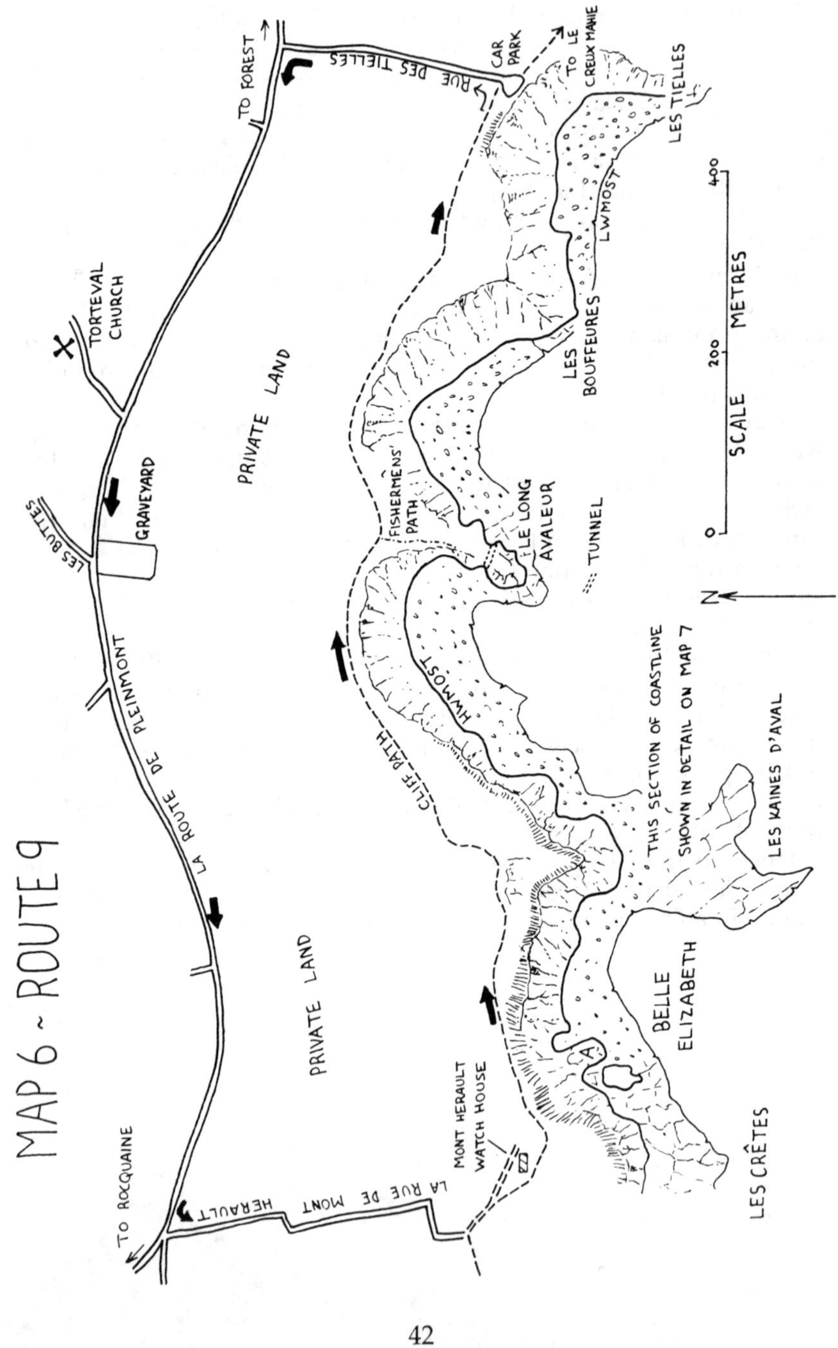
MAP 6 ~ ROUTE 9
TO ROCQUAINE
LA ROUTE DE PLEINMONT
LES BUTTES
GRAVEYARD
TORTEVAL CHURCH
TO FOREST
RUE DES TIELLES
CAR PARK
TO LE CREUX MAHIE
PRIVATE LAND
PRIVATE LAND
LA RUE DE MONT HERAULT
MONT HERAULT WATCH HOUSE
CLIFF PATH
FISHERMENS' PATH
HWMOST
LWMOST
LE LONG AVALEUR
TUNNEL
LES BOUFFEURES
LES TIELLES
A
BELLE ELIZABETH
LES KAINES D'AVAL
LES CRÊTES
THIS SECTION OF COASTLINE SHOWN IN DETAIL ON MAP 7
SCALE
METRES
0
200
400
N

ROUTE 9 A cliff walk returning along the lanes

MAP 6

MONT HERAULT TO LES TIELLES

DISTANCE — 2 miles

A HIGH level route taking us above some of the largest cliffs on the island, and past Le Long Avaleur where the sea has gouged out an enormous tunnel. Our return brings us through Torteval and along the roads and lanes to Mont Herault.

ACCESS — The turning to Mont Herault is about half a mile west of Torteval, on La Route de Pleinmont. It is possible to park near Mont Herault Watch House, a well-preserved relic of the Napoleonic Wars (see Route 5).

MONT HERAULT WATCH HOUSE

From the watch house we should take care to join the cliff path rather than taking a short cut across the field. There are good views down into Belle Elizabeth and below us there is a tottering stack (A), joined to the mainland by a loose coupee. The boulder-strewn bay sweeps underneath high loose cliffs which are covered in nesting seabirds during the spring and early summer, to a small headland. Beyond this we can pick out the huge slab of Les Tielles, with its distinctive sills of black dolerite, the headland at Les Ecrilleurs and the German tower at La Prevôté.

Belle Elizabeth is said to be named after a beautiful unmarried Torteval girl who gave birth to a child. Thrown out of the house by her father, and in a slough of despond, she leapt off the cliffs with the child in her arms. Legend has it that they were both turned into rocks, La Belle Lizabeau and La P'tite Lizabeau at its foot.

LOOKING EAST FROM CLIFF PATH, MONT HERAULT

Hemmed in between a fence and an earth wall (which is soon replaced by some fearsome-looking Occupation barbed-wire stakes), we head east along the cliff path. After cresting a rise we have impressive views of Torteval's cliffs. In the foreground is an un-named bay, bounded on its east side by a ridge. This is Le Long Avaleur, or "The Long Slope". On all recent maps this name has been incorrectly Anglicised to a meaningless Le Long Cavaleux, perhaps by English cartographers who were no doubt confused by the intricacies of Guernesiase! The name is also mistakenly applied to the large tunnel which cuts through the base of "The Long Slope": this is the largest arch in Guernsey, but is not visible from our present position. Beyond the ridge is the bay of Les Bouffeures ("The blow-holes").

A little further on an abeurveure or trough has been built to catch the water from a small spring, and beyond this we can clearly see the arch, where powerful waves have cut through the fractured doloritic intrusions. Those who want a little more excitement can descend a path down Le Long Avaleur to the arch, but care is required (see Route 11). From the top of the ridge there are good views to the pointed rocks of Les Bouffeures, which despite their name never seem to be blowing! Passing a small quarry, we reach the car park at the end of La Rue des Tielles. From the far side of the wall we can look down the vegetated cliffs, which are unfortunately a favoured dumping spot, to the fallen rocks in L'Herbe Baie. Les Tielles ("The Steep Places") are the cliffs on the headland to the south.

We can either return along the cliff path to our starting point, or engage in some road walking. Heading down La Rue des Tielles we reach La Route de Pleinmont, where there is an old water pump and a granite trough. Turning left we soon reach Torteval, where there is a larger pump, in good working order. A short diversion to the distinctive church is recommended.

WATER PUMP NEAR LES TIELLES

The original Ste Marie du Torteval, constructed around 1250, was the smallest of all the Channel Islands' parish churches. Unfortunately it could not be kept in good repair, perhaps due to the meagre resources of this thinly-populated parish. The church was demolished in 1816, and the Victorian replacement, with its sturdy granite buttresses and tall circular tower, is the only Channel Island church to have a Medieval bell (dating from 1432). There is a monument to the Torteval men who died in the two world wars, with Guernsey's shield of three lions and broome leaves.

TORTEVAL CHURCH

Continuing along La Route de Pleinmont we pass a graveyard and Les Buttes, where in the Middle Ages one would have practiced one's archery! There are several pathways and lanes on the left which lead back to the cliff path. Unfortunately these are not rights of way, and we should avoid them. We must return to our starting point by turning left down La Rue de Mont Herault. From here it is possible to see the large tower of Fort Sausmarez and Lihou Island.

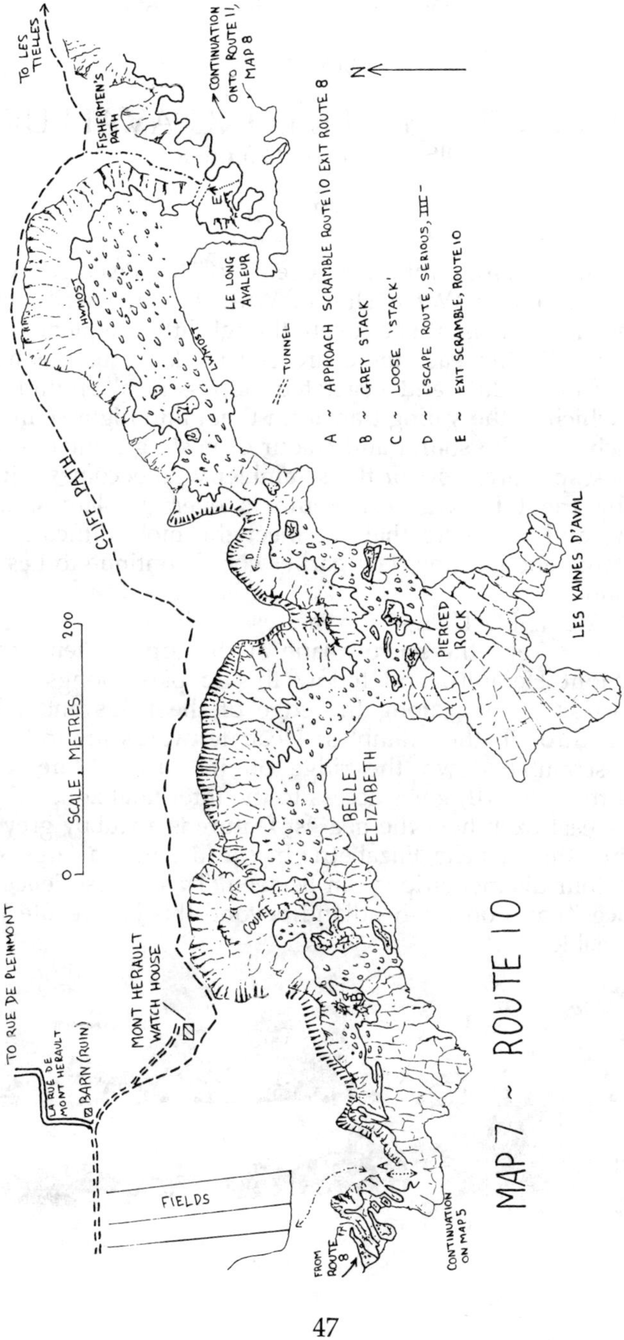
TO LES TIELLES
FISHERMEN'S PATH
CONTINUATION ONTO ROUTE 11, MAP 8
N
HWMOST
LWMOST
LE LONG AVALEUR
TUNNEL
A ~ APPROACH SCRAMBLE ROUTE 10 EXIT ROUTE 8
B ~ GREY STACK
C ~ LOOSE 'STACK'
D ~ ESCAPE ROUTE, SERIOUS, III-
E ~ EXIT SCRAMBLE, ROUTE 10
CLIFF PATH
LES KAINES D'AVAL
PIERCED ROCK
SCALE, METRES
0
200
BELLE ELIZABETH
COUPEE
TO RUE DE PLEINMONT
LA RUE DE MONT HERAULT
BARN (RUIN)
MONT HERAULT WATCH HOUSE
FIELDS
FROM ROUTE 8
CONTINUATION ON MAP 5
MAP 7 ~ ROUTE 10

ROUTE 10 A sea level scramble

MAP 7

LES CRETES TO LE LONG AVALEUR

DISTANCE — 0.75 miles

GRADE — II

OUR scramble starts from Les Cretes ("The Peaks or Crests") below Mont Herault Watch House. With its steep walls, intricate gullies and rock pools, it is a lovely though little-frequented stretch of coastline. To the east there are several large bays which are flanked by loose cliffs and vegetated slopes, ideal ground for the seabirds which in the spring transform them into highrise maternity wards, rich with the sound and colour of nesting fulmar, shag and gull. No escapes are easy for the scrambler who becomes injured or cut off by the tide. Our exit route is over the largest arch in Guernsey, and it is here that we meet the most difficult section. Given a large enough tide, fast parties could continue to Les Tielles and beyond.

RECOMMENDED TIDE — 7.5 metres

ACCESS — Take the narrow lane at the top of Pleinmont Hill (signed Mont Herault), and follow this to park alongside fields. Walk towards the sea along the edge of the fields and follow a faint track through the brambles. Head leftwards around a small bay and scramble down the ridge on its eastern side. A final awkward rock step (II) gives access to the inter-tidal zone.

Looking east from here the nearest feature is a stubby grey stack, and behind this is Belle Elizabeth. In the distance a large slab of rock with four distinct stripes can be seen. This is Les Tielles ("The Steep Places") and on the headland beyond this La Prevôté Watch-tower is visible.

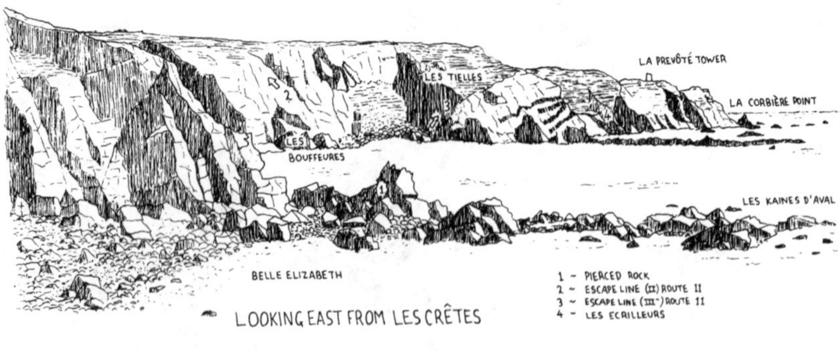

LOOKING EAST FROM LES CRÊTES

THE TRAVERSE — The first 100 yards is quite sustained at II−, with many gullies to cross (the larger the tide, the easier these become). The grey stack (B) can be skirted on either side and to the landward it is possible to crawl, with fingers crossed, under jammed boulders which are poised above the gully like Damocles' sword.

We then enter the broad bouldery bay of Belle Elizabeth, named after a local beauty who threw herself over the cliff after giving birth to a child out of wedlock. Passing a vegetated "stack" (C) which is joined to the mainland by a crumbling ridge, we meet a large cliff of loose and vegetated rock. There is a small cave at 70 feet, a five star nesting spot for the shags which move in every spring! At its foot are five small caves.

More boulder-hopping takes us to a small point where the sea has eroded several holes in the rock. The offshore reefs are known as Les Kaines d'Aval. After rounding the point we cross large smooth boulders and there is a possible escape route (D) on the left where a grassy runnel bounded by rocks leads up the cliffside, which is known as La Carriere Torode (Torode's Quarry). This is quite a serious escape (III−) and should only be considered by those with experience of steep ground.

Beyond is a second bay and visible on its far side is a long ridge with a tunnel cut clean through its seaward end: the largest arch in Guernsey! The point is called Le Long Cavaleux on recent maps, but this is probably a corruption of Le Long Avaleur which means "the long slope", an apt description of the ridge. It is possible to walk through the arch or make a harder traverse to the right around the point (II+/III−).

Our exit (E) is over the top of the arch, and this can prove quite awkward (II). A short section of scrambling leads to a track which is followed to the main cliff path. Heading back west we soon arrive at Mont Herault Watch House.

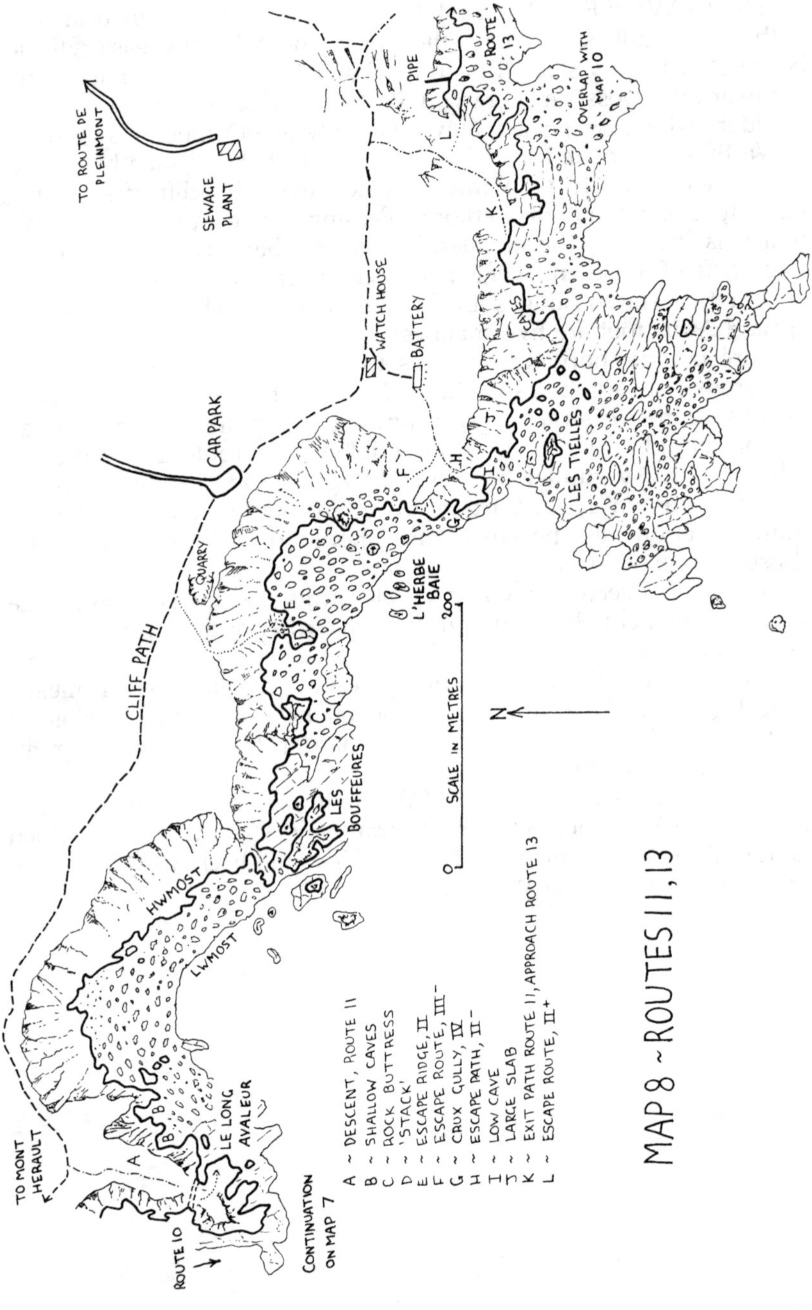
TO ROUTE DE PLEINMONT
SEWAGE PLANT
PIPE
ROUTE 13
OVERLAP WITH MAP 10
WATCH HOUSE
BATTERY
CAVES
CAR PARK
QUARRY
CLIFF PATH
LES TIELLES
L'HERBE BAIE
SCALE IN METRES
0
200
N
LES BOUFFEURES
HWMOST
LWMOST
TO MONT HERAULT
LE LONG AVALEUR
ROUTE 10
CONTINUATION ON MAP 7
A ~ DESCENT, ROUTE 11
B ~ SHALLOW CAVES
C ~ ROCK BUTTRESS
D ~ 'STACK'
E ~ ESCAPE RIDGE, II
F ~ ESCAPE ROUTE, III⁻
G ~ CRUX GULLY, IV
H ~ ESCAPE PATH, II⁻
I ~ LOW CAVE
J ~ LARGE SLAB
K ~ EXIT PATH ROUTE 11, APPROACH ROUTE 13
L ~ ESCAPE ROUTE, II+
MAP 8 ~ ROUTES 11, 13

ROUTE 11 A sea level scramble

MAP 8

LE LONG AVALEUR TO LES TIELLES

A WORTHWHILE expedition taking us from the largest arch in Guernsey to the island's biggest cliff. A careful choice of tide is needed to complete the entire section. Much of the route is very straightforward, crossing two large bays, though the final part has a sting in the tail and needs not a little rock climbing skill.

DISTANCE — 0.75 miles

GRADE — IV

RECOMMENDED TIDE — 9 metres minimum

ACCESS — 100 yards west of Torteval Post Office is a turning to Les Tielles (by Chateau des Tielles). Follow this to the cliff edge. From here we can look westwards towards Mont Herault Watch House. A jagged ridge, Le Long Avaleur, can be seen emerging

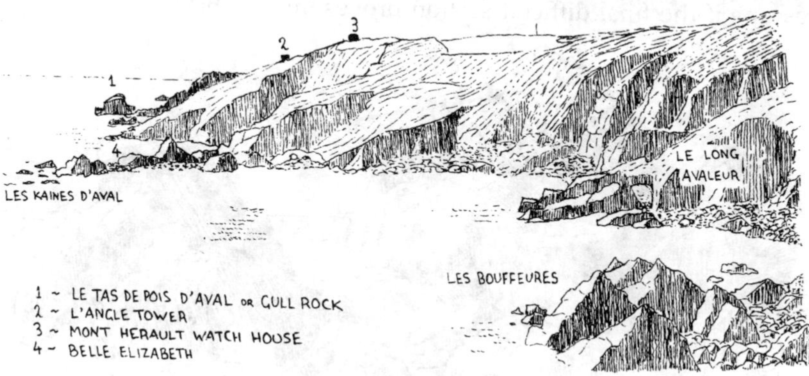

WEST FROM LES TIELLES

from a large bay: our descent path (A) takes us down this ridge, which is the first one we meet heading west along the cliff path. The descent path is quite visible, and well-used by fishermen.

THE TRAVERSE — A depression in the path near the seaward end of the ridge means we are above the large tunnel that cuts through the headland. We should then head down to the left; several options exist, the easiest being at the seaward end of the point (if tide permits).

TUNNEL, LE LONG AVALEUR

A huge ampitheatre of steep loose cliffs skirt Les Bouffeures (The Blow-holes), the bay before us. On its far side are a cluster of pointed rocks, the largest of which is La Noir Rocher (The Black Rock). Behind these are the steep slabs above L'Herbe Baie. Les Tielles, our objective, is beyond these slabs though it is possible to escape if the final difficult section proves impassable.

LES BOUFFEURES

Heading into the bay we pick our way through the huge boulders which litter the shore, passing two shallow caves (B). We leave Les Bouffeures Baie and pass La Noir Rocher to reach a rock buttress (C). If its base is flooded the easiest option is to traverse around it at half height, using the large ledge. There are some excellent rock pools a little further on, then boulder-hopping takes us past a low stack (D). A large rock fall has ensured the stack is no longer cut off at high water. About 50 yards further on is a rocky ridge (E) which provides the first escape route: climb the ridge (II), then take a right-to-left rising ramp below the slabs of the cliff, to regain the main cliff path.

Continuing on we cross some huge boulders to reach an overhanging prow of rock on the far side of the bay. It is possible to escape (F) up the vegetated slope to the left of the prow. This is quite serious and exposed (III−), with difficult moves over the slimy rocks below the vegetation.

Continuing beyond the escape we pass under a large overhanging prow which forms a shallow cave, and down the shingle to sea level. On a 9 metre tide it will be necessary to climb the rocks at this point (III), to the righthand side of a large square-cut overhanging block, and then descend to an inlet. On a larger tide it is possible to avoid this short climb by traversing at sea level.

Escaping from the inlet (G) proves an awkward problem, and we must climb the not-too-steep but smooth rocks right of the grey sill. This is best achieved by a series of "mantleshelf" moves from the often greasy rocks at the base (IV).

We then reach a rocky ledge where several metal tubes have been hammered into the cracks by fishermen, to use as rod stands. We can escape at this point (H) up the rocks on the left (II−) and along a fishermans' track to Les Tielles battery. Continuing on we can stay high in an exciting position and follow a ledge system some 40 ft above the beach (III−), or drop (literally) down to beach level, where a low cave (I) can be explored.

A large slabby cliff (J) then comes into view, the highest continuous cliff in Guernsey. This distinctive face has several sills of black dolerite cutting across it. Small caves and ledges have been formed high up the cliff, possibly during one of the warm inter-glacial periods some 100,000 years ago, when the sea level was 100 feet higher. These caves make perfect nesting spots for shag, which move in during the spring. The pink rock is gneiss, one of the oldest rocks in Europe. It is granite that was changed by heat and pressure some 2,500 million years ago into the rock we see today. It is structurally weaker than granite and tends to shear off along weaknesses to form slab features such as the one above us.

Rounding the point (there is a fascinating reef to seaward) we pass several caves and reach our exit point (K), if we are not continuing on to Le Creux Mahie. A wide rising ledge is followed to a good path which leads us above a cliff of light-coloured rock and past an ivy-clad outcrop to the main cliff path.

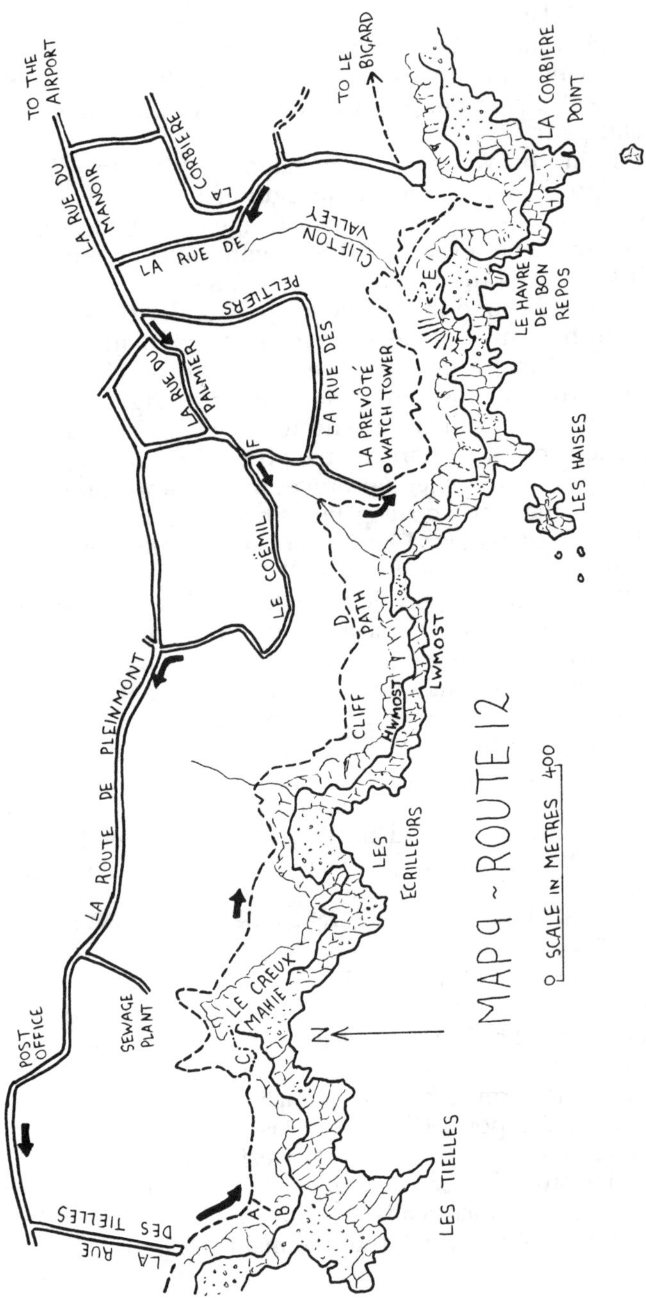
MAP 9 ~ ROUTE 12
0 SCALE IN METRES 400
TO THE AIRPORT
LA RUE DU MANOIR
LA CORBIERE
TO LE BIGARD
LA CORBIERE POINT
LA RUE DE
CLIFTON VALLEY
PELTIERS
LA RUE DES
LA RUE DU PALMIER
LA PREVÔTÉ WATCH TOWER
E
LE HAVRE DE BON REPOS
F
LES HAISES
LE COËMIL
D
CLIFF PATH
HWMOST
LWMOST
LA ROUTE DE PLEINMONT
LES ECRILLEURS
LE CREUX MAHIE
N
SEWAGE PLANT
POST OFFICE
C
LES TIELLES
LA RUE DES TIELLES
A
B

ROUTE 12 A cliff walk, returning via the lanes

MAP 9

LES TIELLES TO LA CORBIÈRE

DISTANCE — 3.75 miles

AN EXHILARATING walk, starting above Guernsey's highest cliffs and passing Le Creux Mahie, the island's deepest cave, and the huge tower at La Prevôté. La Corbière has magnificent views of the coastline.

ACCESS — Start from the end of La Rue des Tielles, which is between Torteval Post Office and the Church, on La Route de Pleinmont.

Heading east along the cliff path above the cliffs which give Les Tielles (The Steep Places) its name, we pass the few bricks which are all that remain of Les Tielles Watch House (A). A diversion on the right leads to Les Tielles Battery (B), which was constructed during the French Revolutionary Wars towards the end of the 18th century. There are excellent coastline views in either direction. To the west we can see Le Long Avaleur and the large arch which cuts through its base. In the far distance Gull Rock, Mont Herault Watch House and L'Angle Tower are visible. To the east below La Prevôté Tower are Les Ecrilleurs, and in the far distance the seaward tip of La Corbière Point, our destination.

Continuing along the cliff path we can look down on the right to the reefs below Les Tielles. These dry out towards low water and the exposed gullies are rich with life and fascinating to explore. A path leads down to the cliff foot (see Route 13). We then descend steep steps to a narrow valley where a buried sewage pipe takes effluent down the cliff and a short distance offshore, a spot usually marked by a flock of gulls and ominously coloured water . . .

Resisting the temptation to swim, we pass two wire fences. At the second fence a track (C) leads down to Le Creux Mahie, Guernsey's largest cave. This makes a worthwhile exploration, but the descent track is more difficult than the main cliff path, and caution should be exercised (see Route 14).

After deviating inland the main path takes us along the cliff-top slopes, thick with bracken and gorse. Views are limited until we crest a rise and La Prevôté Watch Tower becomes visible. We can look down into the bay below Les Ecrilleurs, where there is a dark rift, the entrance to a large overhanging cave. A steep and difficult rock climb called "Stratasfear" wends its way up the far wall of the cave and along the slanting black sill: not for the faint-hearted!

We then cross three valleys, the last being quite large. It is noticeable that the stream in this valley is a mere trickle, hardly enough to carve out the feature. In fact the stream is a "misfit", too small for its valley, and a relic of the Ice Age some 10,000 years ago when Guernsey had a tundra climate. Powerful meltwater streams would have formed in the spring and carved out the deep valley which we see today. There are several such valleys which disect the south coast, with Clifton Valley, Petit Bôt, Saints and Le Gouffre among the largest. They often form sheltered havens for woodland and wildlife, more than adequate compensation for the extra strain which they impose on our legs!

From the far slopes of the valley we can look back to the headland at Les Tielles, and in the far distance to Gull Rock and Pleinmont. Further on we pass a dry stone wall, where there is a large ants' nest by the side of the path. Tread carefully: walkers take a daily toll of these hard-working creatures in the summer months!

Beyond this is a bench and views acrosss the cliffs of La Prevôté to the Germanised tower. A narrow path on the left at this point leads to an open area (D) where close examination reveals numerous flint fragments. The sharp chipped edges of the stone reveal this to be a flint factory: Mesolithic Man may have handled the very fragments we hold in our hands.

We then cross the steep Clifton Valley to reach Le Prevôté Watch Tower, a distinctive landmark of the south coast. Perched above a

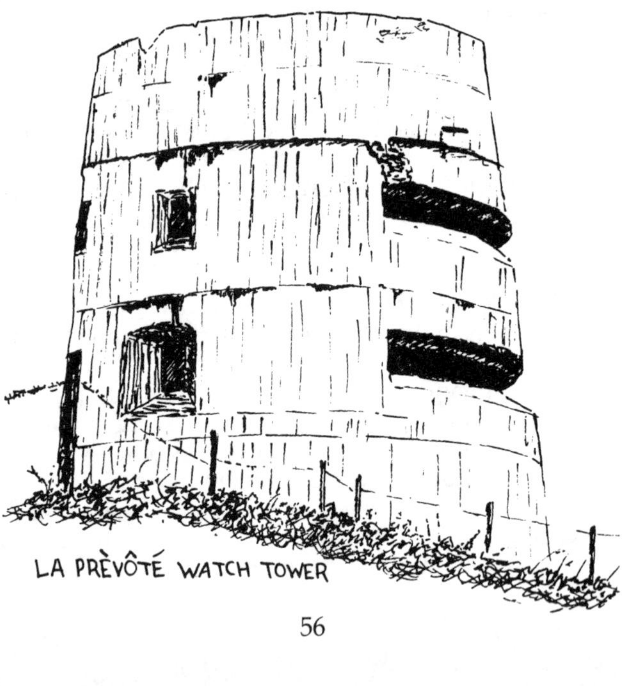

LA PRÈVÔTE WATCH TOWER

small quarry, its original Napoleonic watch house has been all but obliterated by a German range-finding tower (see note in Route 1). Traces of the old walls can be found to the east of the tower. There are good views from here of La Corbière headland, which rises above the rocky bay of Le Havre de Bon Repos or "Harbour of Good Rest". Perhaps this was named in jest, as it would be one of the most dangerous bays on the south coast for a vessel to seek shelter. From the valley floor a path (E) leads down to the bay: it is badly eroded in places, and demands care. On the east side of the bay is a Venus Pool: close examination reveals it to be no product of nature, but of clever use of cement!

Climbing out of the valley we arrive at La Corbière, a name which translates to "Rookery" or "Crow's Nest". Numerous German bunkers riddle the headland, but little remains of the medieval castle which once stood here, guarding the weakness formed in the cliff's ramparts by Le Havre de Bon Repos. The castle was derelict by the end of the 17th century, and all that remains are some of the foundations which can be seen along the edge of the car park. A low earth rampart cuts across the headland, and it is thought to be the remains of an Iron Age fort. It is well worth walking to the end

WELL, LA CORBIERE

of the point where there are superb views east to the cliffs of Le Bigard which rise above a distinct "X" of black doleritic sills. The headland in the distance is Point de la Moye ("Point of the Stack"), and on the far horizon is the southern tip of Little Sark, with the islet of L'Etaq ("The Stack") off its tip. In the far distance to the west we can see the large stack of Gull Rock, and the coastline of Pleinmont.

Those with plenty of energy could take the loop around Le Plaine des Camprôts to the picturesque hamlet of Le Bigard (see Route 21).

For our return we must engage in some lane-walking, and we head inland down the rough lane and take the left fork. Collingwood bungalow will be of interest to shell-lovers: it is adorned with numerous ormer and scallop shells. Arriving at La Rue du Manoir we turn left, then take La Rue du Palmier which leads behind La Prevôté Watch Tower. Another left turn takes us to two granite troughs (F), where we head up a small rise on to Le Coemil. This eventually brings us to La Route de Pleinmont. Almost immediately on the left is a parish boundary marker erected in 1845 between

Torteval and St Pierre du Bois. Further on is a water pump, where those of us who tire of road walking could take a left turn here to join the cliff path by Le Creux Mahie. Those who continue along the road pass Torteval Post Office and shopper to a left turn by another old pump, where we rejoin our starting point.

ROUTE 13 A sea level scramble

MAPS 8 and 10

LES TIELLES TO LE CREUX MAHIE

DISTANCE — 0.4 miles

GRADE — II+

A RELATIVELY straightforward section if the correct tide is chosen. With less extreme tides the grade can rise to a committing III+. This is not a picturesque expedition, and the highlight is Le Creux Mahie, the deepest cave on Guernsey. It is worthwhile taking a torch to explore the cave.

RECOMMENDED TIDE — 8.3 metres

ACCESS —Start as for Route 12, and head east along the cliff path past the remains of a watch house and battery which are shrouded in blackthorn. After about 100 yards cut down a faint track (K) on the right past an ivy-covered outcrop and down an easy ramp to beach level.

THE TRAVERSE — If there is time it is worthwhile scrambling to the right, where there are several caves and the main cliff of Les Tielles (The Steep Places), a slab over 200 ft high and layered by four bands of black dolerite. The reef below the point has much sea life in its gullies and pools, a fascinating place to explore.

Heading west from the foot of the path we pass a small cliff. Beyond this three caves are squeezed into a gully on the left and there is a huge perched block up to the right of these. We soon enter a small bay, where an old sewage pipe hangs down the cliff side. It is possible to escape (II+) at this point, up the gully to the left of the pipe (L). This should only be used in an emergency: its right wall is unstable, and the grass is steep.

Further on we meet a cave. If it is low water on an 8.3 metre tide this should present no problems as the gully at this point will be dry enough to boulder hop. If the gully is flooded, some committing climbing will have to be made over the lip of the cave and down into the rear of the gully (II). The far wall is some 35 ft high and quite smooth. It can be climbed by a left-to-right rising line III+. If in doubt head back to the descent path.

Easier scrambling then leads to a deep narrow gully (II+) which becomes a blow-hole at half tide. Crossing this we reach the concrete foundations of the old sewage disposal point. From here we can descend to the wide debris-filled gully below a scarred headwall and at the foot of this is the entrance to Le Creux Mahie (Mahie's Cave), the largest cave in Guernsey (see Route 14).

An easy path leads from the cave entrance to the main cliff path. Follow this in a westerly direction to Les Tielles. A diversion can be made to Les Tielles Battery, a superb viewpoint (see Route 12).

PATHWAY TO LE CREUX MAHIE

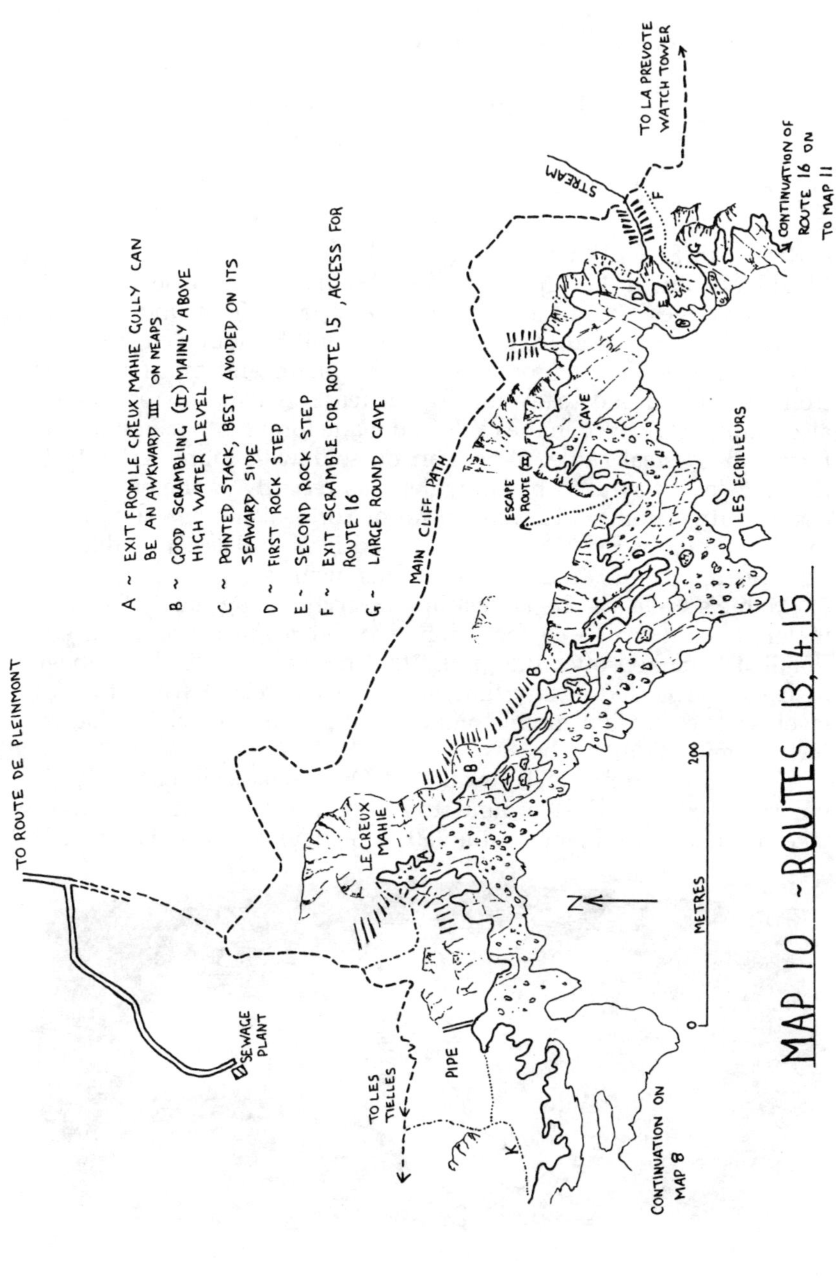
A ~ EXIT FROM LE CREUX MAHIE GULLY CAN BE AN AWKWARD III ON NEAPS
B ~ GOOD SCRAMBLING (II) MAINLY ABOVE HIGH WATER LEVEL
C ~ POINTED STACK, BEST AVOIDED ON ITS SEAWARD SIDE
D ~ FIRST ROCK STEP
E ~ SECOND ROCK STEP
F ~ EXIT SCRAMBLE FOR ROUTE 15, ACCESS FOR ROUTE 16
G ~ LARGE ROUND CAVE
TO ROUTE DE PLEINMONT
SEWAGE PLANT
TO LES TIELLES
PIPE
K
CONTINUATION ON MAP 8
LE CREUX MAHIE
A
B
B
MAIN CLIFF PATH
C
ESCAPE ROUTE (II)
CAVE
LES ECRILLEURS
D
E
G
F
STREAM
TO LA PREVOTE WATCH TOWER
CONTINUATION OF ROUTE 16 ON TO MAP 11
N
0
METRES
200
MAP 10 ~ ROUTES 13,14,15

ROUTE 14 A walk with a short easy scramble

MAP 10

LE CREUX MAHIE

DISTANCE — 0.4 miles

GRADE — I+

RECOMMENDED TIDE — Non tidal!

LEGENDS about Le Creux Mahie abound: a smuggler's haunt, secret passages and a haunt of elves and fairies! An underground passage is said to lead from the cave to Saint Saviour's church, and according to folklore it contains a table, plates and mugs all made from stone and laid ready for a great feast. A band of robbers are also said to have lived in the cave, and made forays into neighbouring farmland to steal cattle. What can be said with more certainty is that the cave was used by smugglers, as recently as the end of the last century. Thomas Picot, the rector of Torteval and Forest parishes in the middle of the 17th century, used it as a place of meditation until his unorthodox methods led to his dismissal.

"Mahie's Cave" is the largest in Guernsey, being nearly 50 yards in length and up to 60 feet high. It used to be called Le Creux Robilliard, named after the family that owned the cliff land above it. It can be visited at any time since it was created when the sea level was some eight metres higher, and it is no longer flooded by the incoming tide.

ACCESS — From the Torteval Post Office take the road towards the sewage plant (just around the bend). After a short distance take the unsurfaced lane on the left to a small car park. Head right

INSIDE LOOKING OUT, LE CREUX MAHIE

along the cliff path to a fence, then follow the track behind this down a ridge and then back left. The cave can be seen at the foot of the cliff. There have been large rockfalls in the past, so don't hang around the entrance admiring the view!

A set of neat steps lead under the narrow entrance (the relics of guided tours which took place in Victorian times). Once inside the cave we are relatively safe from rockfall. At the back of the cave is a talus slope and near the top of this are several tunnels through the blocks which are fun to explore. One of them has a particularly memorable tight squeeze, the nearest thing Guernsey has to potholing! Old clothes are essential for exploring the cave. The guides illuminated the cave with torches made from dried furze, and the soot is still grimed everywhere.

If the tide is low enough there is pleasant scrambling east towards Les Ecrilleurs, or west a short distance towards Les Tielles. Here, if there is a swell and the tide is around the halfway mark, the waves create a blow-hole effect as they crash into the undercut rocks.

EAST FROM LE CREUX MAHIE

ROUTE 15 A sea level scramble

MAP 10

LE CREUX MAHIE TO LES ECRILLEURS

DISTANCE — 0.5 miles

GRADE — II+

A RELATIVELY easy traverse, initially quite sustained but nowhere desperate. There is an escape route near the halfway point, and this section is a logical continuation to Route 13.

RECOMMENDED TIDE — 6.8 metres. On a large spring tide the section is more straightforward.

ACCESS — As for previous section.

THE TRAVERSE — Exit from the gully below Le Creux Mahie (difficulty varies from III on neaps to a slippery I+ on large springs). Interesting scrambling (II) mainly above high water level takes us past a stack to a pinnacle (C) which is joined to the main cliff by a broken ridge. This is best avoided by traversing along the pinnacle's seaward side.

Beyond this we reach a wide bay, the area generally referred to as Les Ecrilleurs (The Stakes). The large cliff on the far side of the bay has several very difficult rock climbs, and the traverse beneath these is described in the next section. Descending into the bay, we immediately pass a cliff and an escape can be made up the grassy slope just beyond this (II). The bay is easily crossed until we reach the first of two rock steps (D). The base of this may be flooded on neaps, in which case it is best climbed from the left. The second step (E) is encountered almost immediately and this can be tackled on its seaward end (spring tides) or by climbing to the square notch near its seaward end on neaps (II+).

Emerging from this obstacle, we reach a slab above a cliff with a large cave at its base. This is the start of the next section, which requires a 9.1 metre tide, if it is to be completed in full.

Our exit is at the very left hand end of the cliff where it diminishes to a 15ft step (II). There has been recent rockfall here, and care is necessary. We emerge in a valley to rejoin the cliff path, and we head west to our starting point.

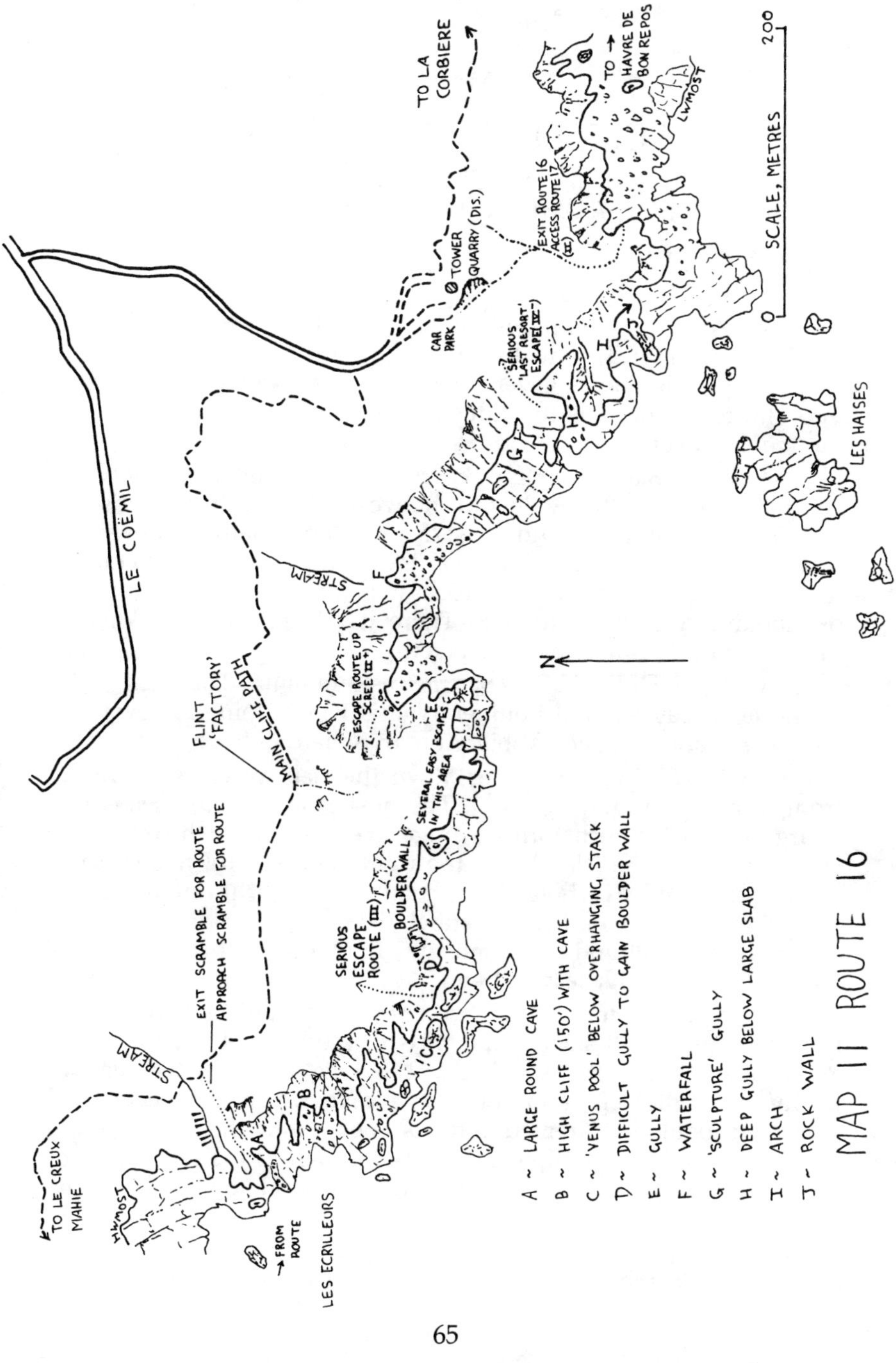

MAP 11 ROUTE 16

ROUTE 16 A sea level scramble

MAP 11

LES ECRILLEURS TO LA PREVÔTÉ WATCHTOWER

DISTANCE — 0.7 miles

GRADE — III+

A FINE expedition with plenty of interesting features including arches, caves and a waterfall. Coupled with some difficult scrambling, this makes a very worthwhile trip which can be split into shorter sections if the tides are not low enough to complete the whole traverse.

ACCESS — Start from La Prevôté Watchtower and follow the cliff path across Clifton Valley to the west. The path then leads to a second valley and descends a series of steps. Halfway down the second set of steps head leftwards to a promontory. Scramble down on the right to a short rock step (II) which leads to a slab overlooking a gully with cave. There has been recent rockfall on the descent and care should be taken.

RECOMMENDED TIDE — 9.1 metres minimum. The route as far as the large bay beyond Boulder Wall is worth doing by itself and has the advantage of accessibility on an 8-metre tide.

THE TRAVERSE — Heading down the slab we cross a gully in front of a large round cave (A). The next gully we meet leads into a large cave (B) which forms a huge overhang beneath one of the largest cliffs on the island. On the right-hand side of this cliff is a narrow cave and two holes have been worn right through the cliff (unfortunately too narrow to crawl through!). A ridge now cuts down to sea level and we climb the short rock wall (II) to a ledge and follow this to its seaward end.

Dropping down to sea level we cut through gullies between the mainland and small stacks, and pass to the right of a large Venus Pool. Beyond this the sea has cut a long fissure which slopes upwards on the left, and there is a cave which can be crossed using the boulders jammed into its roof. From the top of these boulders a gully (tight squeeze) leads through to the next inlet, or there are alternatives on the left (II) or around the stack on the right (II).

Escaping from the inlet up a short wall (II+) we reach an overhanging stack above a Venus Pool (C). The easiest option is to continue through the main gully; a more taxing excursion (III+) can be made by climbing up right of the Venus Pool to traverse the two stacks on their seaward sides.

Whichever way we take a small bay is reached: the blank-looking cliff with an overhanging arch in its centre is known as Boulder Wall and the traverse of this section is hard(ish!). An escape can be made at this point by taking a rising right to left line up the slabs to the left. This 80ft escape is not technically hard, but serious due to its height (III).

A gully (D) cuts into the left-hand side of the cliff: gain the far side by bridging to some holds and pulling over (III+). Traversing onwards close to low water level is sustained in difficulty (smooth barnacle-encrusted rock — not the place to slide off wearing shorts!). An alternative is to climb up to the arch and traverse under this (easier but more serious due to height above sea).

Beyond Boulder Wall easier progress is made along ledges above a gully, and along the crest of the rocks above high water level. Several easy escapes are possible in this area. La Prevôté Watchtower comes into view, and a grey sill is then descended to skirt the base of a slabby cliff with a large red bulge on its right-hand side. Passing through a notch we confront a gully (E).

After crossing this we move leftwards into an inlet below a wide gully with scree slope. This can be used as an escape (II+), but it is a little unnerving as the slope moves down almost as quickly as

ROUTE 16
BELOW LA PREVÔTÉ TOWER

one moves up! Below the slope is a veritable playground of tunnels and squeezes formed by large stable jammed boulders. We pass beneath a short cliff and easier scrambling takes us round into the main bay. On the left is a cave and waterfall (F), complete with rainbow on a sunny afternoon. Continuing on we pass a huge fallen block which has formed several squeezes, a large jammed boulder hanging in a fissure and a gully (G) sculpted from the dark dolerite into smooth rock pools and strangely eroded shapes.

We soon reach a major obstacle: below us is a wide gully (H) and a large slab yellow with lichen in its upper part and smooth and black at sea level. Wave action has contrived to create a problem as the gully does not totally dry out on many occasions. If escape is the only option it is safest to reverse our steps and exit on the far side of the bay. It is possible to escape from our present position by climbing the grass left of the loose rocks which hang over the headwall of the gully, to a perched boulder and finish up the slab behind this. This route is not technically hard, but a slip could be fatal. It can only be recommended for those who climb regularly and have a head for heights. We emerge from this escape at La Prevôté Watchtower.

We can tackle the gully on a 9.1-metre tide (with a short paddle), or totally dry on a 9.4-metre tide. It is easiest to descend the seaward end of the gully and exit up the weedy rocks also at the gully mouth. Continuing on beyond the gully we reach an inlet where there is a low arch (I). Heading around the landward side of the rock barrier which faces us, we pass beneath a cliff which is initially very undercut at its base. At the far end of this cliff we can scramble up (II) and join a faint path which leads through the disused quarry below the tower, and so back to the car park.

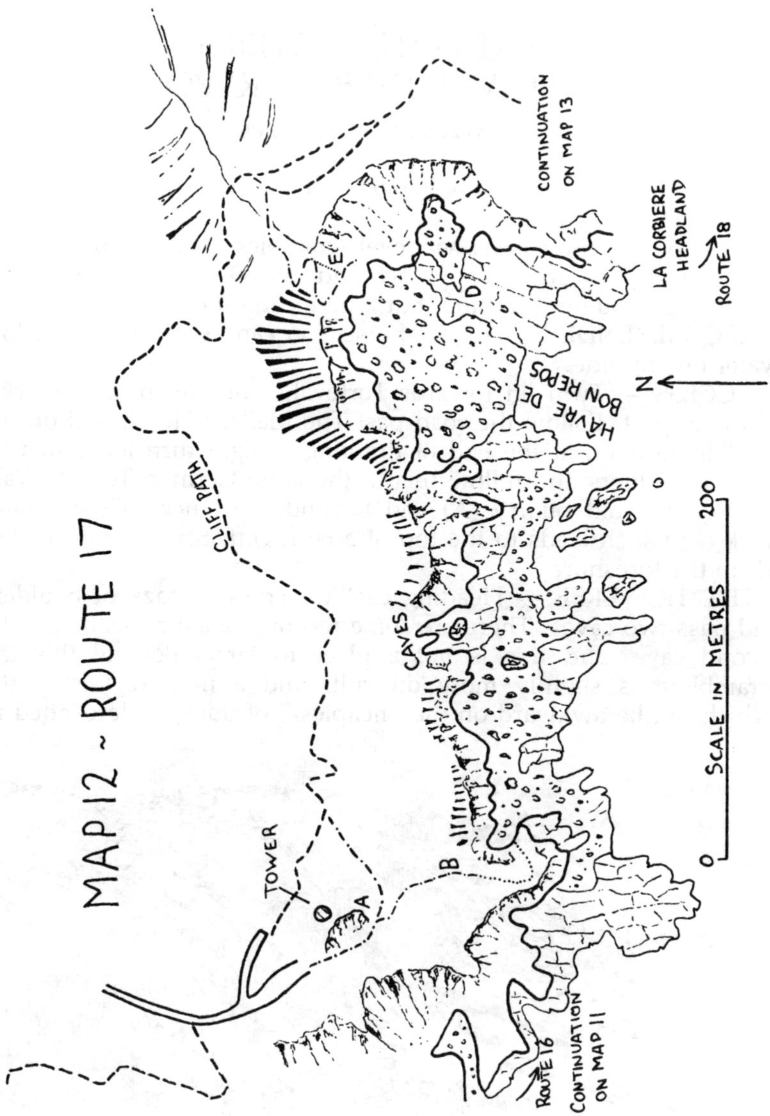
MAP 12 ~ ROUTE 17
CLIFF PATH
TOWER
A
B
CAVES
C
D
E
HÂVRE DE BON REPOS
N
SCALE IN METRES
0
200
LA CORBIERE HEADLAND
ROUTE 18
CONTINUATION ON MAP 13
ROUTE 16
CONTINUATION ON MAP 11

ROUTE 17 A sea level scramble

MAP 12

LA PREVÔTÉ TOWER TO LE HAVRE DE BON REPOS

DISTANCE — 0.3 miles

GRADE — II

THIS is one of the easiest sea level scrambles in the guide. Indeed the hardest parts are the approach and exit! Once at sea level there is plenty of boulder jumping, but little technical difficulty.

RECOMMENDED TIDE — The section can be completed at low water on any tide.

ACCESS — Turn off towards Torteval, a quarter of a mile west of the airport. Follow the road past The Mallard Hotel, and on the right hand bend at the end of the long straight turn left down La Rue des Peltiers and follow this to the large German Tower. Walk through the old quarry (A) and beyond the fence follow a faint track (B) which leads to the top of a 60 ft cliff. Scramble down left (II) to the foreshore.

THE TRAVERSE — Heading east we cross a maze of boulders and pass two caves. There are some recently fallen rocks below the second cave, and this is not a place to tarry! Beyond this the scrambling is slightly more difficult, and a final rock step (C) (which can be awkward on the "neapiest" of tides) is descended to

WEST FROM LA CORBIERE

the shingle of Le Havre de Bon Repos. "The Harbour of Good Rest" was surely a name given in jest: the rock-studded bay is a maelstrom of crashing waves in a southerly gale. On the far side of the bay is a Venus pool (D) artificially created with careful use of concrete!

Our exit path can be seen zig-zagging up to the skyline "V" at the rear of the bay. The path is suffering from erosion and care is required (II−). About halfway up cut directly up an easy slab (E) to a low drystone wall, thus avoiding the badly collapsing section. The cliff path is joned in a small valley.

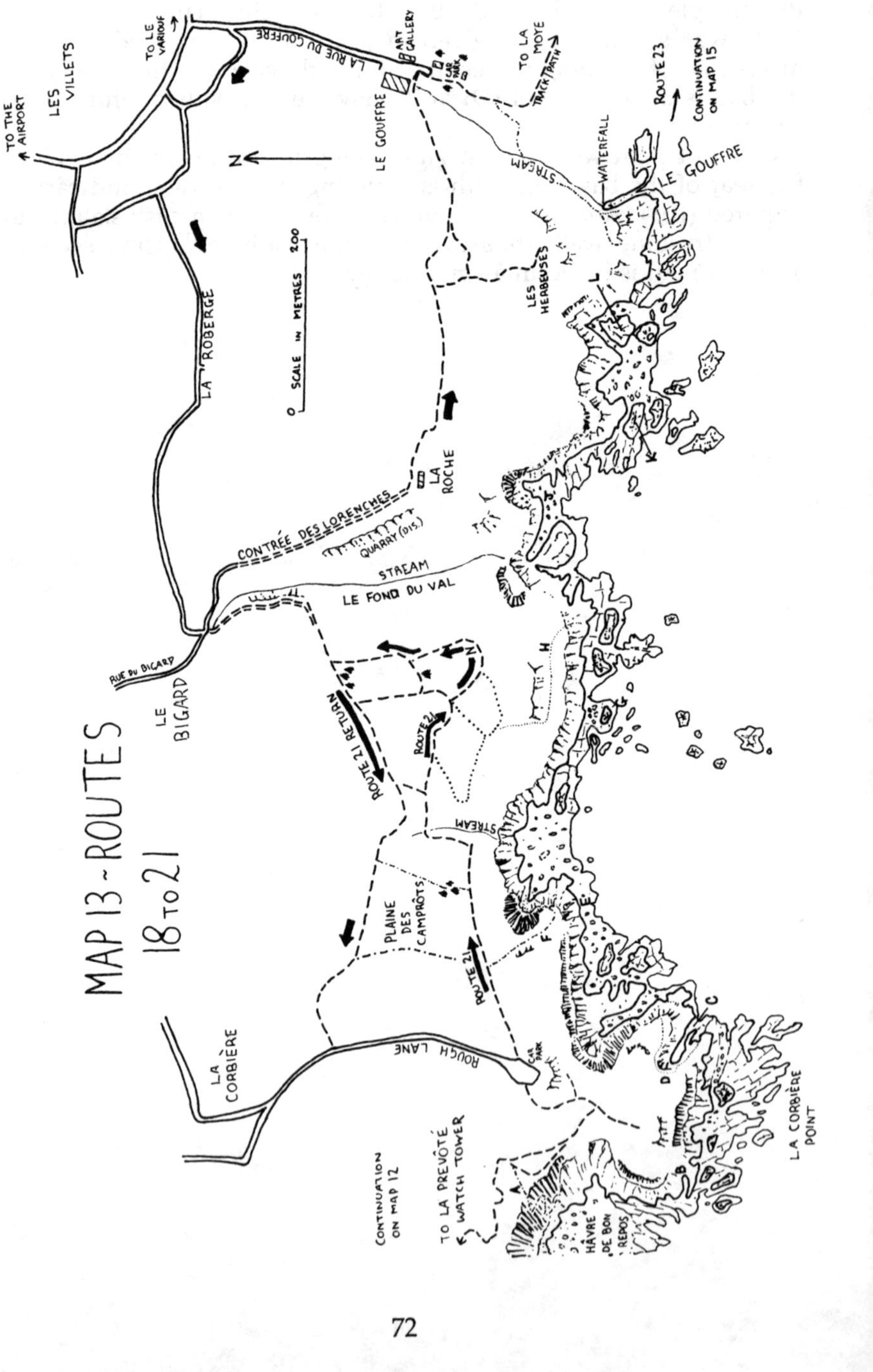
MAP 13 ~ ROUTES
18 TO 21
TO THE AIRPORT
LES VILLETS
TO LE VARIOUF
LA RUE DU GOUFFRE
ART GALLERY
CAR PARK
LE GOUFFRE
TO LA MOYE
TRACK/PATH
N
STREAM
WATERFALL
ROUTE 23
CONTINUATION ON MAP 15
LE GOUFFRE
LES HERBEUSES
0 SCALE IN METRES 200
LA ROBERGE
LA ROCHE
CONTRÉE DES LORENCHES
QUARRY (DIS.)
STREAM
LE FOND DU VAL
RUE DU BIGARD
LE BIGARD
ROUTE 21 RETURN
ROUTE 21
STREAM
PLAINE DES CAMPRÔTS
ROUTE 21
LA CORBIÈRE
ROUGH LANE
CAR PARK
CONTINUATION ON MAP 12
TO LA PREVÔTÉ WATCH TOWER
HAVRE DE BON REPOS
LA CORBIÈRE POINT

ROUTE 18 A sea level scramble

MAP 13

LA CORBIÈRE HEADLAND

DISTANCE — 0.7 miles

GRADE — V

A short but very challenging route! The views from the tip of La Corbière Point are among the most impressive on the island, and a short diversion is recommended. To the east are the cliffs of Le Bigard, above a distinctive black "X" of doleritic sills, and in the distance is the headland known as Pointe de la Moye (Point of the Stack), with its pair of rising black sills. On the horizon beyond the point is the southern tip of Little Sark, with the islet of L'Etaq (The Stack) off its tip. Le Gouffre, the objective in a later section, is tucked in between Le Bigard and Point de la Moye. To the west we can pick out the stack of Le Tas de Pois d'Aval, or Gull Rock, at Pleinmont.

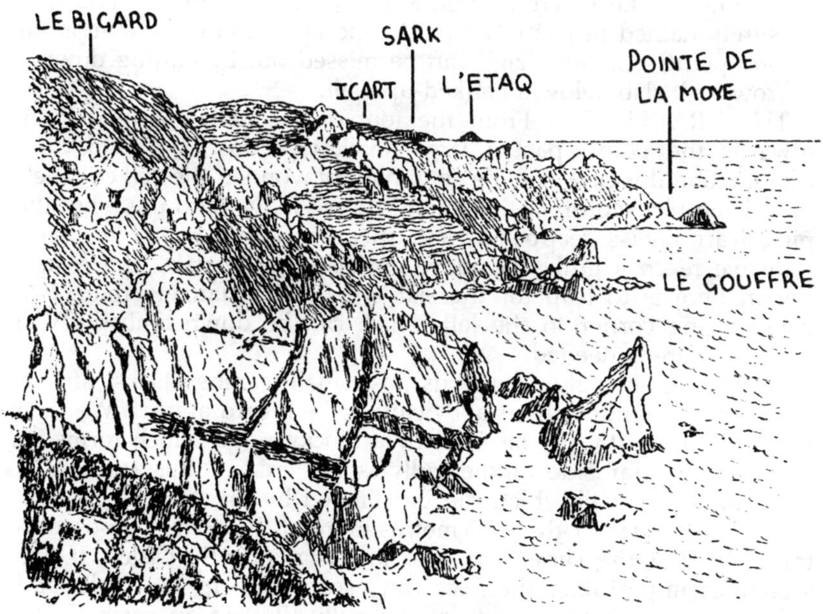

EAST FROM LA CORBIÈRE HEADLAND

A close examination of the rocks in front of the car park reveals some ancient foundations. These are all that remain of La Corbière castle, a Medieval fortress. There is also a low earthern rampart across the headland, possibly the remains of an Iron Age fort. More recent additions are the numerous bunkers and gun placements from the German occupation. La Corbière translates to "The Crow's Nest", or "Rookery".

As to the scramble itself, there is one very hard but short section up an undercut wall. However, it is possible to detour up the cliff to avoid this and the grade of the traverse drops to a more ameniable III−. There are several points of escape, so if the tide is picked carefully, the chances of becoming cut off are minimal.

RECOMMENDED TIDE — 8.2 metre minimum. If the tide is less extreme, the crux section will be awash. Set off about 40 minutes before low water.

ACCESS — Turn on to La Rue de la Villiaze, a quarter of a mile west of the airport. Continue past The Mallard Country Club and around the bend; La Corbière is signed on the left.

From the car park on the point follow the cliff path west into the valley towards La Prevôté Watch Tower. Before the valley floor is reached, take a path on the left, which zig-zags down to the rocky bay known as Le Havre de Bon Repos (The Harbour of Good Rest — surely named in jest!) The path is decayed and quite dangerous at one point, but this "zig" can be missed out by cutting down a narrow rock slab below a banked-up wall.

THE TRAVERSE — From the foot of the path we head back towards the point, past a large shallow Venus Pool. On close examination this proves to be an unnatural wonder: the exit channels have been blocked off with cement! As we move onto the point the pink Icart gneiss reappears, and the scrambling is not technical until we reach a gully (B) above an easy-angled slab. The easiest option here is to leap for the slab (III−). Alternatively there is a overhanging corner to the left which can be downclimbed (IV−) but great care is needed.

Easy scrambling then takes us past small leaning stacks, and as the point is rounded, the slabby cliffs of Le Bigard appear. We then reach a wide gully (C) bisected by a blocky ridge which forms an arch. On the far side of the gully is the crux of this traverse: a short undercut wall which can be climbed by the vertical grey sill (V). On a tide larger than 8.2 metres more of the wall is exposed to the right, but the climb does not look significantly easier. If this section is impassable, then we can escape (D) up the rocks and steep grass on the west side of the gully (II−) to an earthy bowl with a dry stone retaining wall. To regain the car park continue upwards; to rejoin the traverse beyond the hard section cut across the back of the gully, then down the ridge beyond. On the east side of this a faint track leads back down to sea level.

Beyond this we enter an inlet, and thread our way through a maze of small stacks and large boulders below the cliffs of Les Carriers (The Quarries). Exiting from these, we pass under a small red-coloured crag (E). In March 1913, an 86-ton French ketch, *Jenne,* en route from Spain to Dunkirk, hit the rocks at this point. The vessel was beyond repair; all of value was taken off her, including the 40-ton cargo of ore. Scrambling beyond the rocks, we reach a large bay, backed by impressive but loose and vegetated walls: a high-rise tenament for nesting birds in the spring.

If the difficult section was completed at low water, then we have enough time to complete the traverse of Le Bigard (description continued in Route 19). If we are calling it a day, then we must escape at this point. On the west (near) side of the bay is a large combe full of scree and rocks. A path cuts across the scree and then back leftwards up the side of a grassy slope. At the top of this a track (F) leads to the cliff path, and a short walk brings us back to the headland.

ROUTE 19 A sea level scramble

MAP 13

LE BIGARD

DISTANCE — 0.5 miles

GRADE — II or II+, depending on tide state.

THE traverse of Le Bigard cliffs is a tremendous outing, nowhere particularly hard but with lots of interest. It passes beneath some of the most impressive cliffs on the island, and the lack of escape routes gives a sense of isolation. In the spring the rock walls are dotted with nesting seabirds, and the clifftops are a blaze of colour with flowering campion, furze and sea thrift.

A fast party will be able to complete the logical continuation to Le Gouffre, or even traverse from La Corbière to Le Gouffre given a big tide.

RECOMMENDED TIDE — 6.6 metres, which makes this possible on most low tides. If in doubt as to whether the tide is suitable for the traverse, descend part of the way down descent route F. On the far side of the bay a stack forms a "V" notch with a small slab on its left. If the foot of this "V" is dry, then the route is feasible.

ACCESS — Start from La Corbière as for previous section.

THE TRAVERSE — Turn east along the cliff path, and after about 100 yards (just beyond a small rise) take a faint track on the right through the bracken. This takes us beneath an outcrop to a small grassy point. A track then leads down leftwards across a grassy slope to a scree-filled combe, which is descended to the bay. Here we are dwarfed by the towering (and tottering) cliffs which form the backwall. Several caves cut into the base of the cliffs and a small stream tumbles down over 200 ft to the beach.

We exit from the bay through a gully between a stack and an undercut slab. The first boulder in the gully can be a little awkward, though it is just possible to squeeze underneath it! Emerging from the gully we have two options: we can descend to beach level and climb a short rock step (II) to gain a higher platform. The beach will just be dry at low water on an 8.2 metre tide. Alternatively if the beach is flooded we can follow a rising grey sill which cuts up from the base of the cliff, and over the top of a small black slab beneath a large quartzy bulge. Beyond this we down climb to a black ledge (II+, quite exposed).

CLIFFS OF LE BIGARD
ROUTE 19 FEASIBLE
IF THIS AREA IS CLEAR

We then pass under the main slab, undercut at its place. Some of the island's best rock climbs thread their way up these walls, and indeed this was the birthplace of Guernsey rock climbing in the early 1970s. The fracture planes in the gneiss are in evidence here. The rock beneath the slab has slid away, and the massive slab above our heads will surely follow it to a watery grave some time in the future. Let's keep moving!

Beyond the slab is a gully which forms a cave under the cliff foot. This has formed a blow-hole (which no longer works), and it is possible for climbers to emerge from the cave halfway up the cliff. Beyond the gully we can climb up higher, or alternatively traverse near sea level. If the water is clear you might see the occasional flash of silver in the depths. These are mullet: a large shoal frequents this area, where they can be seen grazing on the algae-covered rocks. The stack on our right (G) can be reached two hours either side of low water, when it can be traversed and there is excellent climbing on its seaward face.

Ahead is a "V" notch. Here we can either go down and to the right and follow a blocky gully beneath a small vertical cliff (low water on spring tides necessary). Alternatively a high level route takes us along a knife-edge and through the notch, where we can either descend a gully to sea level or a traverse along an eroded channel leads above the gully (II+) in quite an exposed position. Here we reach the end of Le Bigard traverse. Those who want to continue to Le Gouffre have no time to relax: that section lies within the next 150 yards.

For our exit route we scramble off at this point, and follow a faint track (H) across the top of an earthy bowl and through some rocky outcrops. Beyond these we head up and right and we eventually arrive on Le Plaine des Camprôts, which is criss-crossed by numerous paths. Follow your nose to La Corbière!

ROUTE 20 A sea level traverse

MAP 13

LE BIGARD TO LE GOUFFRE

DISTANCE — 0.6 miles

GRADE — III–

THE first 150 yards can give some exciting moments if the tide is reaching a critical point. After this the difficulty relents and more rapid progress can be made. There are no escapes once the initial crux section is passed. The views across to Pointe de la Moye are superb, and Le Gouffre (The Gulf or Chasm) is a beautiful spot. Here a waterfall tumbles from a little-frequented valley over the lip of a cave into the narrow rift which gives the place its name.

ACCESS — Start from Le Gouffre. This can be reached by taking the first turning west of the airport entrance, La Rue du Mort, and following it to the restaurant and art gallery. Head west along the cliff path to the picturesque hamlet of Le Bigard (The Sheep Pen). It is quite difficult to find the start of the traverse from here: the heath has a myriad of paths and so the description here is necessarily detailed.

From Le Bigard we take the lane signed to La Corbière. As we emerge in the open the valley of Le Fond du Val is on our left. This is a delightful place in the spring when the bracken is relatively dormant and the daffodils are rampant. Continuing along the cliff path, there are three pines ahead. Turn left just before these, pass

PINE TREE, LE PLAINE DES CAMPRÔTS

a single pine and then reach another solitary pine. We are now on the foundations of an old house and around us are the stumps of the pines' companions, which demised in the hurricane of 1987. Passing the pine on its right, we reach a "crossroad" after 30 yards. Turn left, and at the next crossroad go straight over past a small granite block with a carved "P", to a "T-junction". Turn left and after 20 feet turn right down a faint track to a small rocky outcrop. Head left 30 feet to a second outcrop then go down the far side of this (poor track) to the cliff top. Follow a better track left through rocks, then curve around an earthy bowl and head down to a white flat-topped boulder. From here we can see much of the traverse. We will pass through the bay below the scarred brown cliff, under the grey and pink slabs and across to a triangular-shaped stack in the middle distance. This is near Le Gouffre, our destination. In the far distance is the rugged ridge of Pointe de la Moye ("Point of the Stack").

RECOMMENDED TIDE — 8.2 metres

THE TRAVERSE — Ahead of us is a grey face, and the first problem is to reach the gully on its far side. The easiest way is to crawl under a boulder choke which has formed between the foot of the face and the small rounded stack to the right. Emerging from the crawl we see a cave on our left. We can climb out of the back of this via a small hole, or alternatively climb above the cave from the right (II). An awkward descent is then made down a smooth narrow chimney (III−) to the next gully. If this is followed we arrive at the foot of Le Fond du Val, where a stream falls to the beach. We then make easy progress past a grey wall, over a bouldery bay (J) to reach an elongated knife-edge stack (K). Past this there is a wide gully and pointed stack (L) on the left. There are several options here, the easiest of which is to follow the gully round the landward face of the stack.

Beyond this some excellent traversing can be made across the bottom of several slabs (II+) until we arrive at the inlet of Le Gouffre, which can be crossed on an 8.4-metre tide. At the back of the gully is a cave with a stream flowing over its lip and it is possible to scramble behind the fall when the gully is dry. This is a lovely spot, and it is rare to meet other people here. To the left of the inlet is a white cliff (M). The easiest option here is to scramble around its left-hand side and then down to the head of the fall. A harder variation can be made by traversing across the slab below the cliff, to escape up small slabs just left of the fall (III−), with a loose finish.

LE GOUFFRE

Our exit route is to follow the left-hand bank of the valley upstream. Cross on to the right-hand bank beyond the blackthorn bushes, and 30 feet before a thicket head up the valley side to a lane which leads to the car park.

ROUTE 21 A cliff walk returning along lanes and paths

MAP 13

LA CORBIÈRE TO LE GOUFFRE

DISTANCE — 2.3 miles

A LOOP walk taking us over the heathland at La Corbière to the hamlet of Le Bigard, and along the cliff path to Le Gouffre. We return via quiet lanes, and take a different route over Plaine des Camprôts to La Corbière.

ACCESS — La Corbière (The Crow nest or Rookery) is one of the larger south coast headlands, and can be reached by turning onto La Route de Pleinmont, about a quarter of a mile west of the airport, and then taking the signed turning on the left; there is ample parking on the point.

The views from the seaward end of the point are excellent, and well worth the short diversion (see notes in Route 18). Heading east along the cliff path there are good views of Pointe de la Moye, and on a clear day Jersey and L'Etaq, the stack off the southern tip of Sark, can be seen. The path skirts inland around a small valley, and beyond the barrier we head right across the heath, Plaine des Camprôts, past log benches. Continuing straight on at the path junction takes us around a loop path with fine views. From the memorial bench (N) we can look down to the eastern cliffs of Le Bigard and across Le Fond du Val with its old quarry to the house at La Roche. The loop continues to a clearing where there is a solitary pine, all that remains of a stand that demised in the hurricane of 1987. The trees once surrounded a house and the foundations can still be seen.

The gorse-covered heath is rich in bird life. Keep a lookout for the rare Dartford Warbler, a bird which is resident all the year and suffers greatly in hard winters. It is now very scarce on the British mainland, but Guernsey still has several nesting pairs. A pair of cuckoos frequent this area, and they can often be seen flying hawk-like over the bushes. On Guernsey April 19th is Le Jour du Coucou, traditionally the date when this harbinger of spring is expected to appear.

From the pine we rejoin the main cliff path, which takes us around Le Fond du Val. This is a lovely valley in the spring when

it is rampant with daffodils. A path leads down to the cliff line where there is a small waterfall and the remains of a ladder constructed from German wire and stakes: a descent can only be recommended for those who tire of life. There are several dry stone constructions in the valley which was intensively cultivated in the past. The path joins a rough lane which curves beneath oak trees and over a marshy stream to the quaint hamlet of Le Bigard ("The Sheep Pen"). Heading rightwards up the road we take a lane on the right which leads us past the beautifully located house of La

Roche, to rejoin the path. Hemmed in by walls, gorse and ivy we have limited views unless we take a diversion to Les Herbeuses. Here we can look east to Pointe de la Moye ("Point of the Stack") and Icart Point ("Rocky Headland" or "Isolated Place"), and from the edge of the rocks we can look down to the gully which gives Le Gouffre ("The Gulf") its name. It is possible to scramble down to this lovely spot, and an exit can be made by following a path up the stream valley (see Route 20).

Continuing along the main cliff path we descend steps past a spring. There is an area of National Trust land on the left where a circular path leads through small trees and heathland rich in bird life (and an enormous ants' nest!). We then descend steps to Le Gouffre Restaurant and an art gallery.

For our return we can head up the road and take the turning on the left, past a small ruin. At the T junction we turn left onto La Roberge, where we pass two tall chimneys, part of the heating system for greenhouses which have long disappeared, and down to Le Bigard. Here we can retrace our steps onto the cliff path, but instead of heading across the middle of the heath we can continue straight past the National Trust stone below the three pines, and along the path to the rough lane at La Corbière.

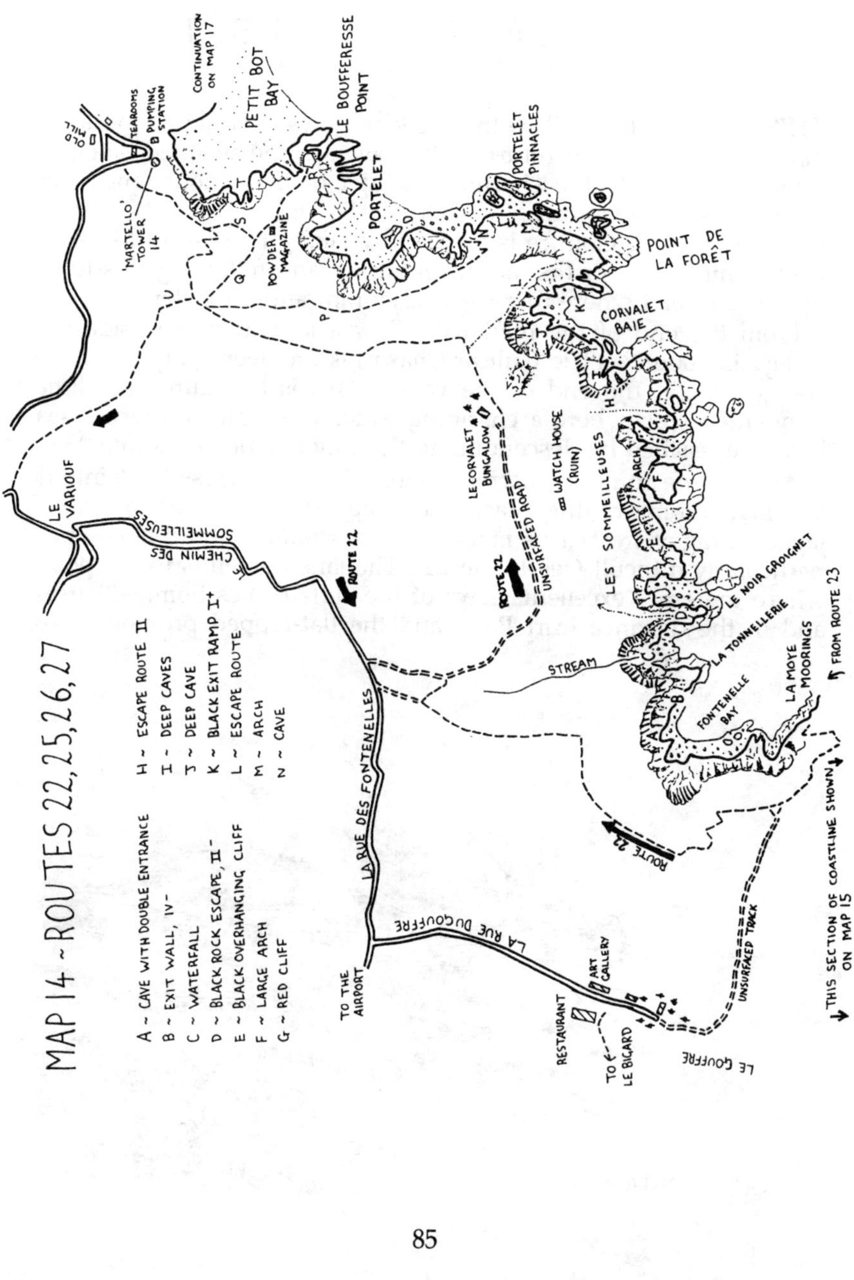

MAP 14 ~ ROUTES 22, 25, 26, 27
A ~ CAVE WITH DOUBLE ENTRANCE
B ~ EXIT WALL, IV-
C ~ WATERFALL
D ~ BLACK ROCK ESCAPE, II-
E ~ BLACK OVERHANGING CLIFF
F ~ LARGE ARCH
G ~ RED CLIFF
H ~ ESCAPE ROUTE II
I ~ DEEP CAVES
J ~ DEEP CAVE
K ~ BLACK EXIT RAMP I+
L ~ ESCAPE ROUTE
M ~ ARCH
N ~ CAVE
LE VARIOUF
CHEMIN DES SOMMEILLEUSES
LA RUE DES FONTENELLES
LA RUE DU GOUFFRE
TO THE AIRPORT
ART GALLERY
RESTAURANT
TO LE BIGARD
LE GOUFFRE
UNSURFACED TRACK
UNSURFACED ROAD
ROUTE 22
ROUTE 23
LE CORVALET BUNGALOW
WATCH HOUSE (RUIN)
LES SOMMEILLEUSES
STREAM
FONTENELLE BAY
LA TONNELLERIE
LE NOIR GROIGNET
LA MOYE MOORINGS
FROM ROUTE 23
THIS SECTION OF COASTLINE SHOWN ON MAP 15
CORVALET BAIE
POINT DE LA FORÊT
PORTELET PINNACLES
PORTELET
POWDER MAGAZINE
LE BOUFFERESSE POINT
PETIT BOT BAY
CONTINUATION ON MAP 17
'MARTELLO' TOWER 14
TEAROOMS
PUMPING STATION
OLD MILL

ROUTE 22 A cliff walk, returning along the lanes and paths

MAP 14

LE GOUFFRE TO PETIT BÔT

DISTANCE — 2.25 miles

THIS is a fine cliff walk with excellent views, leading to the lovely bay at Petit Bôt. The return path traverses the wooded slopes of Petit Bôt valley to the charming hamlet of Le Variouf, and along quiet lanes to Le Gouffre.

ACCESS — Le Gouffre is reached by taking La Rue du Mort, the first turning west of the airport entrance, and following this to the end of the road where there is a restaurant and art gallery.

From the end of the road we follow a lane along the side of a valley. Le Gouffre (The Gulf or Chasm) is the deep gully below the craggy area at the end of the valley. This is a picturesque, little-frequented spot where a charming waterfall cascades into the sea. It can be reached by descending to the valley floor (see Route 23).

As the lane rounds a corner, there are views across to Pointe de la Moye (Point of the Stack), a steep-sided promontory with a jagged, craggy crest. This makes a good scramble and it is nowhere particularly difficult (see Route 24). The lane descends to the point, where there are excellent views of the cliffs of Les Sommeilleuses, and in the distance Icart Point and the flat-topped promontory of

Chateau d'Icart. The dark rift below the skyline trees is Creux au Tchian, or Dog's Cave.

A short diversion can be made down to La Moye mooring, a fascinating little harbour with an ingenious slipway and winch by which boats can be hauled up to the platform constructed on the rocks. It was much frequented by smugglers in the last century. It was one of the planned landing places in Operation Ambassador, mounted shortly after the start of the German Occupation (see Route 34). Towards low water it is possible to scramble round to the caves in Les Fontenelles Bay. The nearest is one of the longest sea caves in Guernsey, but the most atmospheric is on the far side of the bay and needs a spring tide to enter it. Here a hole in the cave's roof creates an eerie glow in the depths, which open out like a bottle behind the narrow tunnel entrance (A).

CAVE, LES FONTENELLES

Continuing along the main cliff path a long flight of steps takes us high up around the back of Les Fontonelles Bay. We then divert inland around a wooded valley where a trough, known as an abreuveur, has been built to catch the spring water, and on to an unsurfaced lane which takes us along Les Sommeilleuses (The Sleepers). At the parking spaces there is a path to the remains of a Napoleonic watch house. In a much better state of preservation is the powder magazine a little further on: the battery which it was built to supply has now disappeared.

After passing Le Corvalet bungalow we reach a viewpoint, with Petit Bôt just visible down on the left. The path then descends towards the bay, and a path (P) leads off on the right and zig-zags down to Portelet (Little Harbour). This was used as a haven in poor weather until the mid-1800s, when the slipway finally crumbled away, never to be repaired. Retaining walls and some mooring posts are all that remain today. The old harbour is worth a visit, and there is a fascinating cave (N) which has one entrance above the other, forming a perfect arch. This can be reached near low water by scrambling round to the south (right). The beach at Portelet has good bathing, and the scramble which is necessary to reach it keeps the crowds away. Watch the tide though: it is easy to become stranded!

Returning almost to the main cliff path, there is a turning on the right (Q) which descends past a powder magazine to St Clair Battery (R) which was constructed on Le Boufferesse Point some 15 years after the "Martello" Tower, at the outbreak of the French Revolutionary Wars. When in use it had two 24-pounder guns. Each battery has a powder magazine situated some distance away in case of explosion. Eric Grimsley suggests in his study of the Martello Towers that this may be a lesson learnt from an accident at Castle Cornet, when lightning struck the magazine and the resulting explosion demolished much of the castle and blew the Governor, still in his bed, on to the battlements.

From the battery we can see Portelet, and an arch just beyond the pinnacle on the headland. Towards low water it is possible to scramble from the battery to the beach at Petit Bôt (look out for a narrow tunnel, where a very tight squeeze gives access to one of the inlets).

Returning past the magazine we can take a right turn (S) to rejoin the main path and descend to the valley floor.

There is much of interest around this attractive, usually-sheltered bay. The wooded valley is another example of periglacial erosion (see note in Route 12), and at one time there were two mills, utilizing the tiny stream to grind corn and make paper from rags.

The latter mill is now the tea room, and several millstones have been built into the terrace behind the building. The upper mill is in ruins amongst the trees behind the terrace and a picturesque waterfall tumbles over a chute where the mill wheel once turned. The miller's cottage is a short distance up the east road. The earliest recording of a mill in Petit Bôt is 1248.

The Luftwaffe had their Guernsey headquarters at Le Manoir Hotel during the Occupation, and the Germans brought many changes to the valley during their years here. The lower mill was at this time the Old Mill House Hotel, and was largely demolished. A second hotel stood just to the west of the "Martello" Tower, and this was completely removed: all that remains now are the foundations around a flat grassy area, a perfect picnic spot.

The "Martello" Tower is the first we have met on our walks, and is worthy of description. These towers are unique to Guernsey, and fifteen were constructed around the island's shores. This is tower number 13, erected in 1778 at a cost of £100. They were built as a "stop-gap" measure, hurriedly thrown up when France became allies of the American colonists who were fighting for independence. The French declared war on Britain in 1778, and half-heartedly attempted to invade Jersey in 1779. They were more successful the following year and marched right into St Helier before being driven off. Fears of an imminent attack on Guernsey led to the hasty improvisation of these structures, which were completed in the remarkably short time of eight months to become the first coastal towers built in the British Isles. Their purpose was to give a height

PINNACLES AND ARCH, PORTELET

advantage to musketry, not to carry cannons (there was a severe shortage of artillery at that time). It was not until 1803 that General John Doyle, the newly appointed Lieutenant-Governor, ordered the addition of a cannonade at the top. It is doubtful whether the towers would have stood up to a cannon attack, with their narrow diameter (20 feet) in relation to their height. They certainly bear little resemblance to the true Martello Towers which were based on the Corsican gun tower at Mortella Point which so impressed the British Navy with its resilience in 1794. Thus Guernsey's towers will always be termed "Martello" Towers, with inverted commas, as they predate the genuine model by some fifteen years. The island does, however, have three true Martello Towers, though they are not generally referred to as such: Fort Grey in Rocquaine Bay, Fort Saumarez at L'Erée and Fort Hommet near Vazon.

VARIOUF

On old documents the area is called Tibo and Petit Bosq. Bosq is Guernesiaise for woody, and the valley must have been wooded since man first arrived here. The bay itself dries out into a sandy beach as the tide falls, and there are no tidal currents for the swimmer to worry about. There is much to explore: on the eastern side of the bay is a cave with a tunnel that provides a rear exit, and there are several sandy gullies with clear rock pools. There are more caves on the western shores of the bay, and particularly interesting is a cave with a double entrance (T). This is known as Le Parleaux de Monsieur Picot (Mr Picot's Parlour), named after the Reverend Thomas Picot, the rector of Torteval and Forest parishes in the mid-17th century, who used the cave as a haven for peace and meditation. His other hideaway was Le Creux Mahie.

For our return path we can follow the cliff path (avoiding the St Clair Battery loop) back west to the junction with the Portelet path. A few feet before this junction we can take a right turn on to a pleasant path (V) which contours across the wooded western slopes of the valley to a road. At the road we can head left past a tiny quarry to a tranquil little hamlet which is to be avoided on the full moon: Variouf translates to werewolf! In fact the "varous" were usually men who dressed up in animal skins during pagan festivals, and indulged in all sorts of mischief.

We leave the hamlet by turning left on to Le Chemin des Sommeilleuses. The steep roadsides limit the view, but these Guernsey equivalent of the hedgerow are rampant with plant life and have much to interest the botanist. Keep an eye open for the spike-topped fencing posts. These fearsome objects once supported German barbed wire during the Occupation, and now have a more peaceful purpose. It is possible to rejoin the cliff path by turning left down a green lane by the large white battlemented house, but it is now much quicker to continue along La Rue des Fontenelles to La Rue du Gouffre. Early Christians erected a cross at this junction, Le Croix Forest, as a comfort to travellers in this densely wooded area. A left turn here leads back to our starting point.

ROUTE 23 A sea level scramble

MAP 15

LE GOUFFRE TO LA MOYE

DISTANCE — 0.6 miles

GRADE — II/III–

LE GOUFFRE is a rarely visited but lovely spot. It means "The Gulf" or "Chasm", which refers to the deep gully at the end of the stream valley. Here a waterfall tumbles over the lip of a cave into

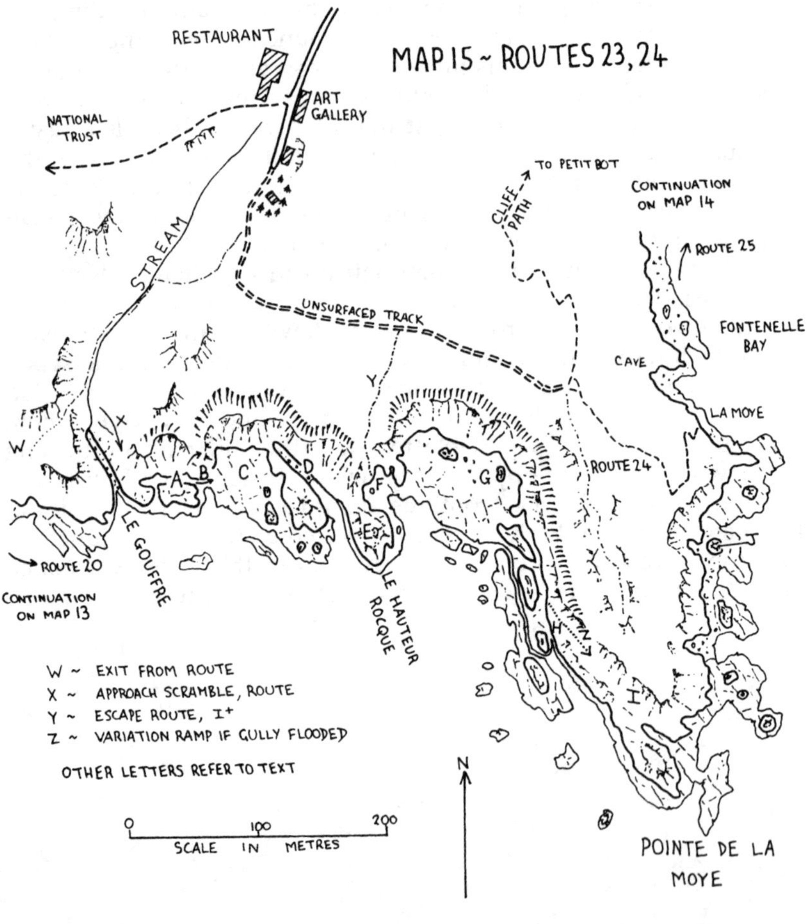

the sea, and when the tide is low enough it is possible to scramble behind the narrow curtain of water.

The stream is very small compared to the size of the valley, which is far too large to have been carved out by today's trickle. In fact, it dates from the Ice Ages when Guernsey had a tundra climate and powerful meltwater streams formed in the spring.

The traverse takes us past caves, Venus Pools, a tunnel and a blow-hole (which hopefully is not working when we arrive!). There are two easy escapes (I+), and the section can be conveniently broken at Pointe de la Moye (Point of the Stack). A fast party could join this section with the previous one from Le Bigard.

RECOMMENDED TIDE — 8.8 metres. With a less extreme tide, short diversions will have to be made around flooded sections, involving scrambles of II+. Le Gouffre to the tip of Pointe de la Moye can be traversed on an 8.3 metre tide.

ACCESS — Take the first turning west of the airport entrance (La Rue du Mort), and follow the road to its end where there is a restaurant and art gallery. Follow the track beyond the gallery and a few yards before the lefthand bend, take a faint path on the right down the valley side to the stream. Follow this to the end of the gully, recross the stream and scramble down on the left to sea level (requires care).

THE TRAVERSE — Heading east we pass a long Venus Pool (A), then drop down below a small cliff (B) with a steep base and narrow cave. If this is flooded, climb up the lefthand side of the cliff, then drop down its far side (II+). We then enter a bay (C) and cross the landward end of a deep gully, and immediately climb down to a second gully (D). The far wall is the crux of the traverse,

POINTE DE LA MOYE FROM LE GOUFFRE

and its difficulty (II to III−) depends on the tide state. Emerging from this we see a "stack", Le Hauteur Rocque (E), which is joined to the mainland at high water. We can make an entertaining traverse around this, or more easily cut through the gap. There is an escape path (Y) on the left at this point (I+).

We now drop down to a gully with a cave (F) tucked beneath large overhangs. A little further is a second gully, best tackled at its seaward end, and quickest progress is made by following this to the high water mark. The rocks here are liberally coated with oil, the worst pollution we will meet on the coast. Halfway across the bay, we pass a rock pillar with a tunnel (G) carved through it, and beyond we can follow a gully running below the cliff.

At the seaward end of this gully are two dark sills of dolerite (H) which rise up from right to left. The gully below these needs a low tide to continue (8.75 metres). If it is flooded we can escape (I+) up the ramp (Z) below the higher of the two sills. A track leads from here, along the crest of the point and back to the cliff path. To continue we can downclimb to rejoin the traverse, and pass to the right of a cliff (I). Beyond this Icart Point comes into view, with its flat-topped promontory known as Chateau d'Icart, or Goat Island.

Rounding the point, we reach a gully with a cave and a blow-hole. If this is flooded, we can make a short diversion on the left. Beyond this we thread our way through gullies and stacks which presumably give the headland its name. One pinnacle of rock (J), has a gravity-defying boss of pebbles and boulders which look to be held together with nothing more substantial than sand. This is geologically known as "head", the product of freeze-thaw erosion during Guernsey's periglacial climate. Beyond this is a platform of rock which hisses loudly if the swell is large enough, and gives quite a start to the unwary! Close examination reveals high pressure air bubbling into a thin rock pool. Given time it may evolve into a fully-grown blow-hole!

Rounding the corner, we can see La Moye mooring a few yards away. Tucked behind the headland, this old harbour provides a haven from the southwesterly gales. Large blocks form a drystone retaining wall which has been used to create a storage area. The winch and slipway are an ingenious method of hoisting up the fishing boats to the platform. The area is said to have been a haunt of smugglers until the turn of the nineteenth century.

Steps lead up to the cliff path, and it is only a short distance along the track, albeit uphill, to the carpark at Le Gouffre.

ROUTE 24 A walk with a short ridge scramble

MAP 15

LA POINTE DE LA MOYE

DISTANCE — 1 mile

GRADE — I+

A SHORT but very enjoyable excursion, without any worries of being cut off or swamped by monster waves! Pointe de la Moye is the closest feature Guernsey has to a mountain ridge, and if you ignore the sea to either side it's possible to imagine oneself to be on a Lake District fell or Scottish peak!

ACCESS — Start as for the previous section, but follow the track to its end above La Moye mooring.

A faint track leads south along the crest of the ridge, with occasional deviations to either side. There are tremendous views: to the east can be seen Icart Point with its flat-topped promontory known either as Chateau d'Icart or more commonly as Goat Island. Further into the bay is the large black hole of La Creux au Tchien (Dog's Cave), Bette Bay and Jaonnet Bay. Petit Bot is out of sight behind the headlands and cliffs of Les Sommeilleuses (The Sleepers). To the west we can see La Corbière Point, and the cliffs of Le Gouffre.

The easiest way back is to retrace our footsteps. Given a low enough tide and scrambling experience, it is possible to descend the higher of the two black sills and head back along the shoreline to Le Gouffre (see Route 23).

ROUTE 25 A sea level scramble

MAP 14

LA MOYE TO PORTELET

DISTANCE — 0.85 miles

GRADE — V

A TREMENDOUS expedition, taking us beneath the wild precipices of Les Sommeilleuses (The Sleepers). It involves a great deal of committment and there are several difficult sections requiring a positive approach. Due to its serious nature, it should only be attempted by relatively experienced rock climbers, and a careful choice of tide must be made.

RECOMMENDED TIDE — 8.8 metres

ACCESS — Park as for the last section, and set off about 50 minutes before low water. Follow the cliff path in an easterly direction towards Pointe de la Moye. The moorings are below the end of the track and we look out onto Les Fontenelle Bay, our first objective.

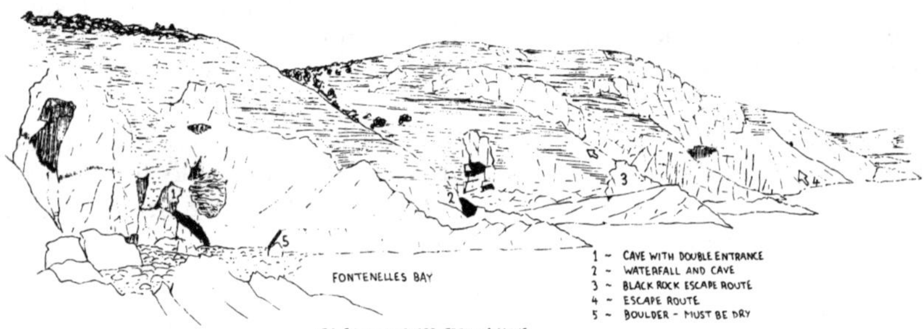

LES SOMMEILLEUSES FROM LA MOYE

THE TRAVERSE — Before setting off check to see if the tide has ebbed sufficiently: on the far side of the bay is a short steep wall. Below this is a large boulder, to the left of which is a right-left trending dyke cutting across the wall. This is the key to the exit, and the rocks at the dyke's base must be dry.

From the moorings scramble down into the bay. There are several caves worth exploring, particularly the one on the far side of the bay where light enters from high up to create an eerie effect (A). The escape up the dyke (B) is steep but there are good holds (IV−). Easy scrambling then takes us round La Tonnellerie and a waterfall (C) comes into view. After descending into the first gully, an awkward climb (III−) can be made up a grey nose between two cracks. A short easy descent gains the foot of the fall which cascades over the mouth of a very deep cave, Le Creux Gravier.

Leaving the gully at this point we round a small promontory, Le Noir Groignet (D). "Black Rock" is painted on the slab at this point, and there is an escape up a faint track (II−). Continuing on we pass a black overhanging cliff (E) and two caves. A superb arch (F) makes a convenient escape to a gully where a major difficulty faces us: the far wall is steep and smooth. It is possible to climb a crack near the left hand (inland) side of the gully wall (V−, very hard low down). On a 9.5 metre tide it *may* be possible to leave the gully at its seaward end (unconfirmed). We then work our way to a gully below a reddish cliff (G) and take a rising left-right weakness (III−) out of this. A few yards further on there is an escape (H) on the left (II−).

We are soon faced by a bay with a veined vertical wall at the back. After a short descent (II) there are two caves (I) immediately on our left. A narrow chasm provides an escape into the main part of Corvalet Baie, where one of the deepest caves (J) in Guernsey is found. Our exit from the bay is up a left-right rising black ramp (I+) below towering cliffs (K).

From the top of the ramp an escape (II−) can be made to the cliff path (L): traverse horizontally along a ledge to a small knoll, then take the grassy gully on the left (a fisherman's rope may be in place). Move up and right, then follow a poor track through the bushes to emerge by La Corvalet bungalow.

Continuing on we descend to pass beneath a small overhanging cliff, then traverse above a gully to reach an arch (M). Passing under this we confront Portelet Pinnacles. The traverse around these is II+, but the quickest exit is through the gully on the left, squeezing past a huge jammed block. There is a cave (N) with an interesting arch feature on the left, and the old mooring posts of Portelet can be seen.

Our exit takes us up the steps to join a good path (P) which leads to the main cliff path, where the signs to Le Gouffre should be followed.

ROUTE 26 A sea level scramble

MAP 14

PORTELET TO LES SOMMEILLEUSES

DISTANCE — 0.6 miles

GRADE — II−

THIS excursion merely takes the last section of the previous route in reverse and takes us past Portelet Pinnacles to the large caves below Les Sommeilleuses. It is a worthwhile scramble and avoids the grade V− horrors of the complete west to east traverse.

ACCESS — Start from Petit Bôt and take the cliff path west (signed Portelet/Le Gouffre). A long flight of steps leads up to a path junction and there are excellent views to Chateau d'Icart, the flat-topped promontory to the south-east. On the west side of Petit Bôt are the sharp rocks of the Portelet Pinnacles. Continuing on we reach a number of paths and follow the sign for Portelet (P).

THE TRAVERSE — From the foot of the steps we turn right, scramble down to beach level (this can be a little awkward) and soon reach an interesting cave (N) with an arch feature. On the edge of the bay we pass Portelet Pinnacles and then head through an arch. Several options of varying difficulty are open to us until we reach Corvalet Baie, below steep cliffs. The bay can be reached by descending a black ramp (I+), and several of the island's deepest caves can be explored. We can either retrace our steps to Portelet, or take escape L, which at present is quite overgrown.

PETIT BÔT

ROUTE 27 A sea level scramble

MAP 14

PORTELET TO PETIT BÔT

DISTANCE — 0.15 miles

GRADE — III+ to VI

THIS short section can prove surprisingly difficult, and care is necessary. The grade varies markedly with the tide.

RECOMMENDED TIDE — 8.2 metres (grade VI), 9 metres (grade IV−), 9.4 metres (grade III).

ACCESS — As for Route 26

THE TRAVERSE — From the end of the path an easy scramble leads leftwards into Portelet, and we cross the bay to a series of gullies. These present no problems until we meet a cleft some 10 feet wide and up to 60 feet deep. On a 9 metre tide it is possible to descend to the gully floor and climb the seaward end of the far wall at grade IV−. On a larger tide the easier chimney further to the right can be used (III+).

On less extreme tides it is not possible to cross the gully, and we can then climb the steep wall 15 feet left of the arete, using an obvious flake. We then make an exciting traverse above the overhanging gulf to safety. Although not technically too difficult (rock climbing grade "Severe") this deserves a grade of VI as the results of a slip would be very nasty. If in doubt head back to Portelet.

Whichever route is taken, we can descend to a wider gully. A surprising exit can be made through a narrow tunnel which leads out of the back wall (not to be attempted after a large lunch). Alternatively we can scramble out the seaward end of the gully, and into Petit Bôt.

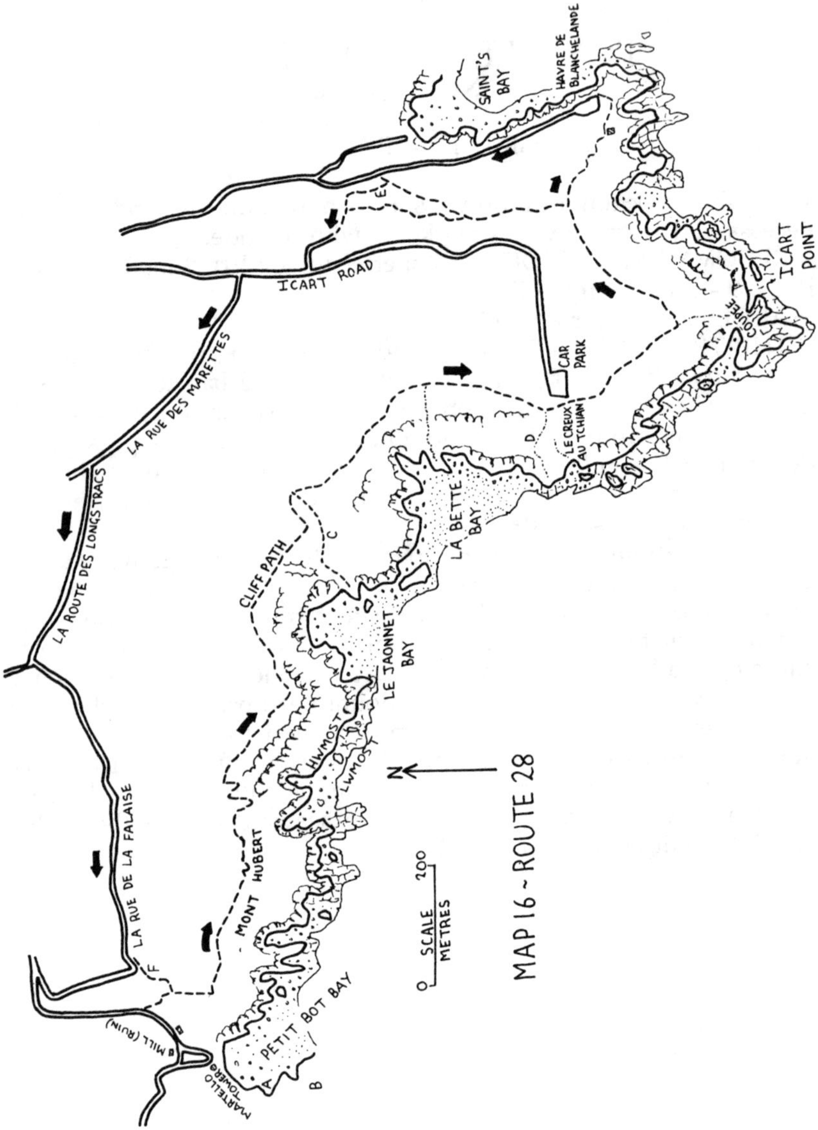
MAP 16 ~ ROUTE 28
SCALE
METRES
0
200
N
SAINT'S BAY
HAVRE DE BLANCHELANDE
ICART POINT
COUPÉE
ICART ROAD
CAR PARK
LE CREUX AU TCHIAN
LA BETTE BAY
LE JAONNET BAY
HWMOST
LWMOST
CLIFF PATH
MONT HUBERT
PETIT BOT BAY
MARTELLO TOWER
MILL (RUIN)
LA RUE DE LA FALAISE
LA ROUTE DES LONGS TRACS
LA RUE DES MARETTES
A
B
C
D
E
F

ROUTE 28 A cliff walk returning along the lanes

MAP 16

PETIT BÔT TO SAINTS BAY

DISTANCE — 3.4 miles

MILLER'S COTTAGE
PETIT BÔT

FIRST we must head up the east road for a short distance beyond the miller's cottage and take the cliff path on the right. At the first junction we head right again to reach the eastern headland of Petit Bôt, where there is a bench. From here we can look west to Portelet, with its zig-zag path, and to St Clair Battery on Petit Bôt's western headland, with the powder magazine nestling in the trees. To the east we can see Icart Point, and the flat-topped promontory known as Chateau d'Icart. To the left of this is the dark rift of Le Creux au Tchian (The Dog's Cave).

Continuing on our way we have good views of the cliffs below Mont Hubert (Hubert's Heights), which although not particularly high, are majestic. We cross two small valleys, and at the second there is a path (C) down to Le Jaonnet Bay. Don't be put off by the "iron ladder" sign, which creates visions of a precarious descent down the cliff: it's only for the last few feet to beach level. When the tide is out the bay has a lovely beach which is never crowded. The bay was the scene of the first raid from England after the Occupation. In July 1940 Guernseyman Hubert Nicolle landed here and collected information for Operation Ambassador (see Route 34).

It is possible to scramble easily round to La Bette Bay, which is perhaps even more picturesque than Le Jaonnet Bay, if the tide is sufficiently low. Le Jaonnet means "Furze Break", a name which dates from the time when furze was a valuable source of fuel to the islanders. La Bette is "Wild Beet".

Returning to the main cliff path we skirt a bracken-filled bowl, where a path leads down to La Bette Bay. This becomes rather steep, and should be approached with care. From the next headland some of the island's magnificent cliff scenery can be enjoyed: it is usually possible to pick out Le Jaonnet and Petit Bôt bays, Les Sommeilleuses and in the far distance the rugged ridge of Pointe de la Moye (Point of the Stack) and Moye moorings. Below our feet are the remains of Icart Battery, constructed during the Napoleonic Wars, and now obliterated by the dense undergrowth.

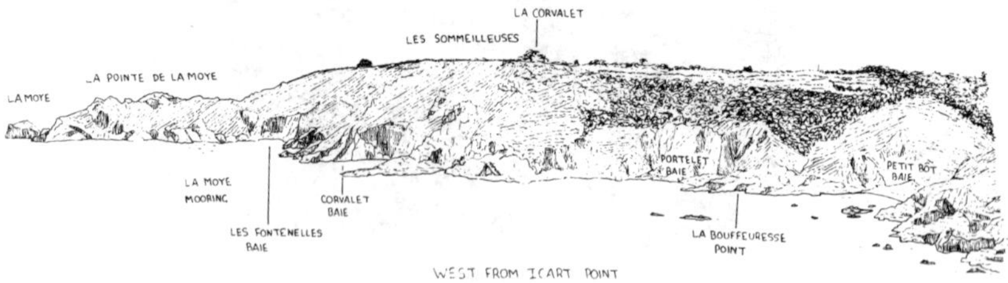

WEST FROM ICART POINT

A rough track (D) leads down from our present position past two rocky knolls to sea level. A short scramble left then leads to Creux au Tchian, which can be reached by a short but difficult rock climb. Although the black sombre walls outside the cave are impressive, the tunnel itself is less than fifteen feet long, and home to a flock of doves. The cave is no longer flooded, and would have been created when the sea level was some eight metres higher during a warm interglacial period.

Continuing along the cliff path we pass a car park and a German bunker (down on the right). The Crown had barracks built on the point when the Napoleonic Wars began in 1804. During the reign of Queen Victoria these were in a state of ruin. In effect Victoria was a tenant, and as such was fined on several occasions for failing to attend the Court of the Manor of Blanchelande, as was her duty! The fine was duly paid until she was granted exemption in 1894! The point was also one of several semaphore signalling stations during the French Wars.

There are excellent views down a rocky coombe to Chateau d'Icart. On Icart Point itself there are some German gun placements, and it is possible to follow a track down to La Petite Coupée, a collapsing ithsmus which now separates Chateau d'Icart from the point. At one time a good path led on to the promontory, but now path and railings have collapsed into the gullies on either side. Local rock climbers still cross the coupée by using ropes, but this is a difficult procedure, which further rock falls are likely to make impossible. An unroped crossing cannot be recommended. There is little evidence of a chateau ever being constructed on the point, but a natural defensive position it must have been. There is an earth wall which looks suspiciously man-made, but this could have agricultural origins. Goat Island is a more commonly-used name for the "chateau": semi-tame goats once roamed the cliffs around here, but unfortunately the minefields of the Occupation wiped them out.

From the top of Icart Point we can look across the wide expanse of Moulin Huet Bay to Jerbourg Point and the stacks of Les Tas de Pois d'Aval (The Pea Stacks), which unfortunately do not reveal their strange shapes from here. In the middle distance and just offshore are two stacks known as the Dog and Lion rocks.

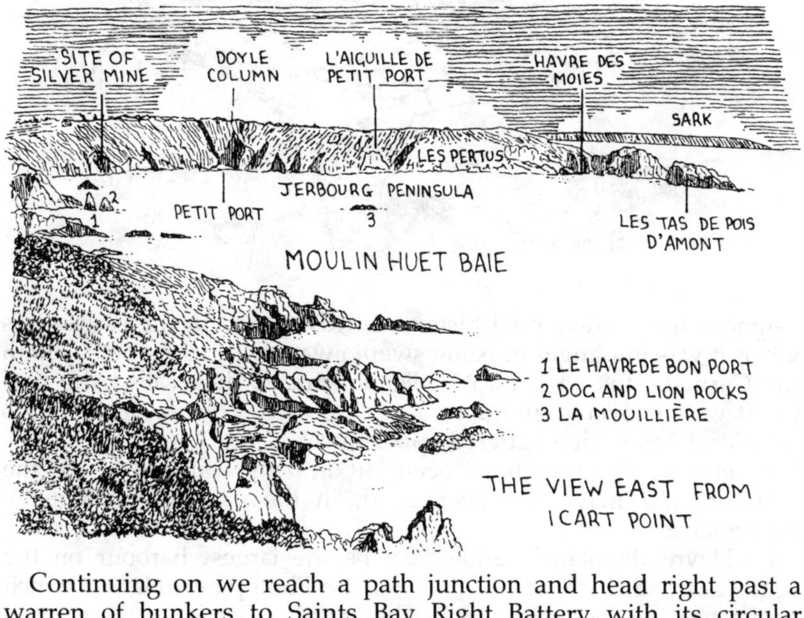

Continuing on we reach a path junction and head right past a warren of bunkers to Saints Bay Right Battery with its circular platform of stone flags and powder magazine, almost obscured with ivy. We soon reach the western shores of Saints Bay, and Le Havre de Blanchelande. With its slipway, tunnel, winch, boats and all the paraphanalia of fishing, the harbour is a fascinating place: don't forget the camera!

Above the harbour is a memorial to Charles le Febvre, Seigneur of Blanchelande in the middle of the last century. He was a generous man who tried to rebuild the harbour for local fishermen in 1868. Unfortunately a gale destroyed the partly-constructed structure on December 12th, and the present harbour dates from 1906. The remains of the destroyed breakwater and slipway can be found just to the south of the present harbour. The granite memorial to the

OLD SLIPWAY, HAVRE DE BLANCHELANDE

Seigneur has a chequered history. It was moved in the early 1900s when it was in danger of being swept away. During the Occupation the Germans tossed it into Heiligenbucht, as they called the bay, but it was recovered and placed in its present position in 1975. No wonder it has such a battered appearance!

Several small caves have been cut into the cliffside above the harbour, and may have been used, in the past, for storage by fishermen.

Le Havre de Blanchelande may be the largest harbour on the south coast, but it was not built for the Philippine freighter which paid a visit on June 13th, 1967. The *President Garcia,* carrying copra from Manilla to Rotterdam, took a left turn into Saints Bay instead of the Little Russel, to become one of Guernsey's most spectacular shipwrecks.

No one is quite sure how Saints Bay came by its name. Some say that two rocks on the far side of the bay are the petrified bodies of saints, kneeling in prayer. However, Saints is probably an Anglicisation of the word Seign, short for Seigneur or Lord. Indeed a 1309 court record refers to the bay as "the waters of the lord king". So perhaps we should talk of Lord's Bay, rather than Saints. Alternatively the name could derive from Baie de Seine, seines referring to the fishing nets which must have been a common sight here at one time.

Beyond the far side of the bay are two prominent stacks known as the Dog and Lion. They bear little relation to those creatures from here and they are the focus of several legends (see Route 34). Petit Port beach can be seen below the white streak of quartz in the far distance. The Pea Stacks appear as two large bosses of rock and their true shapes are not revealed until Moulin Huet Bay is reached.

To reach the beach itself we can either scramble round on the rocks when the tide is low, or walk along the road past the Martello Tower (see notes in Route 22), and down to the beach. During the First World War trenches were dug into the slopes below the Martello Tower, though the dense growth has now obscured these. Saints Bay is an idyllic spot. Towards low water there is a sandy beach, and caves to explore in the cliffs to the east.

For our return to Petit Bôt we must retrace our steps towards the tower, then take the path signed Icart Point. After a short distance a path (E) on the right (signed Bus Route) takes us across the wooded valley slope which has much to interest naturalists. At the path merger we should continue straight on to join Icart Road, where we turn right then left on to La Rue des Marettes (Road of the Small Ponds; the Petit Bôt stream once flooded this land until it was drained). After some 400 yards we turn left on to La Rue des Longs Tracs, where the steep roadsides are rich with plant life. A very modern row of greenhouses are passed, and we take a left turn on Rue de la Falaise (Cliff Road). This takes across Mont Hubert and we begin a steady descent to Petit Bôt Valley. At a stand of pines we can look across to St Clair's Battery, the powder magazine and the path leading up to Les Sommeilleuses. Here we can join a stepped path (F) which leads down to the main cliff path, and so to the road in the valley floor. Descending this we pass the tiny miller's cottage, and opposite can be found the remains of the old mill. Here the stream forms a waterfall as it cascades over a leat. Hardly any of the water reaches the sea; the square granite building opposite the Martello Tower is a Water Board pumping station, piping the stream to the reservoir. The terrace above the café has several mill stones, and is the perfect place to finish our walk and have a cup of tea!

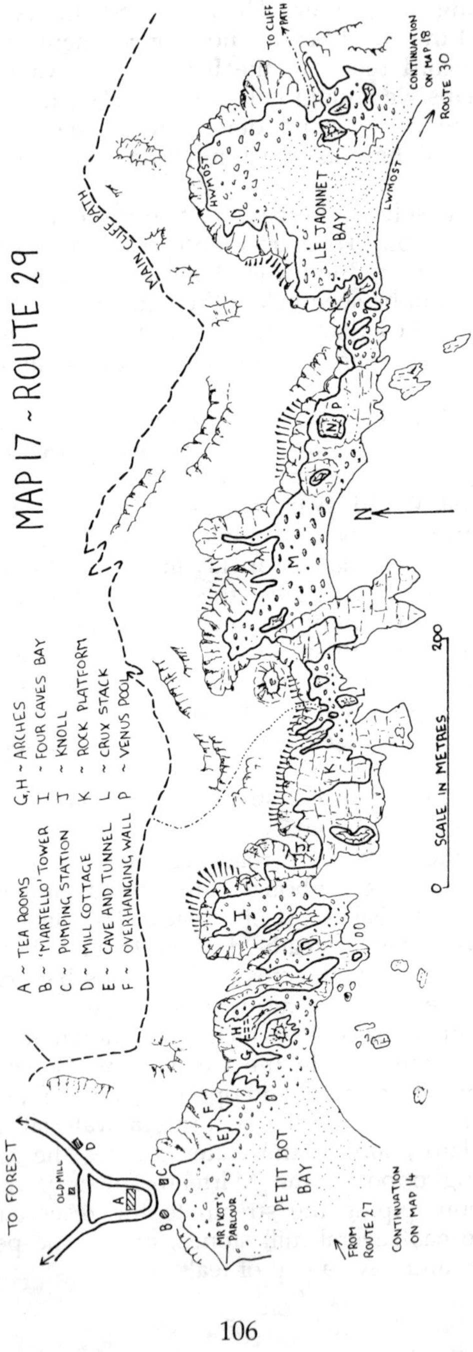
MAP 17 ~ ROUTE 29
A ~ TEA ROOMS
B ~ 'MARTELLO' TOWER
C ~ PUMPING STATION
D ~ MILL COTTAGE
E ~ CAVE AND TUNNEL
F ~ OVERHANGING WALL
G, H ~ ARCHES
I ~ FOUR CAVES BAY
J ~ KNOLL
K ~ ROCK PLATFORM
L ~ CRUX STACK
P ~ VENUS POOL
TO FOREST
OLD MILL
MR PKOT'S PARLOUR
PETIT BOT BAY
FROM ROUTE 27
CONTINUATION ON MAP 14
MAIN CLIFF PATH
SCALE IN METRES
0
200
N
LE JAONNET BAY
HWMOST
LWMOST
TO CLIFF PATH
CONTINUATION ON MAP 18
ROUTE 30

ROUTE 29 A sea level scramble

MAP 17

PETIT BÔT TO LE JAONNET BAY

DISTANCE — 0.5 miles

GRADE — IV–

AN EXCELLENT route, with scrambling at a sustained level, and only one escape. Views are very limited due to the numerous gullies, and the cliffs are steep, loose and capped by gorse and thorns. One feels very isolated, almost claustrophobic, but this only adds to the atmosphere. There are many arches and caves to explore.

RECOMMENDED TIDE — 8.2 metres minimum. A larger tide will make some sections easier, but the grade will still be III. If the tides are neaps it is still worth scrambling as far as the third arch (H) which can be reached without too much difficulty (II–).

ACCESS — Take the turning to Petit Bôt from the Forest Road (opposite Forest Stores). There is limited parking near the bay. Alternatively start from Icart Point and take the cliff path west to Petit Bôt.

THE TRAVERSE — From the beach we head eastwards. In the distance can be seen Icart Point, with the distinctive flat-topped summit of Chateau d'Icart which we meet in a later section. As we round the first rocks we meet a large overhanging wall of rock (F) which doesn't look too solid! By following the narrow cave (E) on the left we can squeeze through a narrow exit into a side gully.

Towards low water it is possible to traverse this initial section close to the waterline but it is more interesting to pick a line halfway between the cliff and the beach, and scramble over rock steps, pools and sand-filled hollows: a useful "warm-up" for the difficulties to come.

Just beyond the overhanging cliff we descend to a narrow gully. Following this we meet a small arch (G), and we can duck through this to a second more impressive tunnel (H) which the sea has carved through a ridge. We emerge from this into a wider gully with a shallow cave on the left. We leave the gully by scrambling easily over its far wall, and we reach an even larger gully (I) — or is it a small bay? Four caves can be found here. The left-most cave is a dove roost, and seems to amplify their noises and fill the bay with an eerie sound. The fourth cave is not so obvious, tucked away above the rock step on the far side of the bay.

The rock step proves an awkward obstacle. On an 8.2-metre tide it will have to be climbed (III+/IV−). On a tide over 8.5 metres it is possible to avoid the difficulties by rockhopping and scrambling up the seaward end (I+ only). After surmounting this problem we see a conical grassy summit (J) ahead of us. At sea level it is guarded by a steep wall, and the easiest solution is to climb the right-hand side of the gully which cuts into the left-hand side of the summit. Confused? We should then immediately descend on the right to gain a ledge system which takes us around the mound.
We then descend into a deep gully, with a cave full of shingle. Easy scrambling (I/II) over platform K leads to the crux section: there is a narrow gully and a large stack (L) in front of us. On a very big spring tide it is possible to skirt the stack on its seaward end. Otherwise climb up to the notch left of the stack and down-climb one of two steep gully/chimneys. The right-hand (seaward) chimney is the easiest. We exit up the gully with a boulder choke on the far side.

That's the hardest part over, and we can afford to relax a little. An easy section well above the sea leads to a wide bouldery bay (M), Le Havre de la Fosse. Prospectors dug a trial adit into one of the gullies in the last century, in search of silver. The bay is easily crossed, and the exit is through a gully with a jammed boulder and stack on its right-hand side. A little further on we come to a large mass of rock (N), La Petite Grande Silleresse, and there are endless possibilities here . . . through the arch on the left, over the arch (adrenaline addicts only), up the face of the rock and so on. Whichever way we choose we come to a large Venus Pool (P), bounded by steep cliffs on its far side.

Beyond this we pass through a square notch, then down and through a narrow gap with a stack on the right (prominent white quartz streak). A short section of scrambling brings us into the beautiful but often deserted Jaonnet Bay. Our exit is up the iron ladder and a good track which leads to the main cliff path.

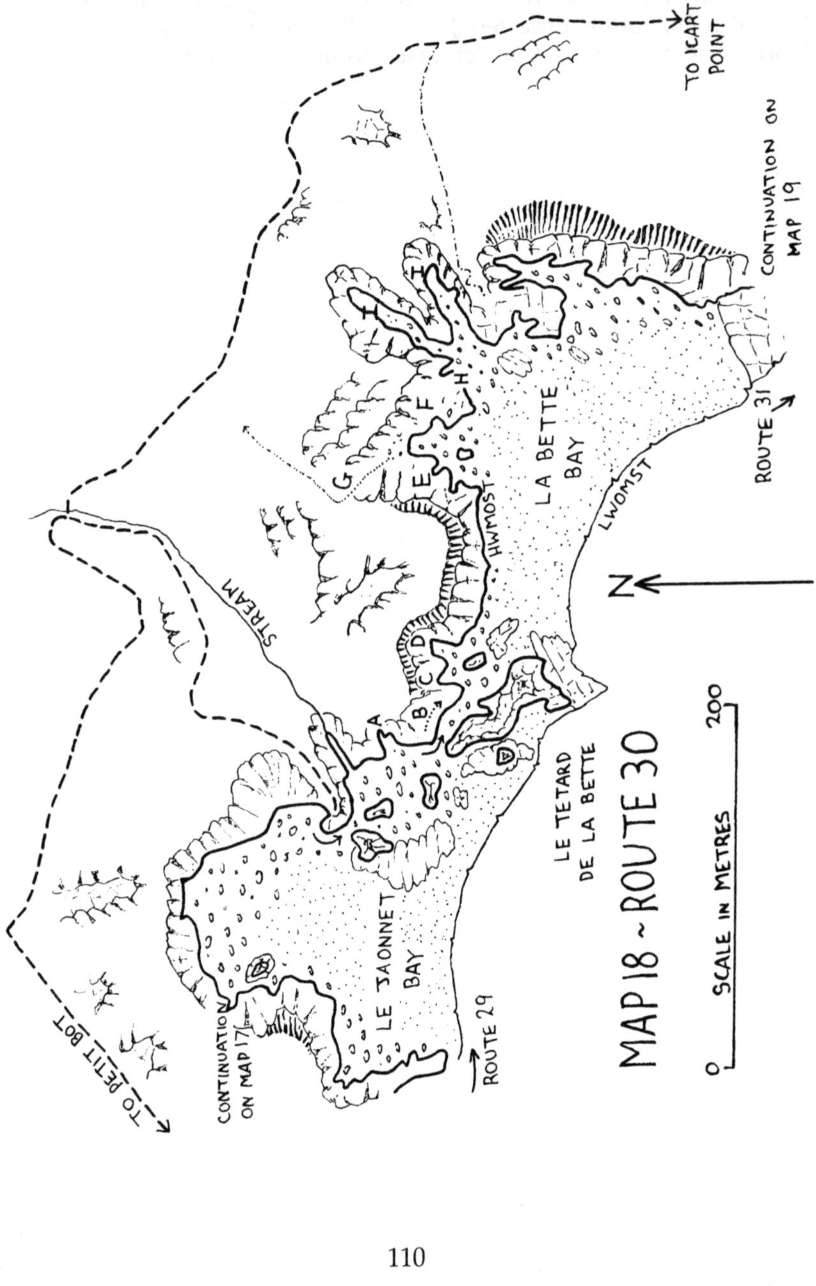
TO ICART POINT
CONTINUATION ON MAP 19
ROUTE 31
LA BETTE BAY
LWOMST
HWMOST
N
STREAM
A
B
C
D
E
F
G
H
I
LE TETARD DE LA BETTE
LE JAONNET BAY
ROUTE 29
CONTINUATION ON MAP 17
TO PETIT BOT
MAP 18 ~ ROUTE 30
SCALE IN METRES
0
200

ROUTE 30 A sea level scramble

MAP 18

LE JAONNET TO LA BETTE BAY

DISTANCE — 0.25 miles

GRADE — I+/II−

DEPENDING on the tide this short route can either be a straightforward beach stroll or a rock scramble. On a low spring tide the two bays dry out into wide expanses of sand, but the long descent is sufficient to deter the hordes which frequent the more accessible beaches. Le Jaonnet means "Furze Break", a throwback to the times when furze was a major fuel on the island, while La Bette refers to "Wild Beet".

ACCESS — Start from Icart Point, turn west along the cliff path and follow it to a path junction where Le Jaonnet Bay is signed. The views west from the point are impressive. In the far distance the long promontary of Points de la Moye (Point of the Stack), and the sands of Petit Bot can be seen in the middle distance if the tide is low. The descent to the bay is along a well-kept track, with a short section of ladder down the final rock step.

RECOMMENDED TIDE — The section is possible near low water on both springs and most neaps, though with the latter tides higher and more difficult variations have to be taken. Above an 8 metre tide the grade is I+, whilst on less extreme tides the grade increases to II+.

THE TRAVERSE — Initially we head through the bouldery gully to the left of the ladder foot, and enter a wider inlet. On the left are two fissures, home to a flock of pigeons and doves and a trickle of a waterfall. The way onwards is clear at low water on springs: ahead is a "V" gully, with the far shore of La Bette Bay visible through it. Before entering the gully take a look at the narrow cave (A) below the dark stripes in the rock on the left. On neap tides a higher route (B) may have to be taken on the left hand side of the gully (II+).

Before emerging into La Bette Bay scramble up on the left to the cliff foot, where a wave-cut platform is pitted with rock pools. The largest is tucked away beneath the overhangs of the cliff, and a cave (D) has formed behind it. A narrow cleft cuts up from the cave to the cliff top, and the beams of light beckon the intrepid explorer. However the gap proves too narrow. The crevices are frequented by a flock of pure white doves. Interesting scrambling can be found by staying high and crossing several gullies. At one point a traverse left leads to a cave (E) which has been eroded from a soft layer of rock, and the roof looks very temporary.

At the back of La Bette Bay is a cliff (F) over 100 ft high with four prominent crack lines on its left hand side, and there is a cave beneath these. A huge ship's rope lies among the boulders beneath the cliff. An escape (G) is possible at this point: 70 ft to the left of the cracks is a steep slab below overhangs. Scramble to the foot of the slab, then leftwards up a grassy rake below the rocks. This leads (II−) to an old path, very overgrown and painful, through the furze.

Beyond the cliff are two gullies separated by a narrow ridge. If the beach is flooded the gullies may have to be gained by down-climbing to two large boulders (H) (II). The far gully has some small caves (I) above high water level. Exiting from the gully can be awkward (II+) when the beach is not clear. Climb the smooth dark rocks to a large wave-cut platform from which a steep eroded path (I+) leads from here to the main cliff path. Care is necessary on the initial steep section.

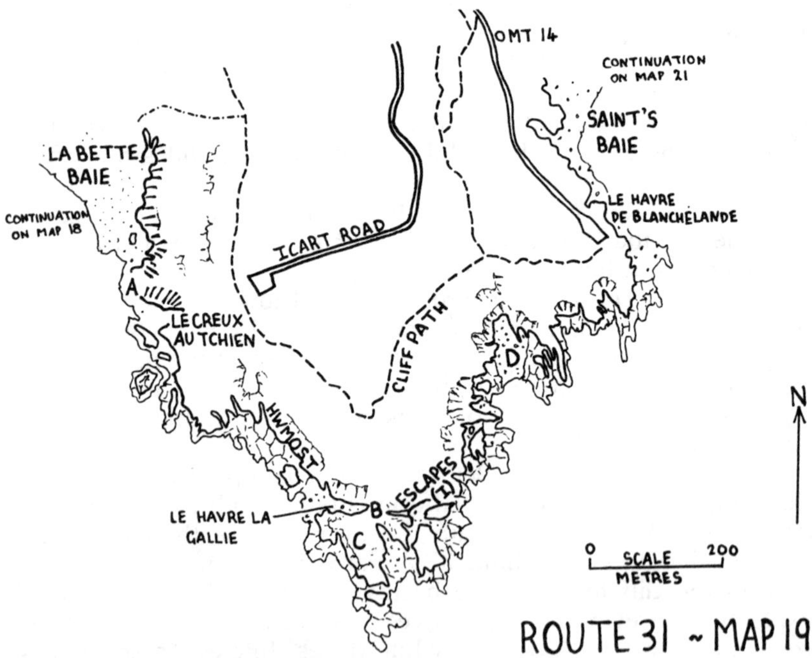

ROUTE 31 A sea level scramble

MAP 19

LA BETTE TO SAINTS BAY

A PLEASANT scramble between the broad sandy sweep of La Bette Bay and the picturesque harbour at Saints Bay, passing the rugged Icart Point. Given a large enough tide there are no sections of great difficulty. However the traverse should not be underestimated as it is quite long and there are few escape routes. Route-finding can also be quite difficult: some of the gullies form a veritable labyrinth!

DISTANCE — 1 mile

GRADE — II+

RECOMMENDED TIDE — 8.6 metres

ACCESS — Start from the car park at Icart Point and follow the cliff path west. After about 200 yards a track (I+) leads down a bowl towards the beach (some care needed on the final section of the path). Towards low tide a wide expanse of sand is exposed to form one of the prettiest and perhaps least-frequented of Guernsey's beaches: La Bette Bay ("Wild Beet Bay").

THE TRAVERSE — Heading back in a southerly direction we thread our way through large blocks to reach the foot of a buttress of rock A (can be an awkward II). After traversing beneath the foot of this a deep dark chasm can be seen ahead. At the back of this rift is Le Creux au Tchien (The Dog's Cave). This can be reached by a short hard climb of III, but the cave proves disappointingly small, and home to a flock of doves. Following a boulder field beyond this we gain height until we overlook a small inlet. Rather than descending down to this it is better to stay high following the ledges and rapid progress can be made until a gully forces us down to the rocks below.

After crossing the small bay beyond this we reach the tip of Icart Point ("Rocky Headland" or "Isolated Place"). It is joined to the mainland by La Petite Coupée (B) which is rapidly crumbling away, and visible on our left. The peninsula formed by the coupée is known as Chateau d'Icart (C) and although its distinctive flat top makes it look the perfect site for a castle, no evidence of one has been found. The point is more commonly called Goat Island, and many ferel goats roamed the area until German mines sent them to pastures new.

We leave Le Havre la Gallie, the inlet below the coupée, and head rightwards up a greasy black slab (II) to gain the point itself. On a large tide it is possible to traverse around the point at sea level. If the rocks at its base are flooded scramble up and rightwards across the point (II), then descend the far side. Here we meet a shingly inlet where the rocks have been washed incredibly smooth by wave action. Continuing on we reach a second gully below a stack. Following the gully we can see the overhanging "cornices" of the remains of the coupée. By staying close to the cliff foot we can avoid difficulties by descending to a gully and following it to the sea's edge. Beyond this the cliffs have degenerated and easy (though thorny) escapes are possible (I).

Crossing the next inlet we surmount a short overhanging wall (II) to reach an easy-angled slab. From here a number of gullies and steps are crossed (nowhere hard but demanding care), until a wide shingly bay (D) is reached. Leaving this we scramble over or around (harder) a rocky promontory until relatively easy scrambling leads around the final point to Saints Bay.

The main cliff path can be gained by following the track up the hillside behind the harbour and past the remains of a Napoleonic battery. Alternatively follow the lane and join the cliff path just beyond the Martello Tower. There are excellent views across Moulin Huet Bay to The Pea Stacks, which from here appear as two large masses of rock, hiding their distinctive shapes.

ROUTE 32 A cliff walk returning via lanes and footpaths

MAP 20

SAINTS BAY TO MOULIN HUET

DISTANCE — 1.6 miles

A FINE cliff walk with wonderful panoramas, taking us to the picturesque bay at Moulin Huet. We return along the lanes and the ancient path of Ruette Tonnelle.

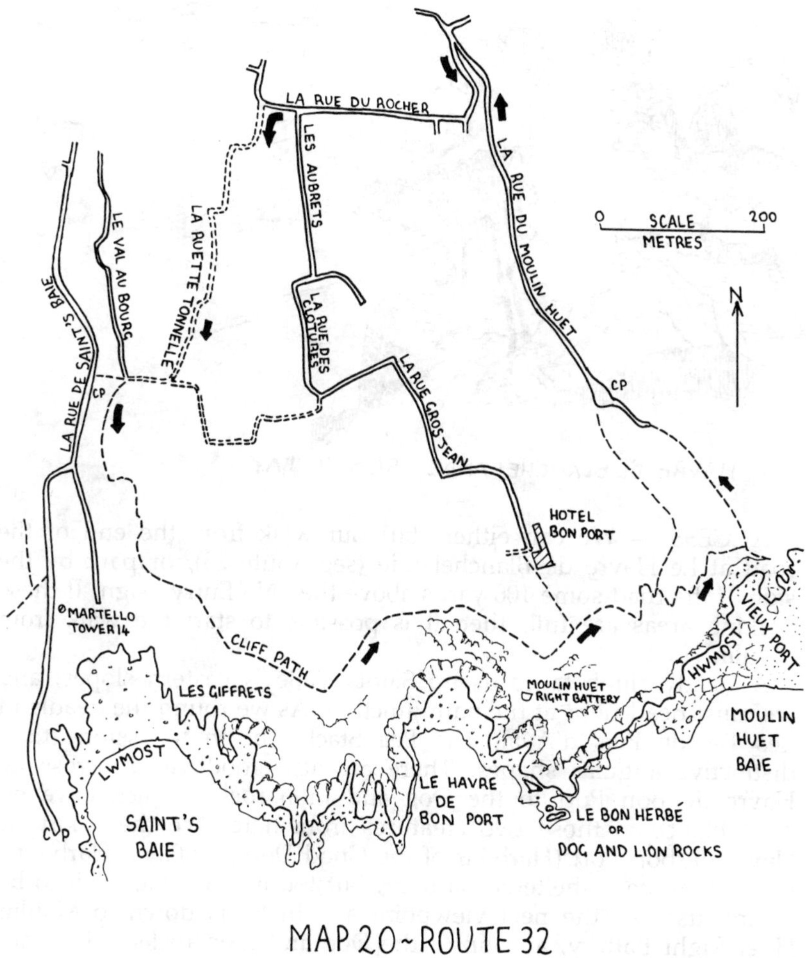

MAP 20 ~ ROUTE 32

HAVRE DE BLANCHELANDE, SAINT'S BAY

ACCESS — We can either start our walk from the end of the road at Le Havre de Blanchelande (see Route 28), or park by the side of the road some 100 yards above the "No Entry" sign. If these parking areas are full, then it is possible to start the walk from Moulin Huet.

A steady climb takes us up Saints Valley's eastern slopes, and we must head right at the path junction. As we round the headland Les Tas de Pois d'Aval, The Pea Stacks, begin to assume their distinctive angular shapes. There are also good views across Le Havre de Bon Port to the Dog and Lion rocks, which have no resemblance to those two creatures from here. We then skirt Le Havre de Bon Port (Harbour of the Good Door, or Good Harbour), which may be a sheltered harbour, but too inaccessible for it to be of any use. At the next viewpoint a path leads down to Moulin Huet Right Battery, and on to the Dog and Lion rocks, which are accessible at low tide. This is not too difficult a climb (II−), and is a recommended diversion. It is also possible to scramble round to the rarely visited Havre de Bon Port, but this can only be recommended to experienced scramblers.

A little further on the left is a path to the Bon Port Hotel, and beyond this we begin our descent towards Moulin Huet Bay. At the next path junction we should head right down the steps, and right again to reach the narrow tarmac lane that leads down to this most delightful of bays. There is much of interest here, for the valley and bay have a fascinating geology which explains the marvellous rock formations and views. A short diversion down to the shoreline is a must. There is excellent bathing and there are many sheltered coves even if there is a strong wind. For more information on this lovely area turn to Route 34.

The narrow lane leading up Moulin Huet valley is a pleasure to walk. The gradient is gentle enough for even the most tired of limbs, and the woodlands and meadows are rich in bird life and wild flowers. Look out for the elusive treecreeper which can be spotted hopping around the tree trunks searching for grubs. These are the continental short-toed treecreeper, a separate species from the British variety. Several of the island's birds, including the blue tits and robins, have small differences to their mainland equivalents.

There is a spring near the top of the road, and beyond this is a crossroads called La Carrière ("The Quarry"). A sharp left turn here takes us on to Le Rocher, and this is followed past Blanchelande College to a footpath which is well signed "Public Path to Cliffs". This attractive path is called Ruette Tonnelle and takes us along several small fields which are alive with rabbits and very peaceful apart from the steady thump of a water pump which never seems to stop! It has been suggested that Ruette Tonnelle was one of several sanctuary paths: if a fugitive gained such a path, they could not be hindered as they fled to the sea and away from the island.

At the path junction we turn right onto Le Val au Bourg, and after a short distance along the road we can take a path down the east slopes of Saints Bay Valley. A concrete bench on the left feels hot in the evening after a sunny day: many a well-known bottom has been warmed here! Lovely views of Saints Bay open up, with the Martello Tower and Le Havre de Blanchelande forming an appealing backdrop to the wooded valley.

A right turn at the path junction leads down to Saints Bay Road and the finish of this fine walk.

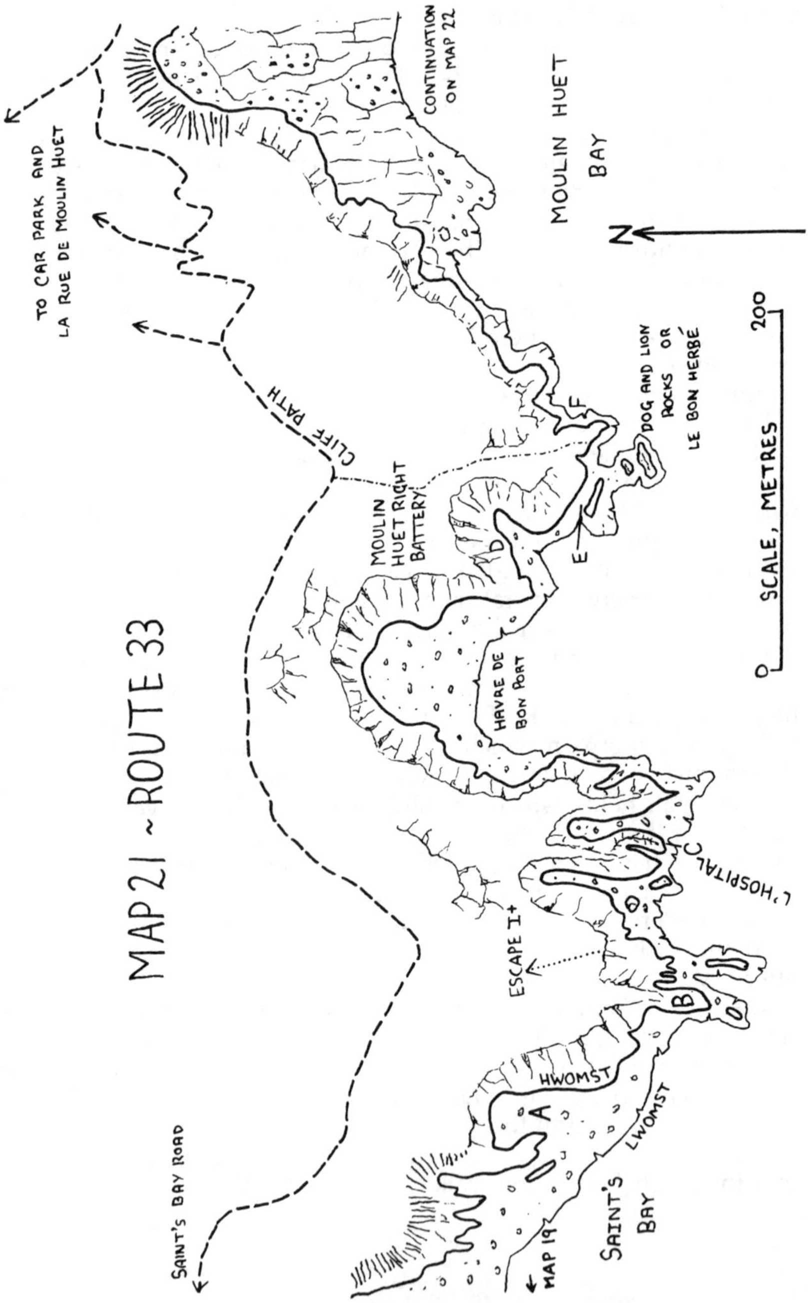
MAP 21 ~ ROUTE 33
TO CAR PARK AND
LA RUE DE MOULIN HUET
CLIFF PATH
CONTINUATION
ON MAP 22
MOULIN HUET
BAY
N
DOG AND LION
ROCKS OR
LE BON HERBÉ
F
E
D
MOULIN
HUET RIGHT
BATTERY
HAVRE DE
BON PORT
L'HOSPITAL
C
B
ESCAPE I+
HWOMST
A
LWOMST
SAINT'S BAY ROAD
SAINT'S
BAY
MAP 19
SCALE, METRES
0
200

ROUTE 33 A sea level scramble

MAP 21

SAINTS BAY TO LE MOULIN HUET

DISTANCE — 0.75 miles

GRADE — III

RECOMMENDED TIDE — a 7.75 metre minimum. On such a tide a gully near the Dog and Lion Rocks will have to be leapt (III). The gully can be crossed without a leap on a 9.3 metre tide.

ACCESS — Follow Saints Bay Road as far as the "No Entry Sign", then turn right and continue past a Martello Tower to a small car park overlooking Le Havre de Blanchelande.

THE TRAVERSE — Relatively easy scrambling leads around from the harbour to the beach. Leaving the beach we immediately pass a small cave on the left, and cross a shingle gully with two caves, the left hand being quite large. Beyond this we reach a small bay (A) with ivy hanging down the cliffs at the rear. There is an old engine which the salt water is gradually eating away. Weed-covered rocks slow progress, until we cross a larger rocky bay with recent rockfall on its backwall. Crossing a small promontory (B), which looks much harder than it proves, we meet a narrow gully, and beyond this it is possible to escape (I+) through the brambles and bracken.

Beyond this we reach a gully with a distinctive backwall: it has the appearance of vertical sand studded with rocks. At low water on a 7.75 metre tide the seaward end of this gully is flooded, but it is possible to climb up the rocks at this point (II) and over a gully to a sharp ridge (B). On larger tides the gully presents no problems. We then pick our way over two more gullies and the encouragingly named promontory of L'Hospital to reach the large bay of Le Havre de Bon Port (The Good Harbour). On the far side are two large stacks, the Dog and Lion rocks. Petit Port is the bay in the distance beyond them, and on the far point are Les Tas de Pois d'Amont, or The Pea Stacks.

On a large spring tide it would be possible to make a low traverse into the bay, but this would prove very weedy and slippery. A higher traverse avoids much of the weed and is grade II: high up and quite serious. There is no escape from the bay, and so we must exit along rocks on its far side, cross a gully D (II) and then round a cliff of creamish rock which has a Venus Pool (E) at its foot. We then meet the Dog and Lion rocks. The nearest is The Dog and can be reached at low water on most tides. The Lion requires a large spring.

Beyond the rocks is a narrow gully which can be jumped, and there is a cave, reached with difficulty from the far side (III). At this point it is possible to escape (I+) to Moulin Huet Right Battery and the main cliff path. As we round the point Moulin Huet Bay comes into view, but we cannot relax yet: we reach a deep smooth gully (F) which is usually flooded. Proponents of the "leap" will probably "go for it" (III), a tactic which will not be necessary on a 9.3 metre tide when it is dry enough to cross (but still an awkward II+).

Once over the gully little of difficulty remains: easy scrambling leads to the delights of Moulin Huet.

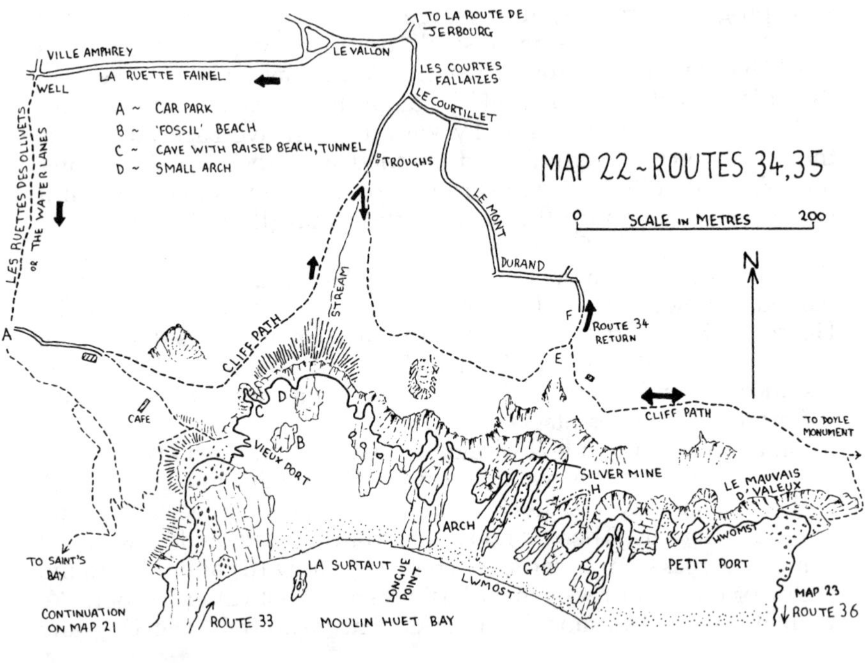

ROUTE 34 A cliff walk returning via ancient and modern lanes

MAP 22

MOULIN HUET TO PETIT PORT

DISTANCE: Approx. 2.1 miles

A high level cliff walk with fine views across Moulin Huet Bay, returning through picturesque hamlets and a wooded water lane.

ACCESS — Follow the signs from St Martin's to Moulin Huet Pottery. Continue past the pottery to the end of the road where there is parking.

ACCESS — Follow the signs from St Martin's to Moulin Huet Pottery. Continue past the pottery to the end of the road where there is parking.

The flat area on which the car park has been constructed was once a beach . . . when the sea level was some 60 metres higher than its present level, during one of the warm inter-glacial periods. In later times it was the site of a pond: the stream was dammed to create a head of water for the mill in the valley below. No stream in Guernsey is too small for the Water Board! Some of the stream water is piped off at this point, for household consumption. The toilet block has been built from Icart Gneiss, the main rock type in this area. It is one of Europe's oldest rocks, over 1,000 million years old.

Heading down the lane towards the bay we soon pass the old mill which gives the area its name, Huet's Mill, originally built in 1372. A wooden leat once guided water down the valley from the pond to the mill wheel. The site is now a house with wonderful views across Moulin Huet Bay to Jerbourg Point and Cannon Rock. The valley sides in this area were not always so wooded: in the last century they were clear of trees and terraced to create potato fields.

A great fault line cuts across Guernsey from Vazon Bay to Moulin Huet, and this weakness resulted in the formation of the valley and the large indentation in the coast. The valley was gouged out when Guernsey had a tundra climate, and powerful meltwater streams formed in the spring. Today's stream is a "misfit", too small to have created its valley.

It is well worth taking a detour down to Moulin Huet Bay, or Vieux Port (Old Port) as it should be called at this point. A narrow tarmac track leads past the tea-house to what is perhaps the most lovely of Guernsey's bays. As the tide falls it dries out into a sandy beach, interlaced with pinnacles and gullies, through which The Pea Stacks form an impressive background.

THE OLD MILL HOUSE, MOULIN HUET

In 1883 the famous French Impressionist painter Pierre Renoir spent a month on Guernsey. When he wrote a letter to his Paris dealer saying "Here I find myself on a charming beach, quite unlike our Normandy beaches", he was referring to Moulin Huet, and all his Guernsey paintings were of this bay. Its beauty and charm have escaped the development and modernisation which has marred much of Guernsey, and our view across to The Pea Stacks has changed little since Renoir's visit.

Much of the bay's attractiveness can be attributed to the sea level changes that have occurred. The area of gullied rock (B) which is revealed as the tide ebbs is a "fossil beach", the remains of a former wave-cut platform, created when the sea was some eight metres above its present level. A cave just beyond the descent steps has one of Guernsey's best examples of raised beaches. It has a layer of rounded compacted stones above the floor of the cave (C), and another near the roof. These are the remnants of the old beaches formed at eight and eighteen metres above the present average sea level. Global warming is obviously not a new phenomenon! A tunnel provides an alternative exit from the cave, and there is a second arch (D) further into the bay.

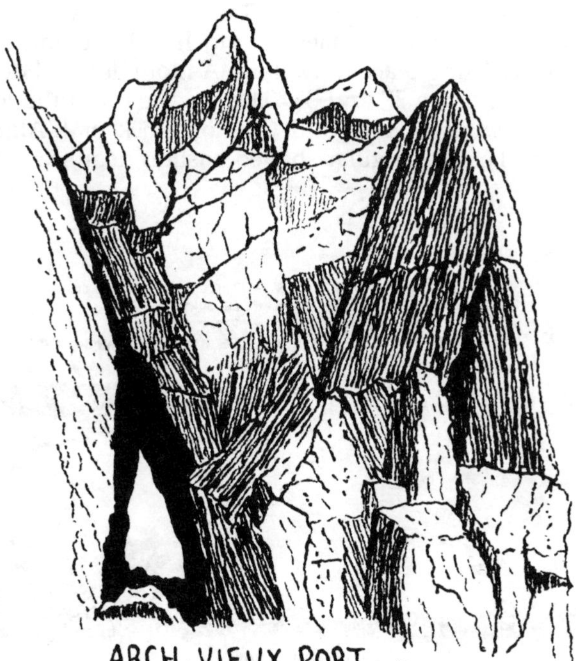

ARCH, VIEUX PORT

The prominent offshore rock is usually called Cradle Rock, or La Surtaut. It used to be called Le Bate des Treis Garces (Boat of the Three Maidens), after three local girls who are said to have gone bathing and sunbathing on the rock at low water. They awoke to find themselves stranded, and unable to swim or raise help they were drowned.

Returning up the path to the mill, we head rightwards along the cliff path, and soon have views of that marvellously jagged row of rocks, The Pea Stacks. A gentle rise takes us up to a viewpoint with benches. The stacks on the headland to the right (south-west) are known as the "Dog and Lion" rocks. The far stack is the lion, but from here has no resemblance to that creature: it will gradually assume the lion's shape as we approach Petit Port. The dog never seems to look like a dog, no matter where it is viewed from! Legend has it that the two rocks are the petrified kneeling figures of a husband and wife, praying forgiveness for murdering their son as he returned with money from the wars. He had disguised himself for a joke, and they were unaware that the soldier was their son. His sister discovered the crime and denounced her parents, who were subsequently executed.

In the centre of the bay is a reef known as Moullière ("The Anchorage"), and to our left are Les Tas de Pois d'Amont (the East Pea Stacks). These are the subject of much folklore and mystique, and make a fascinating place to explore. A more detailed description can be found in Routes 37 and 38. The land mass to the left of the Pea Stacks is Jerbourg Point, and Cannon Rock or L'Alguillon de Petit Port is the large triangular-shaped bastion near sea level.

MOULIN HUET BAIE

We now head inland around a valley and join the road, where there are two granite abreuveurs or troughs. A right turn just beyond these takes us up to the cliff path, and we descend beneath pine and sycamore to an opening where there are views of Moulin Huet Bay and west to Bon Port Hotel on the far headland. The stream in the valley below descends to a waterfall which was formed when the sea dropped to its present level.

Beyond a flight of steps the path levels out and we curve inland around a small valley (E). There is a path on the left which we will follow on our return. Rounding the next small headland, we can look down to Petit Port beach (if the tide is out). A deep chimney-like cleft, jammed with several large boulders, can be seen bisecting the far wall of the bay. Down and to the right of our present position is the site of an old mine, in a remarkable cave which has three separate levels (raised beaches again!). In 1834 an adit was driven up from the lowest gallery in search of silver. None was found, but a large quantity of lead ore was extracted and taken by boat to St Peter Port. However an outcry began that the workings were draining the springs in the neighbourhood, and there were injunctions, arrestings and threatened law suits. In vain it was contended that "there are immense riches in the Manor of Blanche-landes" and the Blanchelande Mines Company was dissolved, just four months after its inception. The adit was blocked with masonry, and although this soon crumbled, there were no further complaints about the diminishing water supply. The affair also led to the cessation of all further mineral exploration in the island. It is dangerous to scramble down to the mine workings from the cliff path, and they are most easily reached from Petit Port itself. Low water on a spring tide is the best time to explore the working; difficulties are much greater on neaps.

We soon meet the Petit Port steps, beneath the slit eye of a German bunker. Petit Port means "Little Door", and this may refer to a long-gone gateway in Le Chateau de Jerbourg. The Jerbourg promontory has been well defended almost since man first arrived on Guernsey. Traces of three banks and ditches stretch from this point four hundred yards across the headland to Pied du Mur ("Foot of the Wall"), following a sheet of quartz which formed a ridge of higher ground. It dates from the Late Neolithic Age, some 4,000 years ago. A castle was constructed on the site of Doyle Column in the 1300s, but little remains of the structure today. The Germans also recognised the strategic importance of Jerbourg, and constructed their Strassburg Battery near the site of the old castle.

Do we descend to Petit Port beach or not? Well, it's less than three hundred steps down, and it is a delightful spot if the tide is out. The beach is never crowded, and it is a safe place to bathe, sometimes with excellent surf. At low water it may be possible to reach Cannon Rock, and explore the tunnel which cuts right through it. With attractions like this, who can refuse?

There are many fascinating stories and legends about Petit Port. It was here that the devil was said to have rowed Duke Richard of Normandy in the legend of the devil's clawmarks (see Route 38).

The beach is said to have been haunted by a ghostly wailing, connected with a brutal murder that had taken place there. A brave farmer, Pierre Thoume, armed with a bible, spent a night in the bay and the haunting noises were never heard again. He promised never to reveal to a soul how he exorcised the spirit.

"Operation Ambassador" is no legend, and it was here that the newly-formed Commandos carried out their first, albeit unsuccessful raid. Those of us who have walked Route 28 will have read how Guernseyman Hubert Nicolle, Second Lieutenant in the British Army, had landed at Le Jaonnet Bay in July 1940 and carried out valuable reconnaissance before being picked up. The information on troop concentrations and strengths was used as a basis for planning the raid: one unit was to land at Petit Port, set up a road block, put the telegraph cable out of action, attack a machine gun post and generally create a diversion. Meanwhile the main unit was to land at Pointe de la Moye and attack the airfield.

Unfortunately bad weather delayed the operation by two days, and the Guernsey tides dealt a blow: instead of landing on the sands of Petit Port, the diversion unit found themselves landing on the boulder-covered upper part of the beach, up to their armpits in water. The steps are bad enough in dry cloths and running up in sodden battledress must have been purgatory! The road below Doyle Monument was duly blocked, the machine gun post was found to be empty, and the telegraph wires were cut. However the fireworks at the airfield never began, as the other units had failed to land on Guernsey. During the ensuing retreat four men were left behind and after several days gave themselves up to avoid endangering the lives of the Guernsey family who had hidden them.

Churchill was scathing about the operation, saying "Let there be no more silly fiascos like those perpetrated in Guernsey". Lessons were learnt though, and more successful raids were later mounted on Les Casquets (when the entire lighthouse crew was captured!), Sark, Herm, Burhou and Jersey.

Upon regaining the cliff top, we can retrace our steps west along the cliff path (those with lots of energy could join Route 38, or cut across the peninsula to join Route 41). If we head back it gradually becomes obvious why Lion Rock is so named, as it does resemble a couchant lion. Unfortunately we cannot say the same of the dog. Taking the path (F) on the right we head past a walled terraced field to the end of Le Mont Durand. We follow this to a junction, and turn left down Le Courtillet and reach Courtes Falaises.

This name is a corruption of Croute Falaises. In the past cattle were grazed on the common land of the cliffs, and they would occasionally stray and cause much damage to crops. A croute was an enclosure where stray cattle were held until their owners paid a fine. Falaises translates to cliffs.

A right turn here, and a quick left takes us past the fine granite arch of Le Vallon, and then we can follow a right of way through Le Vallon, where there is an ancient wooden pump, to La Ruette Fainel (Fennel Lane, named after the herb which was once cultivated for its aromatic qualities). Sandwiched between vegetated walls, this takes us to Ville Amphrey. This hamlet is probably named after Amfreville in France, the family home of the Buarts, Normans who held a fief in this area during the Middle Ages. Here we turn left on to the Water Lane, where there is a spring and well.

The Water Lanes or Les Rouettes des Ollivets, is a delightful path, shrouded in trees which at times almost block out the sun. The stream sides are rich with ferns and other lovers of the dark and damp. Too soon the path opens out and we descend more steeply to the car park in Moulin Huet Valley.

ROUTE 35 A sea level scramble

MAP 22

MOULIN HUET TO PETIT PORT

TUCKED away at the end of a narrow wooded valley, Moulin Huet is a delightful place. Towards low water wide stretches of pristine sand appear, and there are several caves and gullies to explore. The views across to The Pea Stacks are remarkable, and it is little wonder that Renoir found them so fascinating.

The traverse takes us the short distance to Petit Port, which also has an excellent beach, occasionally with good surf. The grade of the expedition varies enormously with the state of the tide.

DISTANCE — 0.5 miles

GRADE — On the largest tides of the year the traverse can be a simple beach walk. On 8.6 metre tides the grade is III.

ACCESS — From Saint Martin's follow the signs to the Moulin Huet pottery, and park at the end of the road beyond this. Follow the lane and path to the beach.

RECOMMENDED TIDE — The traverse is just possible on a 6.8 metre tide, with one short diversion around a gully. Larger tides are recommended to give more leeway, though a tide approaching 9.5 metres will remove all technical difficulty.

THE TRAVERSE — Setting off across the beach we pass several caves, one of which (C) has a narrow tunnel exit, to reach a cliff which is almost orange in colour. A dead tree, which once stood on the point to our left until the hurricane of 1987, is jammed into a cave at the cliff foot. On the right hand side of the cliff is a small arch (D). Leaving the bay we cross weed-covered rocks and pass a large rock pool to reach an ivy-clad cliff above a small bouldery bay. Beyond this a series of narrow gullies cut across our path, and these can prove a little awkward on neap tides. There is an excellent arch, and then two wider inlets are then passed. The second has a cave in the backwall, with three entrances. This is a site of an old silver mine (see Route 34).

Leaving this via a large platform we reach a wide gully (G) which only dries out on springs. On neaps it is possible to either escape to the cliff path (I+) or follow a faint track (H) around the rear of the gully to descend its far side. This brings us to our final difficult section, another smooth wide gully which is just feasible on neap tides when a downclimb from right to left (III−) leads to the gully floor.

Relatively easy scrambling then leads to the sand of Petit Port where we have time to relax and explore the caves before tackling the steps (nearly 300!) which lead up Le Mauvais d'Valeux to the cliff path. A pleasant walk west along the path leads to Moulin Huet.

ARCH BELOW MONT DURAND

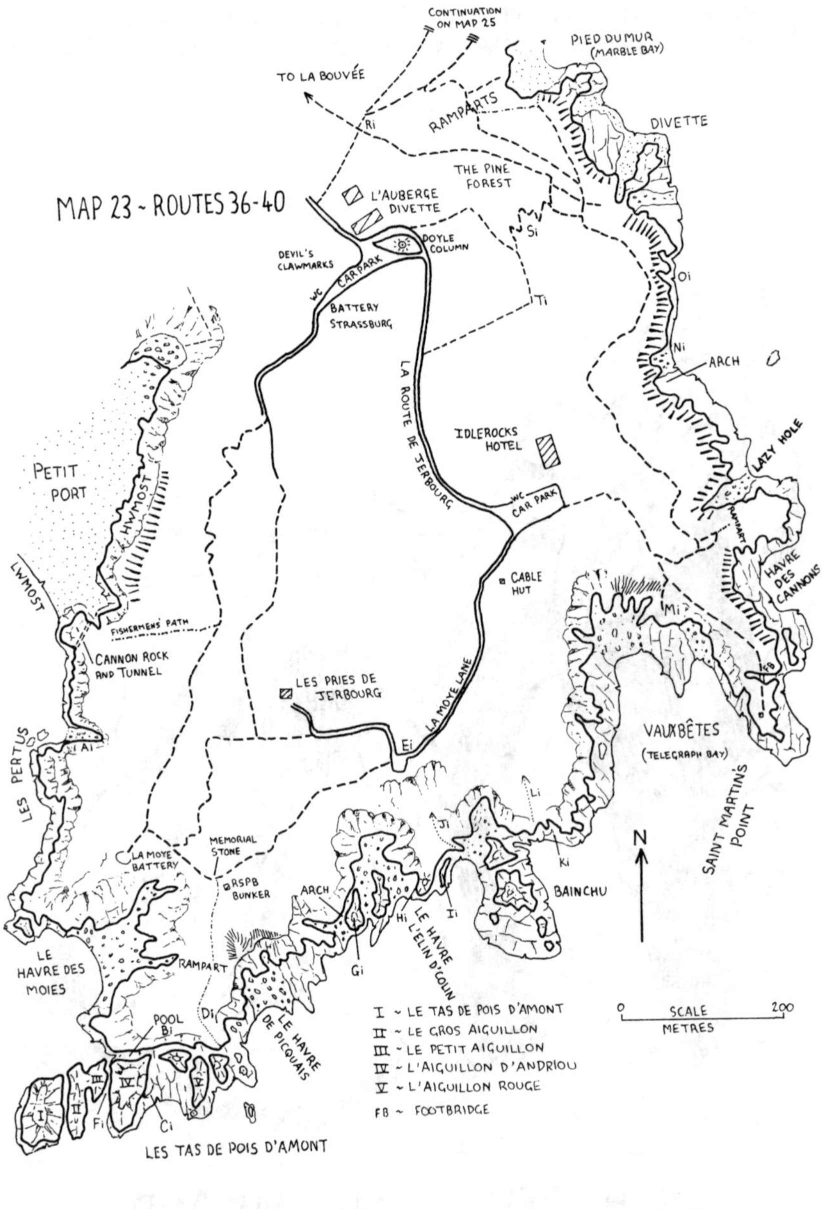
MAP 23 ~ ROUTES 36-40
CONTINUATION ON MAP 25
TO LA BOUVÉE
PIED DU MUR (MARBLE BAY)
RAMPARTS
DIVETTE
THE PINE FOREST
L'AUBERGE DIVETTE
DOYLE COLUMN
DEVIL'S CLAWMARKS
WC CAR PARK
BATTERY STRASSBURG
LA ROUTE DE JERBOURG
IDLEROCKS HOTEL
WC CAR PARK
ARCH
LAZY HOLE
RAMPART
HAVRE DES CANNONS
CABLE HUT
PETIT PORT
HWMOST
LWMOST
FISHERMENS' PATH
CANNON ROCK AND TUNNEL
LES PRIES DE JERBOURG
LA MOYE LANE
VAUXBÊTES (TELEGRAPH BAY)
SAINT MARTIN'S POINT
LES PERTUS
LA MOYE BATTERY
MEMORIAL STONE
RSPB BUNKER
ARCH
BAINCHU
LE HAVRE L'ELIN D'COLIN
LE HAVRE DES MOIES
RAMPART
POOL
LE HAVRE DE PICQUAIS
LES TAS DE POIS D'AMONT
N
I ~ LE TAS DE POIS D'AMONT
II ~ LE GROS AIGUILLON
III ~ LE PETIT AIGUILLON
IV ~ L'AIGUILLON D'ANDRIOU
V ~ L'AIGUILLON ROUGE
FB ~ FOOTBRIDGE
0 SCALE 200
METRES

ROUTE 36 A sea level scramble

MAP 23

PETIT PORT TO THE PEA STACKS

STARTING from the wide sands of Petit Port ("Little Gate") we pass the prominent buttress of L'Aiguillon de Petit Port (usually called Cannon Rock), over numerous gullies at quite a sustained standard (II) to Le Havre des Moies ("The Harbour of the Stacks") and so The Pea Stacks. Here we can continue over these remarkable summits, or escape back to the cliff path. Overall quite a committing traverse as there are no easy escapes between Cannon Rock and The Pea Stacks. The rocks are very weedy and hamper progress.

The name Petit Port may refer to the early Bronze Age defences which have their western limit at this point. Constructed around 2000 BC, a series of banks and ditches stretch nearly half a mile across Jerbourg peninsula to Pied du Mur ("Foot of the Wall") or Marble Bay as it is now known, on the east shore of Guernsey.

DISTANCE — 0.6 miles

GRADE — II+ to III−

RECOMMENDED TIDE — 8.5 metre minimum.

ACCESS — Follow La Route de Jerbourg and turn right opposite the Doyle Column to a parking spot. Follow the lane past the toilets, then turn right onto the cliff path which leads to the steps of Petit Port.

THE TRAVERSE — Set off about 40 minutes before low water. A wide expanse of sand will be exposed in the bay, and we cross this to the large pillar of L'Aiguillon de Petit Port. We can either scramble round the seaward face of this, or find the tunnel which goes under the rock: much more fun! About 30 yards further on we reach a steep-sided gully with a small cave in its headwall. The best way onwards is to jump the exposed rocks at its seaward end. If these are too deeply covered then it is wise to retreat. There is a path leading off from the top of Cannon Rock.

Continuing on below the cliffs of Les Pertus we pass a series of small gullies which all need care (sustained II), to emerge in a small bouldery bay (Ai). We leave this via a gully, and The Pea Stacks come into view. A mast is visible on the far stack: this is no aid to passing boats, but a "No Waiting" sign! Rounding a small point, we descend to an inlet. If a high route is taken here there will be some quite exposed moves (III−). Having crossed the inlet we descend to a gully, and as we emerge we have a superb view of the tooth-like Petit Aiguillon.

The cliffs now start to rear up on our left. The gully below, with its jammed boulder, is best avoided by jumping onto its right hand side, and along this rib to its seaward end. We scramble without major difficulties into Le Havre des Moies. This presents no problems, and after leaving it is best to stay high then descend to the gully separating the nearest stack from the mainland. Once in the gully we meet a large pool (Bi) which is most safely waded, or can be avoided by scrambling up the rocks on the left (II+).

If we are continuing on to Les Tas du Pois d'Amont or The Pea Stacks as they are better-known (there should be enough time) then head down the gully on the right and just beyond the pool. The cracks and chimneys above us can be climbed at II+ to III, though it is easier to traverse the right wall of the gully and scramble up near its seaward end (Ci). We then head rightwards to the grassy hummocks above the chimneys (see The Pea Stacks section).

If The Pea Stacks are to be saved for another day we continue along the main gully, past a Venus Pool and L'Aiguillon Rouge (The Little Red Needle), V. At this point we can join the traverse from The Pea Stacks to Saint Martin's Point. Alternatively we exit on the left, and a faint track (Di) leads up to the RSPB bunker hide and the Osmond Priaulx stone.

Once on the main cliff path it is worth descending the steps to La Moye Battery. All that remains of this Napoleonic defence is a low circle of stones where a bench provides an excuse to relax and enjoy the views. In front of us are the remarkable Pea Stacks, Les Tas de Pois d'Amont, and to the west is Icart Point and the flat-topped promontory of Chateau d'Icart. A martello tower can be seen peeping from the shrubs above Saints Bay. Right of this is the bay of Le Havre de Bon Port, and the Dog and Lion rocks.

The path then takes us above L'Aiguillon de Petit Port and to the Carey memorial stone. Here we can either continue along the main cliff path and descend past a bunker and into a valley. Less energy is expended by taking the path opposite the stone, turning left past the copse and under a fallen pine to the lane.

ROUTE 37 A scramble over a group of stacks

MAP 23

LES TAS DE POIS D'AMONT

THIS fascinating set of stacks provide a short but enjoyable excursion. Difficulties are not great, but care is needed with loose and greasy rock. These are perhaps the nearest to mountain summits that Guernsey has and standing on the top of Le Tas de Pois d'Amont we experience a remarkable feeling of open space and height that is all out of proportion to the altitude of the stack: truly a mountaineering expedition! In the spring the stacks are a haven for nesting seabirds, and they should be avoided until the breeding season is over.

DISTANCE — 0.5 miles

GRADE — II+

RECOMMENDED TIDE — 8 metres minimum. Set off about an hour before low water.

ACCESS — Follow La Route de Jerbourg to the car park on the point. Continue west along the road and join the cliff path just beyond Sea Plane Bungalow (Ei). Follow the path west to the Osmond Priaulx stone, then follow a track past the RSPB bunker hide. Continue down the hillside to the left of a ridge, passing an Iron Age earthwork, then scramble down to a gully.

LES TAS DE POIS D'AMONT (SEE MAP 23)

THE SCRAMBLE — Heading right we pass under L'Aiguillon Rouge ("The Little Red Needle"), which is most easily climbed up its mainland or north face. A small un-named stack is then traversed, and ahead of us is L'Aiguillon d'Androu ("Andrew's Needle"). A perched stone on the stack is known as Le Petit Homme d'Andriou ("the little man called Andrew"). It is possible to climb the cracks and chimneys at grades of II+ to III up the wall in front of us, but an easier and safer route is to skirt left along the gully below the stack. Scramble up its seaward end (Ci), then head rightwards to a large ledge of incredibly springy tussocks. Bouncing round to the west side of the stack, we descend to a gully (Fi) which does not dry out. This can be overcome by a short jump (leaping back is not so easy!) The two pinnacles here are named Le Petit Aiguillon and Le Gros Aiguillon ("The Big Little Needle and the Little Little Needle"!). They are in fact one stack, as they are not separated at high water. The final stack of Le Tas de Pois d'Amont ("The Furthest Pea Stack") is gained quite easily by crossing boulders in the gully. The final climb to the summit is not hard, but the rock is coated with a slippery algae, fertilized each spring by the nesting birds. The feeling of space on the top give it the atmosphere of a mountain summit, though instead of a cairn or triangulation point we have a "No Waiting" sign for company! Many legends of The Pea Stacks have grown over the years, and these are described in Route 38.

ROUTE 38 A cliff walk

MAP 23

JERBOURG POINT

DISTANCE — 1.6 miles

THIS splendid walk takes us around much of the coast of Jerbourg Peninsula. It has marvellous views of The Pea Stacks, Moulin Huet Bay and the other Channel Islands. It can be joined to Route 40 to make a complete circumambulation of the headland.

ACCESS — Follow La Route de Jerbourg from Saint Martin. There is a convenient car park opposite Doyle Column. Before setting off, it is worth exploring a while as there is much of interest in this small area.

The numerous German fortifications here comprised Battery Strassburg, which was equipped with four 22cm guns during the occupation. These had a range of 22 kilometres, and the original Doyle Column was knocked down in 1944 as it was both an obvious landmark for any attacking aircraft and in line with the guns should they wish to fire towards France.

Jerbourg has always been strategically important, and a series of banks and ditches dating from the Late Neolithic Period (some 4,000 years ago) stretch across the peninsula at this point. Little can be seen today around our present position, and the earthworks are

BATTERY STRASSBURG

best observed near Pied du Mur (Foot of the Wall) or Marble Bay as it is now known (see Routes 40 and 41). Ramparts are also visible below the cliff path near The Pea Stacks, and on the small point at Le Havre des Cannons.

Dr Barry Cunliffe has suggested that the Jerbourg area was a fortified trading post on the sea route between St Malo in Brittany and Hengistbury in Dorset. It may have been founded by refugees from Brittany who fled to Guernsey from the wrath of Ceasar after an abortive rebellion in 56BC.

Le Chateau de Jerbourg was built in the early 1300s, but fell into disrepair in the 1600s. Its traces have all but disappeared under Doyle Column. A three storey signalling tower was constructed in 1780, when the island was in danger of invasion from the French, allies of the American colonists seeking independence. This was pulled down in 1816, following Napoleon's come-uppance at Waterloo, and the cessation of hostilities. The construction of Battery Strassburg and, more recently houses, car parks, toilets and an electricity sub-station, have led to the near-obliteration of the area's ancient fortifications, and traces have all but disappeared.

The original Doyle Monument was built in 1816 to commemorate the Lieutenant-Governorship of Sir John Doyle, whose military works did much to improve the island's defences. The tower had an internal stairway leading to a viewpoint. Today's relatively modest column was built in 1953.

Departing from fact into folklore, we can make a short diversion to a rock which bears the clawmarks of the devil himself! In the Cronique de Normandie of 1576, a legend tells how Duke Richard of Normandy was tempted into a boat by a beautiful lady. As the craft neared Petit Port, she turned into an ugly hag with cloven hooves. It was the devil himself, in one of his devious disguises. Jealous of Richards good looks, he grasped the Duke and flew high above Jerbourg before letting go. The devil landed on a rock where the dark imprints are said to be his clawmarks. I suppose the moral of the story is, don't get into a boat with a strange woman without wearing a parachute! The stone itself is the block of quartz in the small stand of conifers behind the car park. It proves disappointingly small, and one assumes souvenir hunters have exacted their toll.

Heading past the toilet block the cliff path is soon reached. If we are not visiting Petit Port we should go through the granite barrier to the cliff edge, where there is a German gun placement and a large outcrop of quartz. This outcrop stretches right across the headland, and the higher ground it formed was used as a basis for the ancient fortifications.

There are fine panoramas from here. In the far distance is Icart Point, with the flat-topped promontory of Chateau d'Icart. To the right, below the skyline trees is Le Havre de Blanchelande, sited on the edge of Saints Bay. The two prominent stacks below and right of the harbour are the Dog and Lion rocks (see note in Route 34). Below us is the bay of Petit Port, which at low water dries out into one of Guernsey's prettiest and least-frequented beaches. Heading south along the cliff path we reach the road, and the impressive pillar of Cannon Rock dominates the view. A right turn takes us onto the cliff path and we cross a dip to a gun placement which can be entered, but the view is largely obscured by bushes. Beyond this is a flat area of land known as the Carey Bequest.

The engraved stone is mounted on the foundations of a German gun position, which in turn may have been sited on the Napoleonic Battery which gives Cannon Rock its name. Look out for a narrow path a little further on the right. This leads down to Cannon Rock (there are brambles: wear long trousers!), which has a tunnel cutting through it. This is fun to explore towards low water, and a torch is unnecessary.

As we approach the tip of the promontory the fascinating rocks known as Les Tas de Pois d'Amont or The Pea Stacks come into view. A literal translation is The East Pea Stacks, distinguishing them from Le Tas de Pois d'Aval, The South-westerly Pea Stack, at Pleinmont. Marie de Garis has suggested that the Pea Stacks is a misnomer, and a more correct translation would be The Weights, or The East Weights, as the Guernesiais word for weight is the same as that for pea. They certainly resemble a row of the old stone weights more than a row of peas, though the name doesn't have the same ring to it.

There are many legends about these rocks. On L'Aiguillon d'Androu (Andrew's Needle) is a perched rock known as Le Petit

BUNKERS, JERBOURG

Bouan Homme d'Andriou (The good natured little man Andrew). It has been suggested that Andriou refers to An Drio or Arch Druid. This old druid was primate of the Unelli, a Brittany tribe who held out against Christianity. St Patrick and his disciples enchanted the druid and turned him into the stone which still stands on the rock.

St Patrick had something of a hard time in Jersey, being pelted with stones and called rude names. Needless to say he received a resounding welcome in Guernsey, and as something of an encore to his petrifying trick, he filled his wallet with snakes, toads and other noxious creatures, returned to Jersey and emptied them there. Perhaps this is why no snakes are to be found in Guernsey, and there are "crapauds" by the thousand in Jersey!

Another legend suggests the stone figure was a man searching for lost treasure amongst the stacks. The treasure's guardian caught the hunter and turned him to stone. Others say that the rock looks like an old monk, dressed in cowl and habit, and up until very recently fishermen would raise their caps to the little figure and say "Watch over all, good man". Sometimes a morsel of bread would be cast on the water as an offering.

A final tale is of three Jerseymen who lassoed one of the Pea Stacks and attempted to tow Guernsey behind their boat to Jersey. Fortunately their plan was thwarted when the rope broke!

A traverse of the stacks is a splendid expedition, involving some awkward scrambling, and details are in Route 37. The sharp-eyed will spy a sign on the furthest stack. No aid to shipping, this is a "No Parking" road sign!

A short diversion down to La Moye Battery, a cannon position dating from the Napoleonic Wars, is worthwhile. The excellent views of the stacks, and Moulin Huet Bay can be enjoyed from a bench.

A little further along the path is a red granite pillar, memorial to Osmond Priaulx. Below this is a bunker which is now used as an RSPB hide. From here we can see another Pea Stack, the pointed Aiguillon Rouge ("Little Red Needle"). In clear weather it is possible to see Sark, Jersey and sometimes France. A path at this point leads down to The Pea Stacks and crosses the banks and ditches of a small earthwork, possibly dating from the Bronze Age.

The main cliff path takes us past another bunker and above a rocky bay, which has a perfect little arch. We then join the road, and there are views down to the fog station on St Martin's Point, and Le Long Pierre with its red and yellow marker. Look out on the right of the road for a well-hidden building. This is the old telegraph hut, whose disablement was one of the objectives of Operation Ambassador (see Route 34).

SAINT MARTIN'S POINT

The views from the top of the point are wide-ranging, from St Sampson's in the far north, to Alderney, Herm, Jethou, Sark, France and Jersey: a perfect vantage point for the guards which were once stationed in the large bunker. The area now covered by the car park was once the site of a parade ground and barracks which were built during the Napoleonic Wars and remained in use until shortly after the end of the First World War.

A third earthwork stretched across here, from Vau Betes (Valley of the Beasts) or Telegraph Bay as it is called nowadays, and down to the inlet at Le Havre des Cannons (Lazy Hole).

From the point we can either walk back along the main road to Doyle Column (quickest), or follow Route 40 as far as The Pine Forest. The alternative shown on the map follows a path which is parallel to the cliff path, and is perhaps the most pleasant way of returning to our starting point:

We must retrace our steps along the road, and continue to Les Pries de Jerbourg. Beyond the barrier a right turn takes us onto a track which rejoins the cliff path near our starting point.

ROUTE 39 A sea level scramble

MAP 23

THE PEA STACKS TO SAINT MARTIN'S POINT

THIS traverse offers some excellent scrambling. Coupled with the superb views of The Pea Stacks, Jersey, Sark, Herm and the Little Russel it is highly recommended. There are few caves to explore, but we will pass a perfect little arch and several impressive rock features.

Although this is a relatively short section, it should not be tackled lightly. It involves some quite technical and exposed moves, where a slip could prove serious. There are two sections of IV, but the route is not too committing as it can be quickly reversed if the first difficulty proves too much. There is also an easy escape before the second crux section, so given the right tide the chances of becoming cut off are not too great. Technical interest is sustained as far as Vaux Betes (Telegraph Bay).

DISTANCE — 0.75 miles

GRADE — IV

RECOMMENDED TIDE — An 8.5 metre tide is the minimum, otherwise the second section of IV will be more serious. A very large tide of 9.5 metres will reduce the difficulty of the two hardest sections.

ACCESS — As for the previous section, all the way to sea level.

THE TRAVERSE — From the gully easy scrambling eastwards leads to the shingle beach of Le Havre de Picouais, where there is a cave. We then continue over a platform, and make a short exit from a gully which can be a little awkward (II+) if the tide is not completely out. Beyond this is a perfect little arch, reminiscent of the pack-horse bridges of northern England. We can cross this to a stack (Gi), then descend the far side to a shingly gully which leads into a bay, Le Havre l'Elin d'Colin. The cliffs forming the backwall must be unstable judging by the landslip scars.

The exit from the bay (Hi) provides the first crux, and is quite a serious proposition (IV) unless we are on one of the year's biggest tides. On the east side of the bay is a prow of rock with a tunnel through its base. We need to find a way up the wall right of this prow, and the best point to start is from the large boulder right of the foot of the prow. Climb up and rightwards on large flakey holds to a ledge. Traverse to the right around an arete, then make balancy moves up a short ramp to the top of a chimney. The climb is not too hard technically, but the exposure is intimidating, and a slip could not be recommended.

Immediately beyond is another overhanging prow (Ii), which is avoided by the gully on its left. Emerging from this we pass on the left-hand side of a stack, which has a tunnel carved through its base. There is an escape route on the left (Ji) at this point (II−).

Continuing on we drop down to a wide gully below an overhanging grey cliff which has two narrow caves. Skirting round this we pass left of a large mass of rock which forms the island of Bainchu at high water, and cross two gullies to reach the final difficulty. This is a narrow gully (Ki) with a cave at its rear and a 50ft cliff which overhangs for much of its base. The safest climb is at its right-hand end (IV but possibly less on a very big tide). If it proves impassable, we can escape (Li) to the cliff path (I+).

As we leave the gully Telegraph Bay and the fog station of Saint Martin's Point come into view. We can breath a sigh of relief as relatively easy scrambling remains. Originally the bay was known as Vau Betes (The Valley of the Beasts), while its modern prosaic name refers to the cable which came to shore at this point. Bring back the beasts! The steps (Mi) leading up from the bay are tempting, but let's finish the traverse to the point proper. Here superb views open up if the weather is clear. In the far distance to the south-east can be seen the outline of Jersey. To the east is Sark and sometimes the coast of France can be picked out between Sark and Jersey. On the far side of the turbulent stretch of water known as the Little Russel is the small islet of Grande Fauconnière (recognisable by its white triangulation point), Jethou, Herm, the Bréhon Tower in the middle of the strait, and to the north we can pick out the power station chimneys of Saint Sampson, and the lighthouse on the Castle Cornet breakwater. In the immediate foreground is a rock known as Long Pierre (Long Stone), with a beacon perched on its summit to warn off passing craft.

From the point we can follow a path over a bridge to the main cliff path, and then slog up the steps underneath Jerbourg bunker to the car park where hopefully the ice cream van is waiting!

ROUTE 40 A cliff and woodland loop walk

MAP 23 and 25

SAINT MARTIN'S POINT TO FERMAIN BAY
returning via Calais
DISTANCE — 3.1 miles

A WONDERFUL cliff path walk along the wooded eastern shores of Guernsey. The views across to the neighbouring islands are memorable and there is much of interest for historians and naturalists.

ACCESS — Start from the car park on St Martin's Point, at the end of La Rue de Jerbourg. This is an excellent viewpoint (see Route 38), and the car park itself was once the site of a barracks, from Napoleonic times until the end of the First World War.

The steps take us below some German bunkers which can be explored, to the point. Here we can take a diversion down a stepped path to Telegraph Bay, or Vau Betes (Valley of the Beasts) as it used to be known. Its modern name refers to the communications cable which once came ashore here.

A more interesting deviation is to follow the path onto the very tip of the point. This takes us across a bridge to the fog station. The rocky promontory is a popular fishing spot, and the angling must be good to compensate for the steep path to the cliff top.

Continuing along the main cliff path we descend a slope where it is said that pirates were once hanged. A path on the right leads down to a flat-topped point where a cannon was once mounted.

THE PINE FOREST FROM LAZY HOLE

The bay to the right is Le Havre des Cannons, and the narrow gully to the north is Lazy Hole. Earthworks, Late Neolithic or possibly Bronze Age, once stretched across the peninsula from the inlet to Telegraph Bay, with a subsidiary bank across the neck of the small promontory at our present position.

A short easy scramble northwards from here leads to a perfect little arch (see Route 42).

Returning to the main path we ascend a gentle slope and views open out to the north. We can see The Pine Forest, Soldiers' Bay, Clarence Battery on Terres Point, Castle Cornet and the harbour at St Peter Port. We soon reach the ambitiously-named Pine Forest, a large stand of Corsican and Monterey Pines. Many of these have been lost in the high winds of recent years, but the planting of saplings should ensure the survival of this Guernsey beauty spot.

A short diversion down a path on the right leads to Divette, an ancient breakwater, possibly the oldest harbour on Guernsey still in its original state. Just beyond the "cauchie" is a gully of golden sand.

Continuing along the main cliff path we take a left turn for Fermain Bay and Le Bec du Nez. Below us is a triangular shipping mark and we emerge from the pines to pass through several embankments and ditches, which are still quite obvious despite their thick covering of undergrowth. These are the remains of the Late Neolithic fortification which once stretched across Jerbourg Peninsula from Petit Port. A path on the right can be taken to the picturesque little bay of Pied du Mur (Foot of the Wall, a reference to the ramparts). Marble Bay is the modern name of the inlet, and there are outcrops of quartz on the beach. It is a fascinating place to explore, with several caves and arches in the vicinity.

We should now use Map 25. The main cliff path takes us out of the valley, and a turning on the right (Pi) leads down to Le Bec du Nez. With its slipway, winch, small fishing boats, and a mass of anchors, lobster pots and floats, this is a charming spot. The harbour is surmounted by a battery constructed in 1803 when the Napoleonic Wars broke out and the island was once again in danger of attack. Behind the battery, half-hidden by trees, is a stone building, and herein lies a tale of subterfuge. Mattieu de Sausmarez, Seigneur of Le Fief de Sausmarez, sold the land to the British Government for the construction of the battery. However he laid the condition that he retained ownership of the hut, and that only the soldiers manning the guns were to be allowed in the area. It has since come to light that he was smuggling wine from the enemy and storing it in the hut until it could be taken at night to Sausmarez Manor!

Continuing along the main path towards Fermain we have good views of the harbour, and traverse a wooded hillside to La Ricou Point, with La Rocque au Peigne just offshore. Further on we pass under a gnarled old oak which forms an arch, cross a stream and up steps to reach a path junction. Here we head right past an old quarry to reach a viewpoint with benches, where we can look down to Fermain Bay and across the Little Russel to the other islands.

The path now begins its descent to Fermain and passes a turning on the left which we will take on our return. In a short time we reach the head of the bay. Fermain is a lovely spot, sheltered from all but an easterly wind and a favoured anchorage for yachtsmen. The "Martello" tower was constructed in 1778 (see notes in Route 22). The terrace behind the sea wall was the site of the North Battery during the French Wars, but the South Battery has disappeared beneath the undergrowth. During the Occupation the Germans dammed the stream to provide hydro-electric power!

In the summer months a passenger ferry operates between Fermain and St Peter Port, with a mobile jetty which is winched up and down the beach with the ebb and low of the tide. There are several caves around the bay, the largest being Le Grand Creux, to the south. This can only be reached near low water on a spring tide, and care should be taken to avoid becoming stranded. The bay is free of strong currents, and makes a fine spot for bathing, though beyond the confines of the bay the Little Russel can flow with the fury of a powerful river.

Returning along the main cliff path we can take the turning on the right (Qi) to Calais. This takes us up the wooded hillside to a lane which joins Calais Road, which we follow to the right hand bend. Some 15 metres before the bend is a lane which leads past lovely cottages and a garden which has a veritable plague of gnomes. (An alternative path, Gipsy Lane or La Ruette sur Fermain is on the bend itself and leads to the hamlet of La Bouvee. Here we can head right at the T junction and so to the main road, or left on to a track which rejoins the main cliff path).

Continuing down the driveway of Le Mont Frie we join the cliff path, which crosses the remains of a German gun placement. An opening on the left provides a excellent viewpoint. On a clear day it is possible to see all the main Channel Islands from here. A little further is an oak which blew over in the 1987 hurricane, but is still just clinging to life.

Ignoring the turning on the left to Le Bec du Nez, we continue to a second junction (Map 23) and head right for Jerbourg Road and St Martin's Point. Steps (Ri) take us up to three paths, where we turn left (the steps behind the National Trust sign is the most direct line back to Doyle Column) and head towards The Pine Forest. An unsigned path on the right then leads to a zig-zag path (Si) which takes us up towards Doyle Column. To avoid more road walking we can turn left at the next path junction, and make a short diversion to a small copse (Ti). There are marvellous views north to Le Bec du Nez, Fermain Bay, Soldiers' Bay and Les Terres Point. In the far distance is Castle Cornet and St Sampson's, and on a clear day Alderney is visible on the horizon. Views to the south are dominated by the Idlerocks Hotel, perched above Saint Martin's Point. Long Pierre is the marker off the point, and in the distance are Jersey and the French coast. Our path leads us back inland, and a small amount of road walking takes us to our starting point.

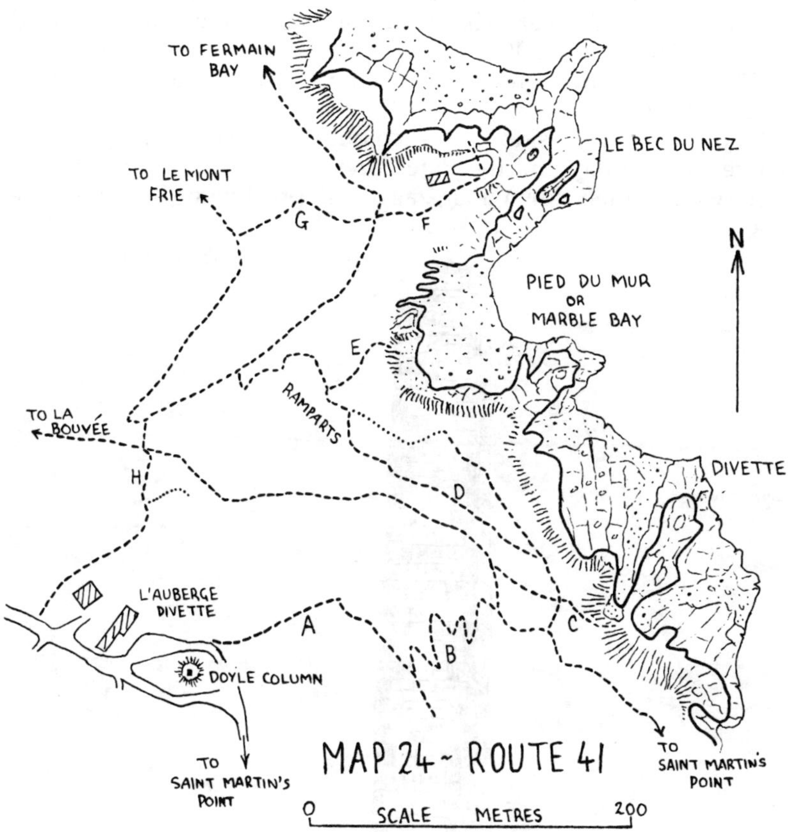
TO FERMAIN BAY
LE BEC DU NEZ
TO LE MONT FRIE
G
F
N
PIED DU MUR OR MARBLE BAY
E
RAMPARTS
TO LA BOUVÉE
H
D
DIVETTE
L'AUBERGE DIVETTE
A
B
C
DOYLE COLUMN
TO SAINT MARTIN'S POINT
MAP 24 - ROUTE 41
TO SAINT MARTIN'S POINT
0 SCALE METRES 200

ROUTE 41 A circular coastal and woodland walk

MAP 24

DOYLE COLUMN LOOP

DISTANCE — 1 mile

A SHORT loop walk through The Pine Forest to Divette, Pied du Mur and Le Bec du Nez. The main points of interest are described in more detail in Route 40.

ACCESS — Start from Doyle Column. There is usually ample parking in the area.

On the north-east side of the column is a path (A) signed for Divette, Marble Bay and the Pine Forest. Follow this to a junction, where we head left down a zig-zagged stepped path (B) to the Pine

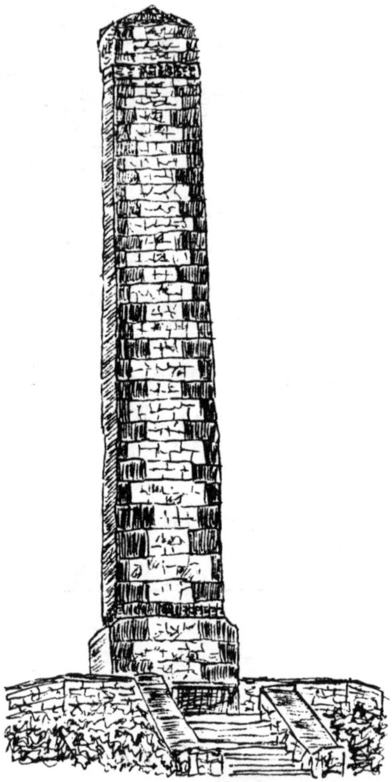

DOYLE COLUMN

Forest. At the junction turn right, then left, and a path (C) leads to the ancient mooring of Divette, with its gully of golden sand.

Returning to the main path we head right, then take the path (D) to Fermain and Le Bec du Nez. This leads us past a triangular shipping mark, and over the banks and ditches which are the barely noticeable remains of the Neolithic/Bronze Age defensive earthworks. A stepped path (E) on the right then takes us down to Marble Bay, or Pied du Mur as it was originally known. Pied du Mur translates to "Foot of the Wall", a reference to the ancient fortifications. There are several interesting caves and arches in the bay.

The main path leads us out of the valley and around a small headland. Here a path on the right descends to the picturesque harbour of Le Bec du Nez.

Returning from the harbour we can take a direct path (G) up the hill to a junction, and head left for St Martin's Point. This recrosses the valley, and if we take the steps (H) by the National Trust sign we cross an open slope to reach the road by L'Auberge Divette, below Doyle Column.

EAST COAST TRAVERSES

AS we round Saint Martin's Point and head north the character of the coastline changes considerably. Here the valleys and hillsides are richly wooded and have a much friendlier aspect than the south coast, with trees, bracken, and shrubs often growing right down to the shoreline. The cliffs are either non-existent or small in stature. However this does not necessarily make the scrambling any easier, and the prospect of escaping through this rampant growth is not very appealing. The east coast is well-sheltered from the south-westerly gales, so these traverses can be achieved in relative comfort when it is difficult to even stand up on the south and west shores.

The Little Russel is a beautiful stretch of water, and the views from the cliff path are memorable. On the majority of days we will see Herm, Jethou, its satellite islets, and the long mass of Sark on the far side of the Big Russel. When the air is very clear we can see the low smudge of Jersey to the south of Sark, and if we are very lucky the French coast can just be picked out between Jersey and Sark.

Ideally these sections would be tackled in the morning when they are in full sunshine. Unfortunately the sun and the moon contrive to make this impossible: low water on a spring tide is essential, but these do not occur until after midday.

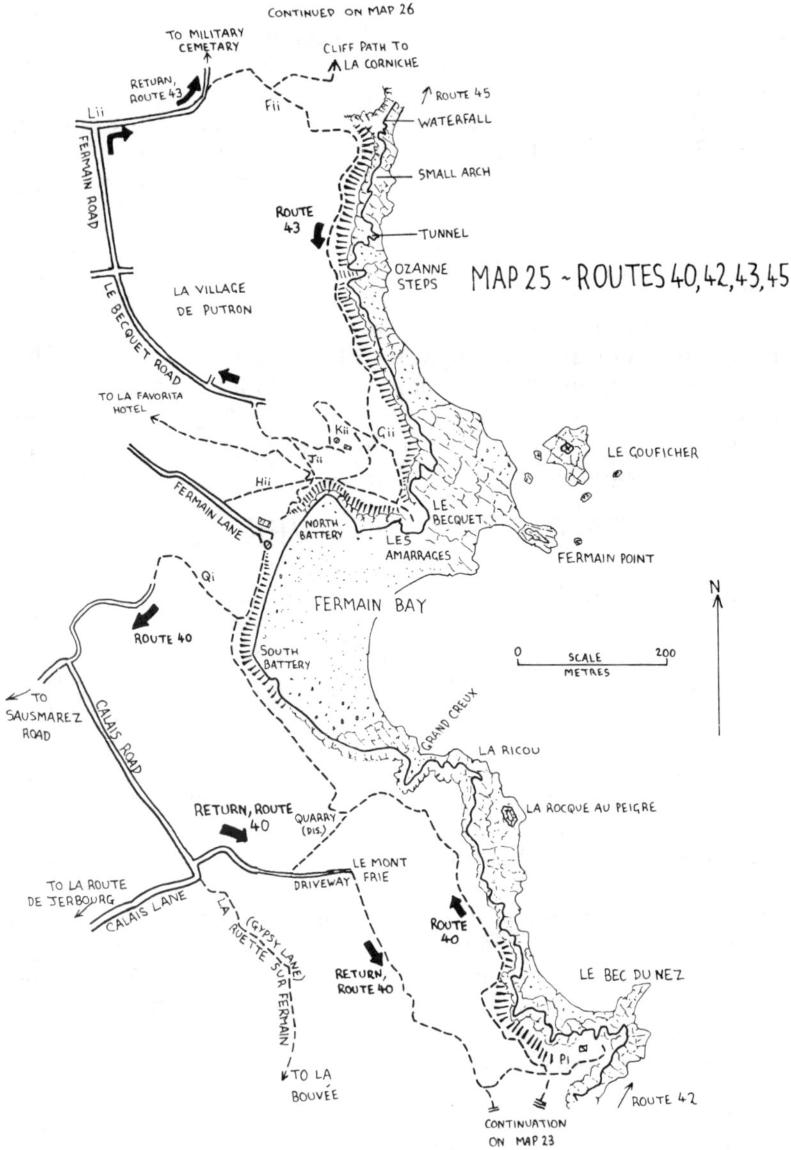
CONTINUED ON MAP 26
TO MILITARY CEMETARY
CLIFF PATH TO LA CORNICHE
RETURN, ROUTE 43
ROUTE 45
Lii
Fii
WATERFALL
FERMAIN ROAD
SMALL ARCH
ROUTE 43
TUNNEL
OZANNE STEPS
MAP 25 ~ ROUTES 40,42,43,45
LA VILLAGE DE PUTRON
LE BECQUET ROAD
TO LA FAVORITA HOTEL
Kii
Gii
LE GOUFICHER
Jii
Hii
FERMAIN LANE
LE BECQUET
NORTH BATTERY
LES AMARRAGES
FERMAIN POINT
Qi
N
FERMAIN BAY
ROUTE 40
0 SCALE 200 METRES
SOUTH BATTERY
TO SAUSMAREZ ROAD
CALAIS ROAD
GRAND CREUX
LA RICOU
LA ROCQUE AU PEIGRE
RETURN, ROUTE 40
QUARRY (DIS.)
LE MONT FRIE
DRIVEWAY
TO LA ROUTE DE JERBOURG
CALAIS LANE
LA RUETTE SUR FERMAIN
(GYPSY LANE)
ROUTE 40
RETURN, ROUTE 40
LE BEC DU NEZ
Pi
TO LA BOUVÉE
ROUTE 42
CONTINUATION ON MAP 23

ROUTE 42 A sea level scramble

MAPS 23 and 25

SAINT MARTIN'S POINT TO FERMAIN BAY

A FUN expedition, without the same sense of isolation as some of the south coast traverses as the cliff path is never more than 100 yards from the shoreline. In addition to the superb views we will pass over and under arches, a deep cave, an extinct blow-hole, ancient harbours and Napoleonic batteries. We may be lucky enough to see the striking green lizard, a Continental species not found on the UK mainland. It inhabits the cliffs around Fermain Bay.

Difficulties are not sustained. There are several sections of II south of Divette, though the more adventurous will find plenty of harder variations. The most difficult point is reached just before Fermain Bay where there is a deep weed-covered gully. Rapid progress can be made along several stretches which follow an ancient wave-cut platform.

In order to complete this section in one trip, speed is essential. A gully quite near to the start needs to be tackled when the tide is near low water, and a point near the end also requires a similar tide state. This leaves little time for dawdling in between! A more leisurely approach can be made by splitting the section, and exiting at either Le Bec du Nez or Pied du Mur. Traverse direction makes little difference, though scrambling south from Fermain Bay will make the grade III− gully slightly easier, and the difficult section is then quickly out of the way.

DISTANCE	— Saint Martin's Point to Le Bec du Nez	0.75 miles
	Le Bec du Nez to Fermain Bay	0.6 miles

GRADE	— Saint Martin's Point to Le Bec du Nez	II
	Le Bec du Nez to Fermain Bay	III−

RECOMMENDED TIDE — An 8.5-metre tide will allow most of the major difficulties to be by-passed. Pick a less extreme tide and be prepared for some rock gymnastics and wet feet at the very least!

ACCESS — As parking is never easy near Fermain Bay it is best to start from the car park above Saint Martin's Point. Follow the steps down to the point, conspicuous with its fog station and light.

THE TRAVERSE — From Saint Martin's Point we scramble easily around Le Havre des Cannons to a small promontory. The ramparts here date from the Bronze Age, and during the Napoleonic Wars a cannon was mounted here. Immediately offshore is the Longue Pierre rock. Upon leaving we descend to Lazy Hole, which has a cave at its head, and then round another small point. Beyond this the sea has crafted a lovely arch from the bedrock, and we can use this as a bridge to reach a shingly gully (Ni) which needs to be dry for us to cross. Exiting from this we head up to the rocks above the high water level and from here we take a rollercoaster route,

ARCH, NEAR HAVRE DES CANNONS

climbing up and down the cliff to avoid awkward sections. The optimistically-named Pine Forest comes into view, and easy escapes are possible from here. Below the first main stand of pines we meet a deep gully (Oi) which does not dry out but here we can skirt around its landward side and over a jammed boulder. Ominous gurgles eminate from the blackness beneath feet . . .

A little further on and we reach the ancient mooring known as Divette. Huge piled blocks are evidence of what James Marr suggests may be the Bailiwick's oldest harbour still in its original state. It probably dates from the fourteenth century, when Chateau de Jerbourg was constructed. Beyond the breakwater is a gully of golden sand.

CAVE AND ARCH, PIED DU MUR

Easy scrambling leads round to the bay of Pied du Mur, which means "Foot of the Wall". This refers to the earthen ramparts of the Bronze Age fort which stretched across the Jerbourg Peninsula from Petit Port to this point. The touristy modern name is Marble Bay, and we descend a rock step of "marble" (quartz in fact) to beach level. If the route is being split, then this is a perfect spot to rejoin the cliff path.

A small stream tumbles down La Tourrehaize, the cliff forming the back of the bay, and to its right is a cave. Continuing on we pass under a promontory via two tunnels, and beyond this is a third arch and a deep cave. The best exit is from the seaward end of the gully (II−), which leads to a flattish area of rock. This is a raised beach, eroded by the waves during a warm interglacial period when the sea level was higher. It can be followed fairly easily to Le Bec du Nez, which is on Map 24.

This charming little harbour has lots of interest. There is always a mass of fishing gear and a flotilla of small boats. A slipway and winch is used to haul up the vessels for repair. Above the harbour is the stonework of a battery which was constructed during the Napoleonic Wars (see Route 40).

We can just see part of the defences of Fermain Bay peeping out from the next headland to the north. We don't have far to go now, but the way is still committing as there are no escape routes other than reversing our steps. Easy scrambling leads over a wave-cut platform, and past a small arch and a huge blowhole which must have been an impressive sight in the distant past when the sea level was higher. We then move around La Ricou Point and Fermain Bay comes into full view. Just as we think we've made it, we reach the sting in the tail: a deep gully with slippery weeded sides and a vertical back wall, known as Le Grand Creux. This is not too technical (III−), but neither is it a place for disco-dancing. Beyond the gully there are no further difficulties. We pass a tiny waterfall below a copse, and soon reach the shingle of the bay. Made it!

Fermain Bay is a popular beach in the summer. Sheltered from all but an east wind, it provides a perfect suntrap in the morning. It is a relatively safe place to swim, though beyond the edges of the bay the turbulent Little Russel can resemble a river. Impressive defence walls and a Martello Tower rear from the beach: a severe obstacle for would-be invaders, and dating from the late 1700s. In the summer a ferry from St Peter Port lands here.

Several different routes lead back to Saint Martin's Point, and these are described in Route 43.

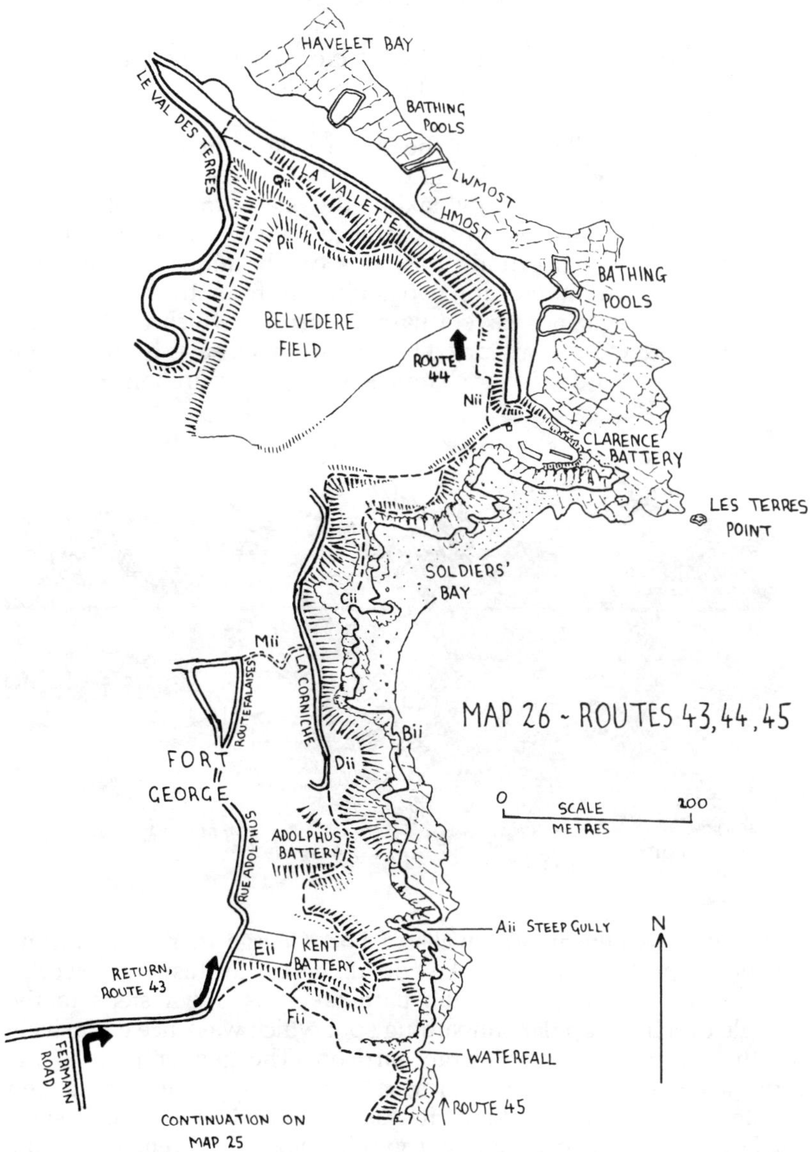
HAVELET BAY
BATHING POOLS
LE VAL DES TERRES
LA VALLETTE
LWMOST
HMOST
Qii
Pii
BATHING POOLS
BELVEDERE FIELD
ROUTE 44
Nii
CLARENCE BATTERY
LES TERRES POINT
SOLDIERS' BAY
Cii
Mii
ROUTE FALAISES
LA CORNICHE
MAP 26 - ROUTES 43, 44, 45
Bii
FORT GEORGE
Dii
0 SCALE 200 METRES
RUE ADOLPHUS
ADOLPHUS BATTERY
Aii STEEP GULLY
N
Eii
KENT BATTERY
RETURN, ROUTE 43
Fii
FERMAIN ROAD
WATERFALL
ROUTE 45
CONTINUATION ON MAP 25

ROUTE 43 A coastal walk returning via Fort George

MAPS 25 AND 26

LA VALLETTE TO FERMAIN BAY

DISTANCE — 2.3 miles

ACCESS — La Vallette is on the south side of St Peter Port, and can be reached by turning left at the foot of Le Val des Terres.

We join the cliff path by taking the steps to the left of the aquarium. These take us up to Clarence Battery, an outlier of Fort George. The original cannon positions can be found amongst the undergrowth, and there are two additions from the Occupation. The powder magazines have a narrow corridor which runs around their seaward walls. This puzzling feature may have been a damp course, forming a dry inner chamber where the munitions could be stored.

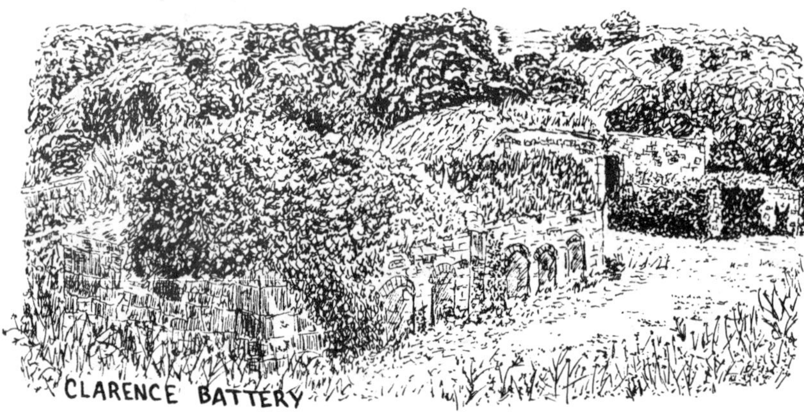

As we pass beneath the walls of Fort George there is a turning on the left to Soldiers' Bay. A short diversion to this bay is worthwhile, and the left fork of the path takes us down steps to the shingle beach, a popular sunbathing spot which was once exclusively for the use of the Fort George garrison. The gentler path to the right leads to a rocky platform, a popular spot for fishing and diving when the tide is high. It was once used as a landing stage for Fort George, and several cut granite blocks still remain. To the right is a brick arch, kiln, and a narrow trial mine adit (Cii) which dates from the 1830s. These can be explored when the tide is out.

Returning to the main cliff path we follow a wide gravelly track up to the road at La Corniche (Clifftop Road), where we turn towards Fermain Bay and South Coast. At the "Private Road" sign we move left onto the cliff path proper, past a clearing (Dii) with three benches where there are wonderful views across the Little and Big Russel to Herm, Jethou, Sark and the smaller islets. Continuing on we meet the imposing ramparts of the Adolphus Battery

which has several embrasures for musket fire. The walls are unfortunately marred by breeze block repairs: granite would have looked so much better! Steps take us a short distance inland beneath Kent Battery, then down to a junction where we head left for Fermain Bay. The turning to the right (signed Ford Road) leads to the military cemetery (Eii) which we pass on our return path. Continuing down a wooded valley we again turn left at a path junction (Fii) to emerge on the cliff slopes, where there are fine views south to St Martin's Point, The Pine Forest and Ozanne Steps. The steps themselves, which once gave access to a private beach, are soon reached. The walls were covered with numerous ormer shells, with their beautiful mother-of-pearl linings, but few now remain.

The next path junction (Gii) is signed The Moorings, Bus Route and Fermain Bay, and a short diversion to The Moorings or Les Amarrages, is worthwhile. The original platform, which was constructed in the 1600s, has been replaced by a modern structure which makes an excellent place from which to swim or fish. The path continues around the headland of Le Becquet to Fermain Bay. Above the bay we have a choice of two routes: the easier right hand route (Hii) taking us down to the road, while the left turn descends steps to emerge on the north battery, atop the impressive granite defence walls. The "Martello" tower pre-dates the battery by several years, and was constructed in 1778, as a stop-gap defence measure when France became allies of the American colonists (see Route 22). The battery was constructed in the early 1790s. The south battery is now hidden in the undergrowth and no longer accessible. During the occupation the ingenious Germans used the valley streams as a source of hydro-electric power! Buried beneath the beach are some large wooden posts that are occasionally revealed by the waves. These could be the remains of a very old pier, possibly dating from the Roman Period.

Fermain Bay is a popular spot. It has a safe beach with good bathing, avoiding the strong currents of the Little Russel, which at times resembles a turbulent river. The bay is well-sheltered from all but easterly winds, and the visiting yachts which often anchor here add to the scenery. For the adventurous there are caves to explore, the largest being Le Grand Creux which is on the south side of the bay and is only accessible at low water on spring tides. Take care not to get cut off! In the summer a boat service operates trips to St Peter Port, and this can make a pleasant return trip for those who do not relish the remainder of the walk. There are regular sailings from mid-morning to late afternoon, and embarkation is via a mobile jetty which is winched up and down the beach with the changing tide.

LE COQUELIN

Our return path takes us up the north slopes of the bay, following our descent route. We must avoid the path signed Main Road, which leads along the slopes of Fermain Valley to La Favorita Hotel, and then up to Fort Road (this is an option for those who wish to return by bus, and there is a convenient watering hole at the top of the road in the form of the Fermain Tavern). Our path is the second turning (Jii) signed Fort Road, and we turn right off this to Le Becquet headland. Here we find the oddly-shaped Pepper Pot or Le Cocquelin ("The Winkle"), (Kii), named after its shell-like outline. The building was a sentry box, constructed at the same time as the Fermain batteries, and there is a spiral inside. The view from the slits is now obscured by trees, and the construction is now painted white to make a useful shipping mark. On the end of the headland is a powder magazine and the stone platform of Le Becquet Battery, which now has a bench where we can sit and enjoy the view.

Retracing our steps past Le Cocquelin we reach Le Becquet Road and follow this onto Fermain Road. At the left hand bend (Lii) we turn right onto a lane guarded against vehicles by three granite bollards. At the junction we pass beneath the inner walls of the old fort which has been a dominant feature of our walk.

Construction of Fort George began in earnest in 1780, and continued for over 30 years. Two years earlier the French had become allies of the American colonists, who were engaged in the War of Independence. An invasion of Jersey, albeit unsuccessful, led to fears of similar attempts on Guernsey, and the large fortification was planned. In many respects it had the characteristics of a Medieval fort, with a moat, drawbridge and a star-shaped citadel similar to a keep, as well as barracks, walls and four batteries. From the time of its construction, and until the British forces abandoned Guernsey in 1940, there was a British garrison continually stationed in Fort George. The Germans used "Georg-feste" until a bombing raid in 1944, and following the end of the war the fort remained in a sad state of repair. The Crown sold it to the States of Guernsey in 1958, who then sold it to property developers in 1961. It is unfortunate that most of the fort was destroyed during the construction of the housing estate, and part of Guernsey's heritage lost forever.

Below the walls is a military cemetery. Here are the graves of British soldiers who died whilst stationed on Guernsey, or in the First World War, and over 100 German soldiers who died during the Second World War. Many of these were injured at the D-day landings and taken to the underground military hospital in St Andrew's. We continue along Rue Adolphus for a short distance to a fork, and then turn rightwards onto Routes Falaises (Cliff Road). A right turn down a narrow walled lane (Mii) takes us back to the cliff path, and we retrace our steps to the Clarence Battery. Here it is possible to join Route 44 and follow this past the Belvedere Field to La Vallette.

ROUTE 44 A short coastal walk

MAP 26

LA VALLETTE LOOP

A CIRCULAR route taking us a short distance up the cliff path to Clarence Battery, and returning via the Belvedere Field and Le Val des Terres. There are excellent views of St Peter Port, the Little Russel and the neighbouring islands.

DISTANCE — 0.6 miles

ACCESS — As for previous section.

Our walk starts from the bathing places at La Vallette. These are generally understood to be the first open-air marine swimming pools in the British Isles, and were constructed in 1844. The aquarium at the end of the road occupies a tunnel dated 1864. This was part of an ambitious plan to construct a road along the east coast to Fermain Bay. Thankfully the project was abandoned to leave an area of 'unspoilt woodland'. The Germans extended the tunnel through Les Terres Point to emerge in a small bay where they constructed a gun emplacement.

To the left of the aquarium a set of steps takes us steeply up towards the Clarence Battery, an outlier of Fort George. Keep an eye open on the left for a narrow track which leads past a man-made cave to the end of Les Terres Point. Near the top of the steps we pass through an arch, where the railings on the left were sawn off as part of the post-war search for scrap. Clarence Battery is well worth exploring: it has several gun tracks and powder magazines which have an unusual narrow corridor which runs around their seaward walls. This was possibly some form of damp proofing. The views to the south take in St Martin's Point, Le Bec du Nez moorings, Doyle Column and the headland of Le Becquet which hides Fermain Bay.

From the battery we take a right turn (Nii) which is signed Val des Terres and Belvedere. Following this there are views down to the bathing pools, and we pass beneath the granite walls of Fort George. The wall has been painted white at one point as a marker for shipping, and behind this is a lighthouse which can be viewed from the Belvedere Field. An arch on the left is the Postern Gate and a short diversion through this takes us into the Belvedere Field, which was used for ceremonies and parading. Its big day was 24th May, Queen Victoria's birthday, when the Grand Review of the Island Militia took place.

When the delapidated Fort George was sold to property developers in 1961 three deputies (the Guernsey equivalent of an MP) fought to save the field, which is now part of Guernsey's green belt. There is a good viewpoint above the car park on the right, no doubt the reason why the Town Point Battery (Pii), with its more recent German addition, was constructed there. The platforms for the cannon can be observed, though the embrasures have been bricked off. There is a panoramic view of St Peter Port, the harbour and Castle Cornet, and the islands of Alderney (in clear weather), Herm, Jethou and the northern end of Sark.

Returning through the arch we have a choice of two ways. A left turn takes us up a short flight of steps, and we can follow the edge of the wall to emerge about halfway down Le Val des Terres (those with an aversion to road walking can take a more direct steep path to the right of the steps). Alternatively we can continue straight on from the arch and follow a wide path (Qii) to the road, and then down steps on the right to La Vallette. Le Val des Terres was constructed in 1929, providing work rather than dole for the rising numbers of unemployed. Returning to the start we pass La Vallette Underground Military Museum, which is open from March to October.

LA VALLETTE

ROUTE 45 A sea level scramble

MAPS 25 and 26

FERMAIN BAY TO LA VALLETTE

DISTANCE	— Fermain Bay to Ozanne Steps	0.3 miles
	Ozanne Steps to Soldiers' Bay	0.5 miles
	Soldiers' Bay to La Vallette	0.2 miles
GRADE	— Fermain Bay to Ozanne Steps	I+
	Ozanne Steps to Soldiers' Bay	III
	Soldiers' Bay to La Vallette	I+

GREAT care needs to be taken on this traverse. The first and last sections present no problems, but the central section needs a careful choice of tide. Here the route is only traversable for a short period of time, there are no escapes and it should only be attempted by a competent party.

The traverse and cliff walk have much of historical interest, and there are marvellous views across The Little Russel.

RECOMMENDED TIDE — 8.7 metres. Fermain Bay to the Ozanne Steps and Soldiers' Bay to La Vallette are possible at low water on neap tides.

ACCESS — Follow Route 43 to Fermain Bay.

THE TRAVERSE — Heading off across the bay we pass a cave on the left, and soon reach the structure known as The Moorings. Originally called Les Amarrages, it dates from the 1600s. Rounding the point we can make rapid progress along a wave-cut platform, before descending to a shingle beach littered with limpet shells. Passing a gully and cave we arrive at the Ozanne Steps and embark on the difficult and committing middle section.

The shingle beach beyond the steps can be left by a tunnel near the high watermark, which takes us through the rock barrier. The rock steps beyond this vary in difficulty from II− to III depending on the state of the tide. Rapid progress is then made along a platform and over a small arch. Scrambling then becomes more sustained and we descend to a gully below a waterfall. Beyond this is an awkward descent to a gully, and the exit from this is hard (III−) if flooding. We then pass under an overhanging cliff; the cliff-top is covered with nesting shags in the spring. Climbing around this, Soldiers' Bay, the houses of Fort George, and the Clarence Battery come into view.

We then meet a steep gully (Aii) which is easily passed at its landward end. Almost immediately we descend to a second gully. This presents no major problems if the boulders at its seaward end are uncovered. If they are submerged, then the best route is to climb up to a broken corner, then descend down to the right (III).

Beyond this gully we gain a platform and there is relatively simple scrambling until we reach the cliff (Bii) which leads into Soldiers' Bay. Given the right tide and enough speed, the base of this should not be flooded. If it is, then an unpleasant traverse of the cliff can be made (III+). Soldiers' Bay was named after the Fort George garrison, who at one time had exclusive use of the bay. It has several interesting features. On its south side a gully has been bricked over to form an arch leading to a ravine with a stream. There is also a kiln (Cii) and a narrow copper mine adit which dates from the 1830s. The rock platform in the centre of the bay was used as a landing place for Fort George, and several stone flags still rest on its top.

Scrambling round from Soldiers' Bay we reach a small rocky bay with a gun emplacement and a tunnel which connects to the aquarium. A gully leads out of this bay beneath the walls of the Clarence Battery, and an exit left from a corroded girder brings La Vallette Bathing places and Castle Cornet into view.

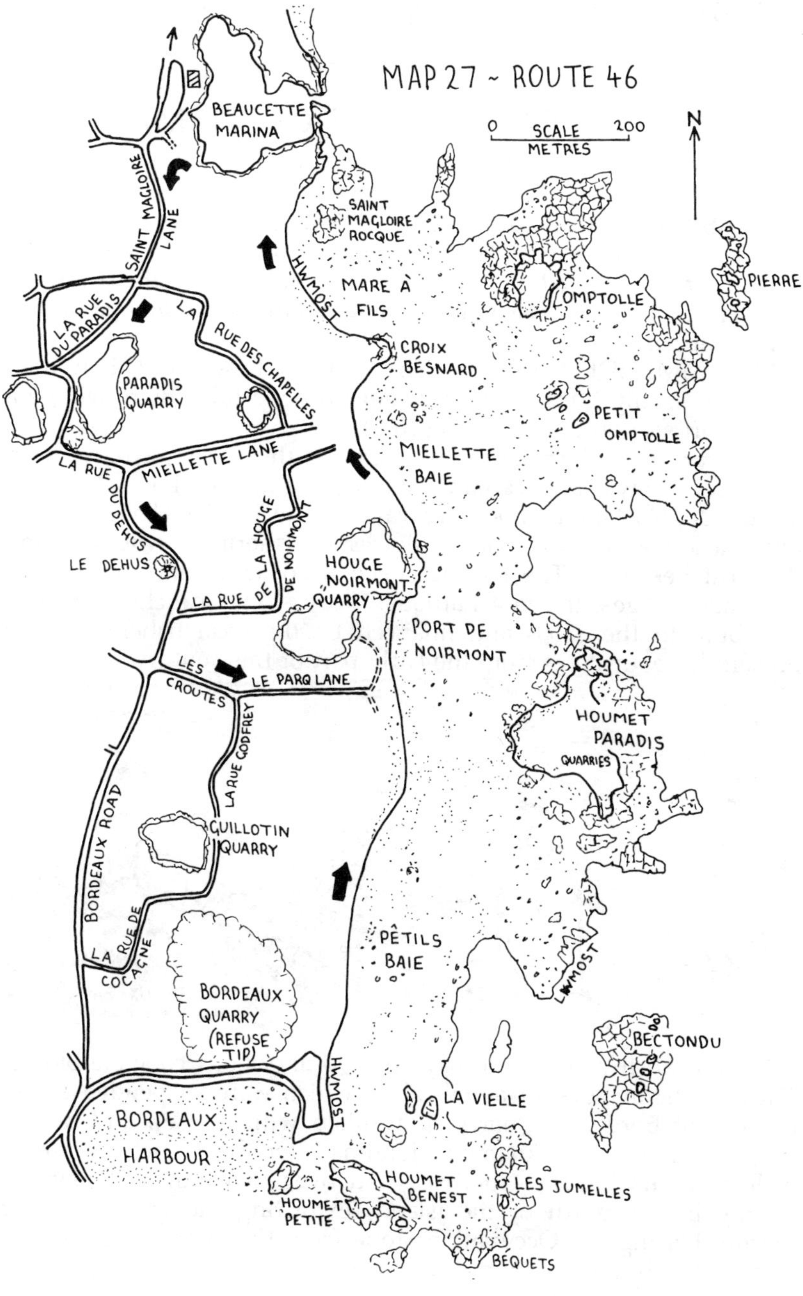
MAP 27 ~ ROUTE 46
0 SCALE 200
METRES
N
BEAUCETTE MARINA
SAINT MAGLOIRE LANE
SAINT MAGLOIRE ROCQUE
MARE À FILS
HWMOST
OMPTOLLE
PIERRE
LA RUE DU PARADIS
LA RUE DES CHAPELLES
PARADIS QUARRY
CROIX BÉSNARD
PETIT OMPTOLLE
MIELLETTE BAIE
MIELLETTE LANE
LA RUE DU DEHUS
LE DEHUS
LA RUE DE LA HOUGE DE NOIRMONT
HOUGE NOIRMONT QUARRY
PORT DE NOIRMONT
LES CROUTES
LE PARQ LANE
HOUMET PARADIS
QUARRIES
LA RUE GODFREY
GUILLOTIN QUARRY
BORDEAUX ROAD
LA RUE DE COCAGNE
PÊTILS BAIE
HWMOST
BORDEAUX QUARRY (REFUSE TIP)
BECTONDU
HWMOST
LA VIELLE
BORDEAUX HARBOUR
HOUMET BENEST
LES JUMELLES
HOUMET PETITE
BÉQUETS

ROUTE 46 A coastal walk with some scrambling at high water

MAP 27

BORDEAUX BAY TO BEAUCETTE MARINA

DISTANCE 2.1 miles

AN EASY, enjoyable walk with fine views across the Little Russel to the neighbouring islands. Our return route takes us through the lanes past the flooded quarry of Paradis, and the burial chamber of Le Déhus. The area also has excellent bird-watching, passing a variety of habitats.

RECOMMENDED TIDE — The walk is best avoided at high water on spring tides. At high water on neap tides there will be a very short section of scrambling (II–).

We start from Bordeaux Bay, perhaps the most picturesque of Guernsey's bays, and certainly its best natural harbour. Much of Victor Hugo's famous book, Travailleurs de la Mer (Toilers of the Sea), described the lives of the Bordeaux fishermen, who still land their catches here. The bay has been used as an anchorage since the Middle Ages; the first harbour, a dry stone "cauchie" or quay was built in the 1800s and financed by the local fishermen. The present harbour dates from the early part of this century.

On the north side of the bay are two enormous concrete blocks. These were anchors for aerial cables which were suspended across the top of Bordeaux Quarry (now filled with refuse), and carried suspended trucks nicknamed Blondins after the French tight-rope walker. In its heyday Guernsey had over two hundred quarries, mainly in the north of the island, extracting the grey and blue diorite. During the Occupation stone from the quarry and pebbles from Petils Bay were taken by rail to the stone-crushing plant on

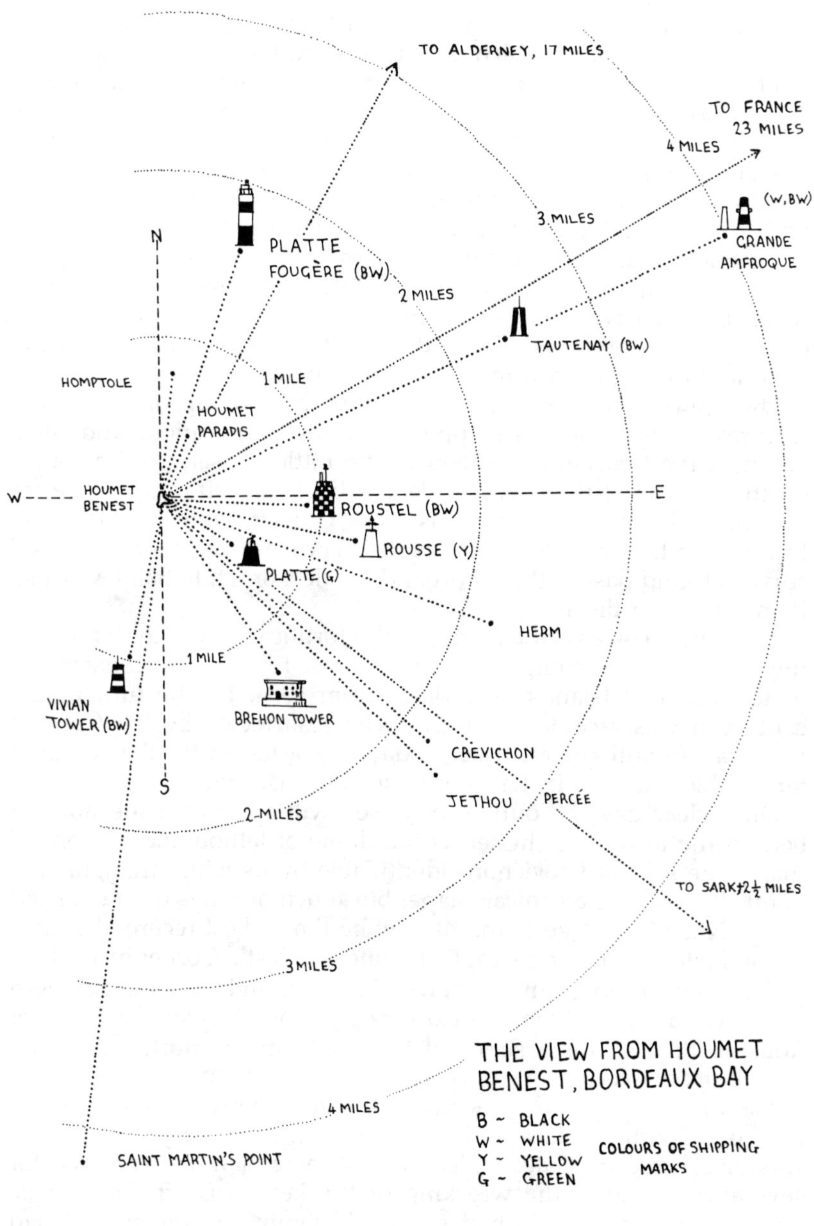
TO ALDERNEY, 17 MILES
TO FRANCE
23 MILES
4 MILES
3 MILES
2 MILES
1 MILE
(W, BW)
GRANDE
AMFROQUE
PLATTE
FOUGÈRE (BW)
TAUTENAY (BW)
N
HOMPTOLE
HOUMET
PARADIS
W
HOUMET
BENEST
E
ROUSTEL (BW)
ROUSSE (Y)
PLATTE (G)
HERM
1 MILE
VIVIAN
TOWER (BW)
BREHON TOWER
CREVICHON
S
JETHOU
PERCÉE
2 MILES
TO SARK 7½ MILES
3 MILES
4 MILES
SAINT MARTIN'S POINT
THE VIEW FROM HOUMET
BENEST, BORDEAUX BAY
B ~ BLACK
W ~ WHITE
Y ~ YELLOW
G ~ GREEN
COLOURS OF SHIPPING
MARKS

the north quay of Saint Sampson, and used in the massive fortification programme.

At the end of the road on the north side of the bay are two houmets (peninsula) which are worth exploring. They are only briefly cut off at high water on spring tides, when the Little Russel, or The Roads as it used to be called, will be flowing northwards as swiftly as a river. The houmets are veritable rockeries, with wild flowers growing in profusion amongst the crevices and boulders. On Houmet Benest ("Simpleton's Peninsula") there was a battery with a 24 pounder cannon during the French Revolutionary and Napoleonic Wars, and a more modern gun placement during the German occupation. The clean-cut nature of many of the rocks reveal past quarrying: few outcrops were left untouched. The patches of yellow soil are loess, glacial dust that was blown over from the continent during the warmer interglacial periods.

The views from the houmet are superb, and full of interesting features, with numerous shipping beacons, fortifications and islets amongst the treacherous waters of the Little Russel. To the south, on the far side of the bay, is Vale Castle. To its left (and on the far side of St Sampson's harbour) is Mont Crevelt, with its "Martello" tower, perched above the oil tanks. The east coast of Guernsey curves around past St Peter Port and Castle Cornet, to Saint Martin's Point in the far distance.

Le Brehon Tower is the large circular fortification which dominates the middle of the strait. This was the last tower to be constructed in the Channel Islands, and dates from 1854. By the turn of the century it was abandoned, only to be resurrected by the German forces as an anti-aircraft base. Today it is a haven for the common terns which nest on its flat roof in splendid isolation.

On a clear day the outline of Jersey will appear on the horizon behind the tower. To the left is the dome of Jethou and in front of this is the islet of Crevichon, identifiable by its white triangulation point. It was once a conical shape, but much of it has been quarried away. Nigel Jee suggests that it may be the earliest recorded quarry in the Bailiwick, having supplied stone for Castle Cornet in 1564.

Sark appears through the Percee Passage, and near the northern tip of Herm are golden sand dunes and the chequered beacon of Roustel. Behind this a series of low islets stretch north; these are the Humps, which were once part of Herm. From south to north these are Godin and Galeauex, Longue Pierre and Le Grand Amfroque with its black and white beacon. In January 1919 a body was discovered on Galeaux. The unfortunate man had survived for several weeks after the wrecking of the ketch *Isis* off Fontennelle Baie (see Route 47). He had survived mainly on limpets and had constructed a shelter from seaweed and wreckage, before succumbing to hunger and cold.

Our walk takes us north along a flat grassy area above Petit Miels Bay, a sheltered anchorage for fishing boats. We soon reach the islet of Houmet Paradis, which is accessible near low water, and proves remarkably wild and deserted considering its proximity to this crowded island of Guernsey. Much quarrying took place here in the past and a rift has been cut through the centre of the island. We should take great care to avoid being cut off by the tide which sneaks up quickly and quietly to create a strong flow in the channel. Do not try to wade or swim back: people have lost their lives here. "Houmet Paradis" may be a corruption of Houmet L'-Eperquerie, which reveals that it was once a place for drying fish.

At the northern end of the bay there is a rock outcrop which, like most of the headlands in the north of the island, has been quarried (look out for the drill holes which were filled with explo-

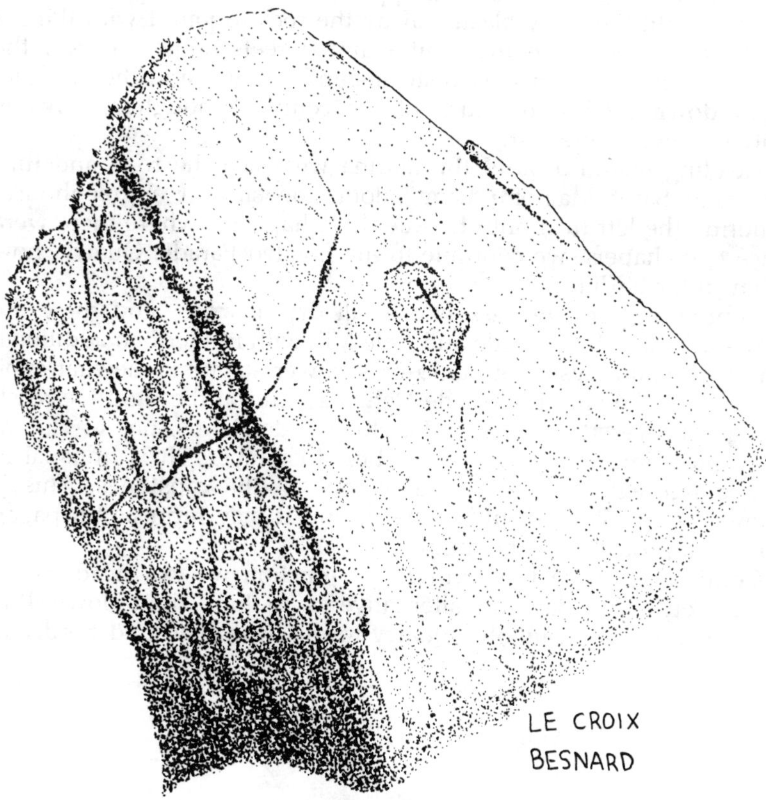

LE CROIX BESNARD

sive). When the tide is clear of the cliff foot, it is an easy matter to walk along the shingle to Miellette Bay. If the cliff base is flooded then we can engage in a spot of scrambling and either work our way along the rocks above the water, or gain the rocky ridge which follows the skyline fence, above Houmet Noirmont Quarry. The quarry is flushed by the sea at high water on spring tides, and is used as a shellfish rearing farm.

If the scramble looks too daunting, an alternative would be to follow the lanes around the back of the quarry to emerge at Miellette Bay.

Crossing Miellette Bay we reach a rocky spur, La Croix Bésnard. Close examination reveals a carved cross, and the drill holes of the quarryman. The path then skirts the bay of Mare à Fils, to reach Beaucette Marina.

An 1802 military survey refers to a battery at Bosuet Point, which suggests Beaucette may be a misnomer. Traces of the battery and its powder magazine have disappeared. The marina was once a quarry, until the army blasted away the rock to join it with the sea in 1969. Offshore are the white-painted reefs of Les Brayes, the scene of several wrecks. Two steamships, the *Ibex* and the *Brighton,* went down around the turn of the century, though remarkably only two lives were lost.

Heading inland around the marina we reach the road and turn left onto Saint Magloire Lane, along the side of a greenhouse. Ignoring the left turn onto La Rue des Chapelles, where there were once two chapels, we continue to the flooded Paradis Quarry, now a haven for birdlife.

Continuing left we pass two small dry quarries, and there are views across to Vale Castle and Vale Mill with its German additions. The twin chimneys of St Sampson's power station somewhat spoil the view! Following La Rue de Déhus around to the right we reach the grass-covered tumulus of La Hougue de Déhus, one of Guernsey's most impressive megalithic burial chambers. It is unusual in that a figure has been carved on one of the capstones. This is known as Le Gardieu du Tombeau, and it may represent a pagan god, or a protector of the tomb.

Continuing on to the second "T" junction we can head left to reach Petit Miel Bay (an alternative is to turn right down Rue Godfrey and past Guillotin Quarry to the main road and Bordeaux Bay).

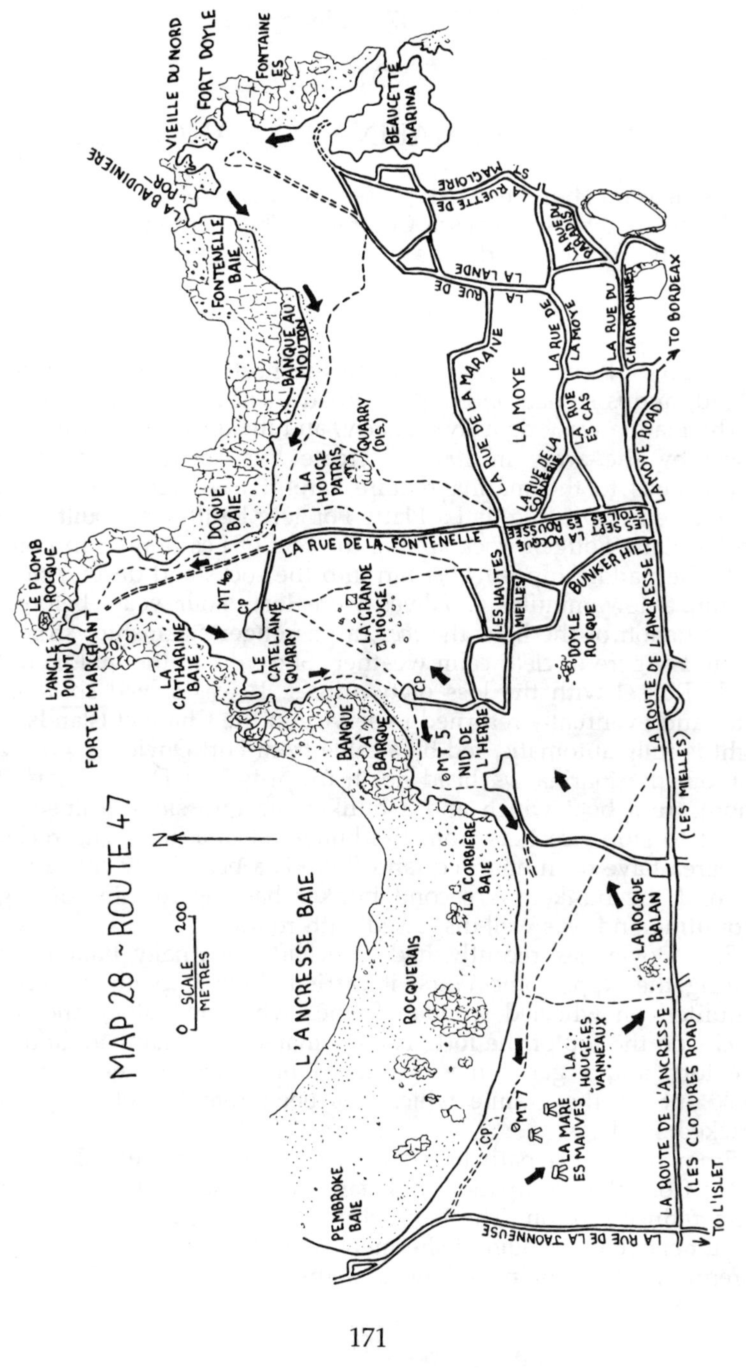
MAP 28 ~ ROUTE 47
0 SCALE 200
METRES
N
L'ANCRESSE BAIE
PEMBROKE BAIE
ROCQUERAIS
LA CORBIÈRE BAIE
NID DE L'HERBE
MT 5
MT 4
MT 7
CP
BANQUE À BARQUE
LE CATELAINE QUARRY
LA GRANDE HOUGE
LA CATHARINE BAIE
L'ANGLE POINT
FORT LE MARCHANT
LE PLOMB ROCQUE
DOQUE BAIE
LA RUE DE LA FONTENELLE
LA HOUGE PATRIS
QUARRY (DIS.)
BANQUE AU MOUTON
FONTENELLE BAIE
LA BAUDINIERE
POR-
VIEILLE DU NORD
FORT DOYLE
FONTAINE ES
BEAUCETTE MARINA
LA RUETTE DE ST. MAGLOIRE
LA RUE DE LA LANDE
LA RUE DE LA MARAIVE
LA MOYE
LA RUE DE LA MOYE
LA RUE DU PARADIS
LA RUE DU CHARDRONNET
TO BORDEAUX
LA RUE ES CAS
LA RUE DE LA CORDERIE
LA MOYE ROAD
LES SEPT ETOILES
LA ROCQUE ES ROUSSE
LES HAUTES MIELLES
BUNKER HILL
DOYLE ROCQUE
LA ROUTE DE L'ANCRESSE
(LES MIELLES)
LA ROCQUE BALAN
LA HOUGE ES VANNEAUX
LA MARE ES MAUVES
LA ROUTE DE L'ANCRESSE
(LES CLOTURES ROAD)
TO L'ISLET
LA RUE DE LA JAONNEUSE

ROUTE 47 A loop walk

MAP 28

BEAUCETTE MARINA TO L'ANCRESSE

THIS pleasant shoreline walk passes many sites of historical interest, and returns over L'Ancresse Common. There are many scrambling possibilities on the headlands.

DISTANCE — 3 miles

ACCESS — Beaucette Marina is on the northern-eastern tip of the island, and is signed on La Moye Road, near L'Ancresse Common.

The marina was originally a quarry, and the quarry wall was blasted away by the army in 1969 to create this sheltered haven. The approaches to the marina require careful navigation to avoid the jagged reefs. Offshore is La Platte Fougère lighthouse, built in 1909 on La Platte Fougère rock among the reef of Les Brayes. In January 1887 the paddleship *Brighton* ran into the rocks and despite sinking within a few minutes, no lives were lost. Four years before the construction of the light the *Ibex*, a passenger steamship, struck La Platte Fougère in clear calm weather. She sank in the middle of the Little Russel with the loss of two lives. It was salved six months later and eventually returned to service in the Channel Islands. The light is fully automatic, fed by a cable from Fort Doyle.

From the marina we head north towards Fort Doyle. Along the shore are a boat winch and a bunker, its gun slit still lined with wood to stop ricochets from the bullets of attackers. The rocks in the area have been quarried, and there is a beautifully-cut capstone beyond the bunker. A second bunker has the remains of a gun mounting and was well-disguised with rocks.

Fort Doyle has recently had a facelift. Originally built in 1803 during the Napoleonic Wars, it carried three 18-pounder cannon, mounted on wheeled wooden frames which ran along the metal tracks on the top of the fort. The Germans made many additions to the fort, and a garrison was housed here. On the descent steps look out for the granite which has been rounded off to prevent cracked skulls.

From the fort a path takes us past a large concrete slab which dates from the Occupation and has been tossed onto the shore to help reduce erosion. The bay before us is generally referred to as Fontenelle Bay, though fishermen refer to the small bay in the foreground as Fontenelle Bay, and the far corner as Docque Baie.

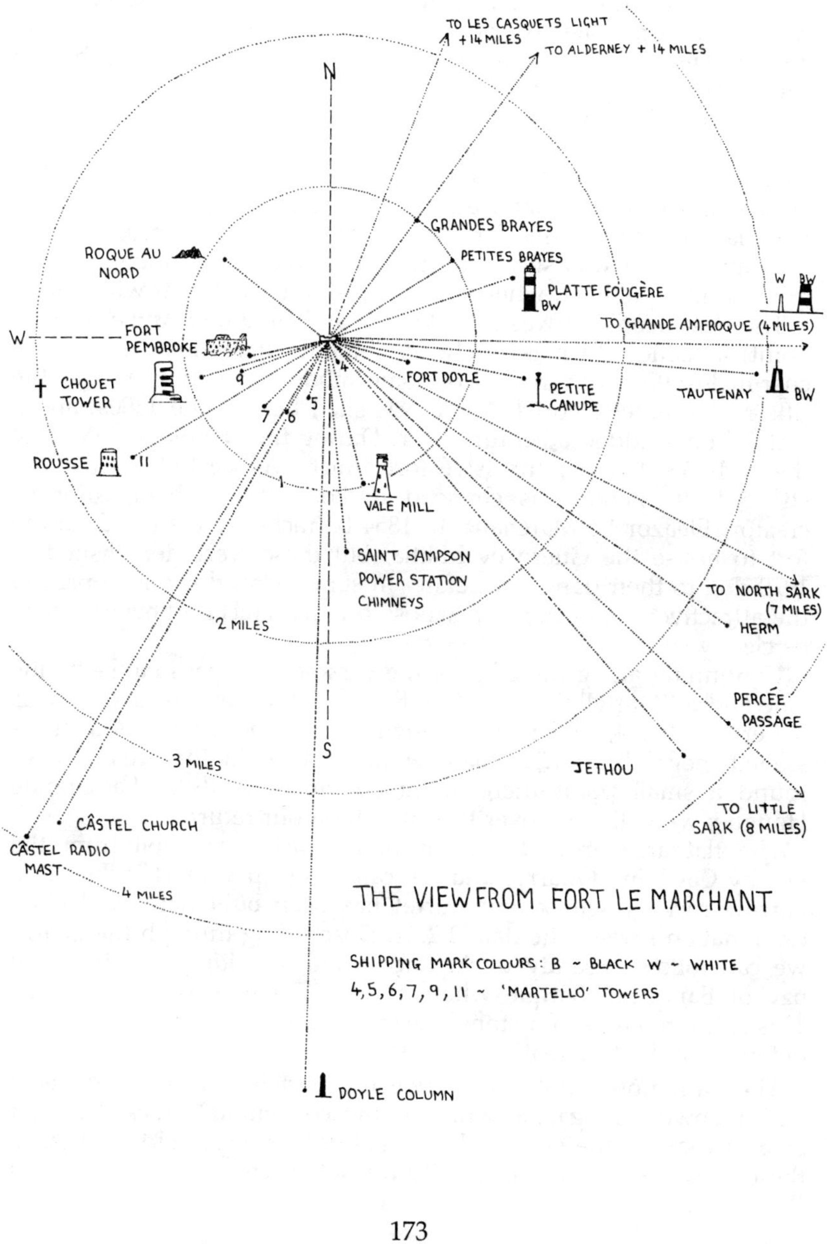
TO LES CASQUETS LIGHT
+14 MILES
TO ALDERNEY + 14 MILES
N
GRANDES BRAYES
ROQUE AU
NORD
PETITES BRAYES
PLATTE FOUGÈRE
BW
W
BW
TO GRANDE AMFROQUE (4 MILES)
W
FORT
PEMBROKE
4
9
FORT DOYLE
CHOUET
TOWER
PETITE
CANUPE
TAUTENAY
BW
5
7
6
ROUSSE
11
1
VALE MILL
SAINT SAMPSON
POWER STATION
CHIMNEYS
TO NORTH SARK
(7 MILES)
2 MILES
HERM
PERCÉE
PASSAGE
S
3 MILES
JETHOU
TO LITTLE
SARK (8 MILES)
CÂSTEL CHURCH
CÂSTEL RADIO
MAST
4 MILES
THE VIEW FROM FORT LE MARCHANT
SHIPPING MARK COLOURS: B ~ BLACK W ~ WHITE
4,5,6,7,9,11 ~ 'MARTELLO' TOWERS
DOYLE COLUMN

Several reefs divide the bay at low water, and it is a good place for snorkelling.

In December 1918 the ketch *Isis* hit the rocks off the bay. A body was washed onto the shore a few days later, and a second body was found on Galeaux, an islet north of Herm, the following month. The unfortunate man had survived on limpets and built a shelter of wreckage and weed. Numerous vessels must have passed within sight, but the sailor succumbed to cold and hunger.

The path leads us below the shingle of Banque au Mouton, and we are now following the tracks of a railway which was constructed around much of the island during the Occupation, and carried the materials for the massive fortification programme. We pass through a cutting which was sliced through the edge of La Hougue Patrie to reach Docque Baie, where there are four ancient boat winches.

The next headland was once known as Pointe de l'Angle (Corner Point) a name which is rarely used today. It retains much of its charm despite the intrusion of some modern storehouses and the rifle range targets. Fort L'Angle was sited here in the 1600s, and a watch house added a century later. During the Napoleonic Wars of the early 1800s the impressive fort which we see today was constructed. Its name was changed to Fort Le Marchant, after its creator, Eleazor Le Marchant. In 1854 barracks were erected on the fort to house the Guernsey Militia, but these were demolished in 1970 due to their dangerous state. In some ways this has improved the attractiveness of the fort, whose original graceful lines can now be clearly seen.

Continuing along the edge of the common we pass La Catherine Baie and a "Martello" tower (see Route 27 for more details). This is tower number 4, and is also known as Trepied Tower as a three-stoned megalithic burial chamber once stood in the area. As we round a small point there are good views south to La Grande Hougue; we will cross over this hillock on our return.

The flat area around the car park consists of spoil from the nearby Catelaine Quarry, and we can head up a short incline to a narrow rocky ridge. A gun turret has been built here, and close examination reveals the date 2.2.44. Descending through the quarry we can follow a sandy track, once a railway siding, to the small bay of Banque à Barque where there is an ugly concrete tower. This is the remains of a stone crushing plant, built for the extensive defences of the Occupation.

The path now climbs up between "Martello" Tower number 5 and a powder magazine which is tucked behind a rock. The flat area of rocks is the site of Nid de l'Herbé Battery. Skirting around the craggy mound of Nid de l'Herbé we reach a car park and can either descend past a bunker to the beach, sometimes called La Corbière Baie at this point, or walk along the edge of the common behind the sea wall, once again in the tracks of the German railway. The sea wall is also of Occupation vintage, originally constructed as an anti-tank wall.

We reach our halfway point at the Sablon d'Or Café, above the western shores of L'Ancresse Bay. Scanning the land around the bay we can see numerous fortifications dating over hundreds of years. No doubt the wide sandy beach and the absence of cliffs made the bay a likely target for an invading force. The chain of "Martello" Towers, and Forts Pembroke and Le Marchant date from the French Wars of the late 18th and early 19th centuries. The occupying German forces added the sea wall, flak batteries, radar stations, numerous bunkers, and the huge observation tower at Chouet(†). The common must have been a hive of activity with huge quantities of sand and stone arriving by rail to our present position, which was a large concrete mixing plant.

L'Ancresse was called Ankerbucht (Anchor Bay) by the occupiers. The origins of its name are uncertain; it may be a corruption of L'Ancrage, The Anchorage. It is said that Duke Robert, father of William the Conqueror, took refuge from inclement weather in the bay. Less likely is the suggestion that Rollo assembled his Scandinavian Viking ships in the bay before heading off for some fun in

LA MARE ÈS MAUVES AND 'MARTELLO TOWER' 7

Normandy. In 1923 the bay was used several times as a landing place for the Sea Eagle Flying Boat, which for a short while offered a passenger service between Guernsey and England.

There are several sites of archaelogical interest in the vicinity. The largest passage grave in Guernsey can be found on La Varde, the hill to the south-west (see Route 48). About 50 yards to the south of the car park is a fallen menhir: close examination reveals it to be christianised by a carved cross. Just to the east is an area of stones which could be the remains of a stone circle. Nearer to La Rue de la Jaonneuses is a cist, or single chambered tomb, called La Mare ès Mauves.

From here we can begin our return walk and head in an easterly direction past La Hougue es Vanneaux to La Rocque Balan (Ballen's Rock). This was once a pagan site, and two cup marks (purpose unknown) can be found on the central stone. It is said that on Midsummer Night it was the scene of naked dancing and orgies. Presumably there was less gorse in those days.

The rock is a good vantage point, and there are fine views of the wide expanse of L'Ancresse Bay, and the "Martello" Towers which guard it. Tower 9 looks distinctly Pisa-ish from here! Tower 11 is visible at Rousse on the west coast, while Chouet Tower dominates the headland to the north-west(†).

Numerous pathways cross the common, and there are several possible routes to Beaucette. A pleasant way back is to head for the knoll beyond the car park on the east side of the bay. This is La

LA GRANDE HOUGE

Grande Hougue, a labyrinth of Germanic defences, some still camouflaged with rocks.

The masts of Beaucette Marina are visible from the hill. We can either descend to Fontenelle Bay and retrace our steps, or head down to La Rue de la Maraive and follow this back to our starting point.

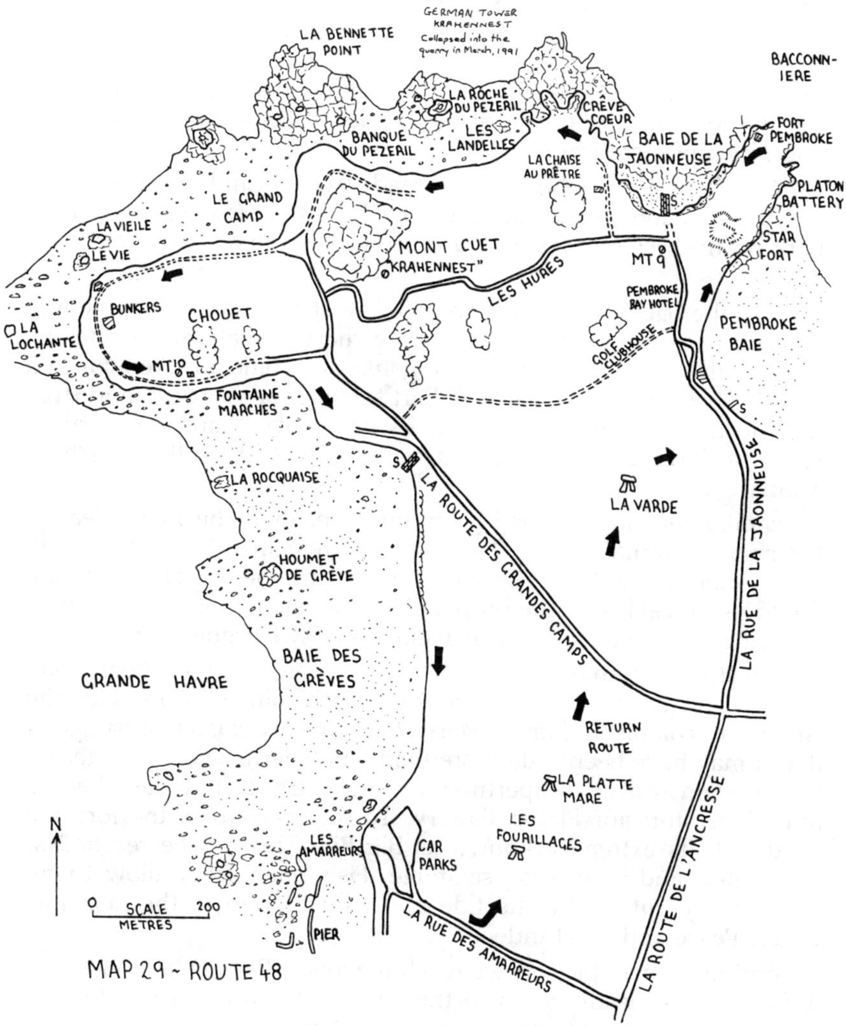

MAP 29 ~ ROUTE 48

ROUTE 48 A shoreline loop walk

MAP 29

CHOUET HEADLAND

DISTANCE — 2.6 miles

THIS easy walk can be cut short at several points. Although this is not the most beautiful part of the island, it has some pleasant bays and much of historical interest.

ACCESS — From Chouet Crossroads (which can be reached from several directions) continue down La Rue de la Jaonneuse to a car park on the western side of L'Ancresse Bay, often called Pembroke Bay.

From the Sablon d'Or cafe we head west around the bay, behind the large sea wall constructed during the Occupation. Beyond the end of the wall the path rises gently to some bracken-covered banks. These are the remains of Fort L'Etoile, or Star Fort, and from the top it is possible to pick out its distinctive shape. Its purpose seems to have been merely as a training ground for the Guernsey Militia.

Examination of the small promontory beyond the fort reveals a flat area of granite blocks. These are the remains of Platon Battery, which mounted a 20 pounder cannon during the Napoleonic Wars. Boulders have been piled up above the shoreline to give extra protection. It is now a popular fishing and swimming spot.

The sturdy granite structure on the point is Fort Pembroke, constructed around 1778 when the French joined forces with the American colonists. James Marr, in Bailiwick Bastions, suggests that it may have been little more than a powder magazine protected by a curtain wall with apertures for musketry. It may have been a munitions store for Platon Battery. To the seaward of the fort is a headland, its extremity known as Big Bill. This can be reached at low water, and is an easy scramble. Fishermen often allow themselves to be cut off by the tide and fish through to the next low water. Peace and quiet indeed!

Continuing past the fort we reach the lovely Baie de la Jaonneuse. A fine slipway leads down to the beach. This was constructed for the harvesting of seaweed or vraic as it is called in Guernesiase. Vraic was once a major source of fertilizer and fuel, and large amounts were loaded into carts and pulled up the slipway by horses. Notice how the blocks have been laid to give the horses a firm grip.

NUMBER 9, THE LEANING TOWER

Near the slipway is "Martello" Tower 9, Guernsey's "Leaning Tower", gradually keeling over to the west. Skirting the bay we pass a powder magazine; there is no longer any trace of the battery which it would have supplied. Martello Tower 8, which was built near to the golf clubhouse, was destroyed by the Germans as it interfered with their line of fire. We then cross the headland of Creve Coeur, and the rock of La Chaise au Pretre (The Priest's Chair) to Les Landelles. Here we can follow a track to the landward of a shingle bank to reach Mont Cuet Quarry, with its huge tower perched precariously on its edge(†).

The occupying forces built these Marinepeilstaende und Messtellungen for observation, signalling and range-finding. Similar towers can be seen at Fort Sausmarez, Pleinmont Point and La Prevôté. They are unique to the Channel Islands, perhaps inspired by the "Martello" towers, and were constructed by the slave workers of the Organisation Todt. In Railways in Guernsey Frank Wilson states that Cuet Tower was cast entirely by hand. A circular stairway ran around the outside of the wooden shuttering, and barrows of concrete tipped in at the top. Some 7,000 bags of cement are estimated to have been used. It was christened "Krahennest" (Crowsnest)(†).

The beach at this point is called Banque du Pezeril. Banque is a beach or shore, while Pezeril may be a corruption of L'Eperquerie, which was a place for drying fish. Further down the coast are Baie des Pequeries and Pointe des Pezeries, also fish drying grounds.

Generally this area is not very scenic, with its dirty track, dumped boulders, fences and signs. In the '80s plans were afoot to create an ice rink and leisure complex inside the quarry, and despite much local support the idea was well and truly squashed by the Board of Administration, who intend to fill the hole with refuse.

We now round the bay of Grand Camp, or Big Open Fields, a name which probably refers to the land on our left rather than the bay. Passing a disused quarry we reach the tip of Chouet Headland. There are two bunkers here, but both are well-blocked. Wide views of Grand Havre (Big Harbour) now open up to the south. On the far side of the bay is "Martello" Tower 11 at Rousse, and in the distance is Pleinmont Tower and Lihou.

POWDER MAGAZINE AND TOWER, CHOUET (†)

To the seaward of the bunker are the remains of a battery, with just a few granite flagstones visible amongst the vegetation. Continuing on we pass "Martello" Tower 10, and the powder magazine which once supplied the battery.

Beyond the metal bar is the Torrey Canyon Quarry, so-named as it contains much of the oil scraped off the beaches after the disastrous shipwrecks on the Scilley Isles in 1967. The oil is to be reclaimed in the near future, to provide another refuse disposal site.

Passing the car park we can leave the road and follow a track which takes us to the seaward of two bungalows. This area was the stamping ground of Gerald Edward's wonderful character Ebenezer Le Page in his novel "The Book of Ebenezer Le Page". To the south is Baie des Greves, Bay of the Sandy Beaches, nowadays touristified to Ladies' Bay. Autocross racing occasionally takes place on the beach. Following the old dune line above the bay we are in the tracks of Guernsey's race course, which has been used since 1830. We soon reach the car park, toilets, kiosk and playground at Les Amarreurs (The Moorings). This refers to the dry stone cauchee or breakwater, and the more solid quay which was added at the turn of the century. During the Occupation a railway siding ran from Chouet crossroads to Les Amarreurs, and much sand was taken to the concrete mixing plant at L'Ancresse.

We have now reached the southern edge of L'Ancresse Common, and can now turn towards our starting point. After following Les Amarreurs Road to the garage we can head left to Les Fouillages, a monument discovered in 1978. Excavations have revealed evidence of its use as a funeral complex, stretching over 4,000 to 5,000 years from Mesolithic and through Neolithic to the Early Bronze Age. Just 100 yards further on, by the 6th tee, is La Platte Mare, a small single-chambered tomb or cist. A "cup-mark" can be found on one of the support stones.

Ahead the common rises to the broad hill of La Varde (The Height). Burrowing into its brow is a superb example of a communal

LA VARDE

passage grave. Aligned to face the rising sun, it is over 40 feet long and the largest grave in the Bailiwick. It was discovered in 1811 by troops digging defences. During the Occupation many bunkers and a radar post were built on the hill, fortunately with no damage to the grave.

From La Varde a short descent takes us down to our starting point.

ROUTE 49 A shoreline walk, with many scrambling possibilities

MAP 30

PORT SOIF TO GRANDE ROCQUE

DISTANCE — 1.4 miles

THIS short walk takes us from the bay of Port Soif to the rugged little peninsula on the northern arm of Saline Bay. It can be tackled at any state of the tide, though towards low water there are numerous scrambling possibilities.

ACCESS — Turn left three-quarters of a mile north of Cobo (signed Port Soif) then take the left fork to a car park on the north side of the bay.

If the tide is low we can cut across Port Soif (Thirsty Harbour, perhaps because a stream which once flowed into the bay was dammed in the past). The bay is bounded by sand dunes which have now been stabilised with granite blocks. The southern side of the bay has some craggy outcrops, the largest being Le Nic au Corbin which can provide some very entertaining scrambling. They are also a favourite spot for cliff jumping, and the waters have excellent snorkelling, particularly when the spider crabs move in to breed.

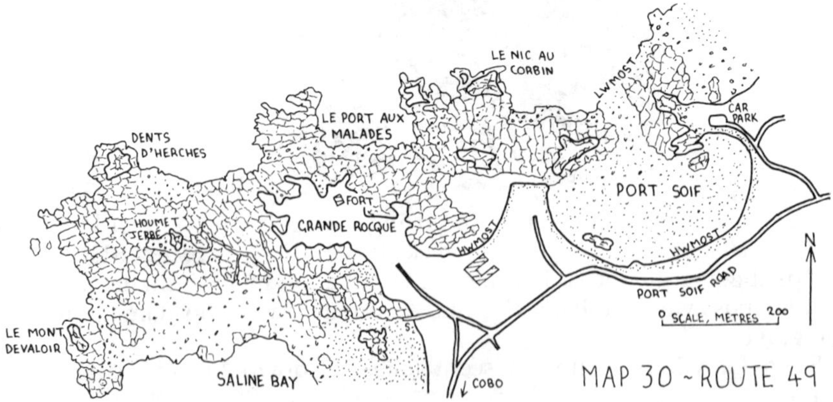

To reach Grande Rocque, we must cross a small bay known as Le Port aux Malades (The Harbour of the Sick People). It is possible that lepers were brought ashore here, as the island had two Maladries (leper hospitals), one near Perelle Baie and the other at L'Islet.

Grande Rocque refers to the promontory to the south, and there is much to explore here. The fort is a complex blend of early nineteenth century and German military architecture, though the recent additions for once almost enhance the character of the fort. The original building dates from 1803 with the outbreak of the Napoleonic Wars, and it carried three cannon. The little powder magazine, which has some hefty granite slab tiles; was added a year later. The fort was rebuilt and strengthened in 1813, and barracks constructed on the headland.

The rocks to the west of the fort have been eroded into strange shapes by the wind and waves, and there is good bouldering and scrambling to be found. The reefs here were the scene of Guernsey's most spectacular wreck in February 1978. A huge oil rig broke loose while being towed from Rotterdam to Brazil, and drifted onto Grande Rocque. It was being carried on a barge with its three hundred feet high legs in the air. These could be seen from much of the island, and the wreck was a great attraction until it was towed off several weeks later. Fortunately no lives were lost.

For our return we can either retrace our steps, or join La Route de Port Soif near the Grandes Rocques Hotel, now a private residence, and follow this to Port Soif.

GRANDE ROCQUE FORT

ROUTE 50 An easy scramble

MAP 31

COBO BAY TO VAZON BAY

A VERY easy, unserious scramble. There are many harder variations, and escape is possible at most points on the route. There are some fascinating rock sculptures, a deep cave and several fortifications.

DISTANCE — 1 mile

GRADE — I+

ACCESS — Cobo (The Wooded Cove) is situated on Guernsey's west coast. There are usually parking spaces below Le Guet, the prominent rock face above the south side of the bay.

RECOMMENDED TIDE — Low water on any tide is sufficient. Much of the section is feasible near high water by taking a higher route.

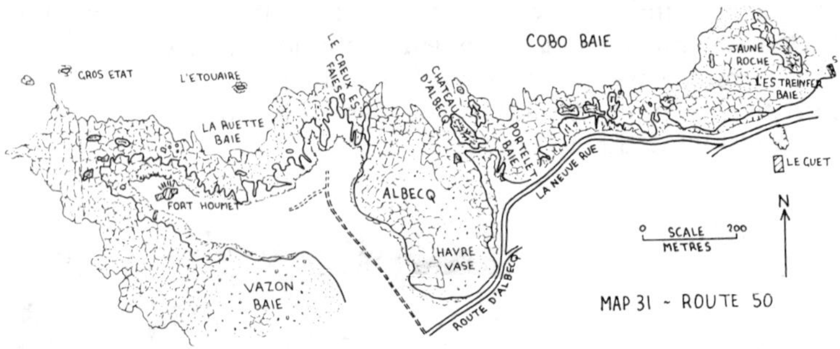

Easy scrambling takes us out of the small inlet of L'Estrainfer Baie (The Bay by the Cow Stable of the Infer Family) to a stack (A). The rocks on its seaward end remarkably resemble a lion and a pig. Difficulties can be avoided by following a gully which cuts behind the stacks, but traversing around them can be great fun in hot weather, when falling in isn't a problem! Between the second and third stack is a large shallow rock pool.

Emerging from the stacks we reach Portelet Baie (Little Harbour). At the mouth of the bay is a large rock; its summit can be gained by a short easy scramble. The stack is called Chateau d'Albecq on early maps, and the remains of a dry stone wall can be seen on its top. It was probably used at most as a lookout, or a position for musketry.

Beyond the chateau is the wide bouldery bay known as Albecq. Here a rock face has been quarried, and there are many gullies and pools to provide interest. Look out for the white-tipped rocks, painted to help guide small fishing craft to Havre Vase (Slimy Harbour).

Leaving the bay we scramble round small quarried outcrops to a wide gully where there is a double cave. This is Le Creux des Faies, Fairies' Cave, and it features in several Guernsey legends.

LE CREUX DES FAIES

One tells of how the fairy king fell in love with a Guernsey girl and took her through the cave to his kingdom. The fairy bachelors all thought this was a good idea, and set off to claim Guernsey wives for themselves. The Guernseymen fought hard to protect their women, but the magical forces were too strong and all were slain. The fairies settled down in Guernsey and married the locals. Their life of bliss came to an end when the call of Fairyland led them back through the cave, leaving their wives and children. This, it is said, is the reason why many of the islanders to this day are short and dark.

The gully below the cave is not difficult to cross, but it can be avoided by skirting behind the fence which is above the cave. Passing another outcrop we cross the rugged Ruette Baie to reach the Houmet Peninsula. Two German bunkers squat on the edge of the promontory, and the camouflage nets and wooden boards to prevent ricochets can still be seen. Easy scrambling takes us around to the tip of the point. Les Grunes lies offshore, and these rocks and reefs have been the scene of many wrecks.

In July 1906 the steamship *Swansea* struck the rocks in dense fog. She was towed off and beached on Vazon Bay where her load of coal was removed and the vessel patched up. In October 1937 the steamship *Briseis* hit Les Grunes while sailing from North Africa to Rouen with a cargo of wine, spirits and phosphates. The captain managed to reverse the ship off the rocks, but it sank just off the peninsula. As it did so the boilers burst, with steam and water spouting high into the air. Many barrels of liquor floated to the surface, and these were pounced on by the large crowd of onlookers. Much of it was consumed on the spot, or carried away in any pots that could be found. There were some wild parties that month! The wreck may have been the inspiration for Compton Mackenzie's novel "Whisky Galore"; the author was in Jethou at the time. In May 1965 the large steamer *La Salle* also grounded on Les Grunes. The crew were rescued but the ship broke up and sank. On Christmas Day 1973 the *Elwood Mead,* a bulk carrier of iron ore, went aground a few miles offshore. This huge ship was stranded for two months before being towed away for extensive repairs.

Fort Houmet is one of Guernsey's three true Martello towers. A fort was sited here in the 1600s, if not before, and the circular tower was added in 1804, with the outbreak of the Napoleonic Wars. Around this central tower, which has two levels, are four gun tracks, with small powder stores. The occupying German forces added several bunkers to the fortification, and a chapel which is presently closed.

Vazon Bay is now before us, and unless we are heading down to this most extensive of Guernsey's beaches, we can head back along the road to Cobo. Spare a few minutes to explore Le Guet, a wonderful vantage point. Its name means "Look-out", and it was an important part of the island's defences during the Middle Ages, if not before. The watch house which still stands on the summit was constructed in 1780, when the French became allies of the American colonists during the War of Independence. Cobo was undoubtedly a suitable landing site for any invading forces, and a battery was later added (its powder magazine is the small granite hut by the road). The German forces must have thought along similar lines as they added a gun emplacement and observation post. In more peaceful times the cliff was quarried for its pink "granite", and the Monterey Pines which surround the area were planted after the war.

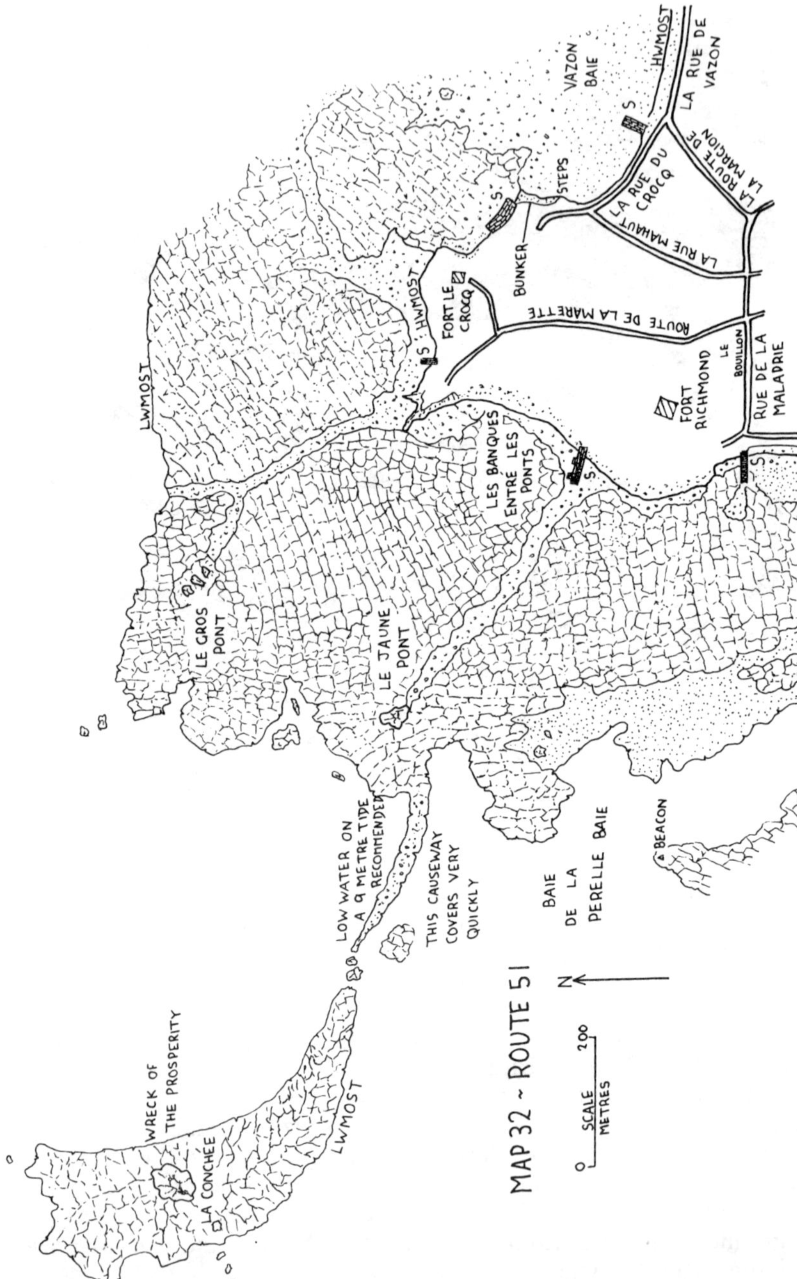
MAP 32 ~ ROUTE 51
SCALE METRES
0
200
N
WRECK OF THE PROSPERITY
LA CONCHÉE
LWMOST
LOW WATER ON A 9 METRE TIDE RECOMMENDED
THIS CAUSEWAY COVERS VERY QUICKLY
BAIE DE LA PERELLE BAIE
BEACON
LE GROS PONT
LE JAUNE PONT
LWMOST
LES BANQUES ENTRÉ LES PONTS
S
FORT RICHMOND
LE BOUILLON
RUE DE LA MALADRIE
ROUTE DE LA MARETTE
S
HWMOST
FORT LE CROCQ
BUNKER
S
STEPS
LA RUE MAHAUT
LA RUE DU CROCQ
LA ROUTE DE LA MARCION
S
HWMOST
VAZON BAIE
LA RUE DE VAZON

ROUTE 51 A shoreline walk

MAP 32

LE CROCQ

THIS short walk takes us round the headland of Le Crocq between Vazon and Perelle Bay. It is feasible at most states of the tide, but should be avoided at high water, particularly on spring tides.

DISTANCE — 1.25 miles

ACCESS — Start from Richmond Corner, near the southern shore of Vazon Bay.

From the end of La Rue du Crocq steps take us down to the beach. Rough walking leads past an extensive bunker and an ancient slipway, all but washed away. In the past this would have been used by the vraic carts. Vraic, or seaweed, was once an important source of fertilizer and fuel on the island, and it was harvested in enormous quantities.

Fort Le Crocq once stood on the point, and guarded this south-western tip of Vazon. James Marr suggests this was probably no more than a Napoleonic battery consisting of two 18 pounders and one 20 pounder cannon. No trace of the emplacement remains, and the present Fort Le Crocq, despite its battlements, is no more than a house. However it is certainly fighting in earnest, something which the battery never had to do. The sea is making inroads into the front garden despite the concrete and bricks which have been dumped as protection.

As we round the headland we can look inland to two large menhirs or standing stones. The largest is known as La Longue Pierre, The Long Stone, which stands some ten feet above the ground. It would have been erected between 1500 and 3000 BC. The smaller stone may have been selected as weathering has given it some of the features of the female form. Just to the north are the scattered remains of a megalithic tomb.

Around the point we cross a shingle beach, Les Banques Entre Les Ponts (the Beaches between the Bridges). Les Ponts are the raised natural causeways leading to the rocky islets of Le Gross Pont and Le Jaune Pont. The rock pools around this last islet are among the best on Guernsey. Beyond the shingle bay are some slipways, and views to the south take in Perelle Bay, Fort Sausmarez and Lihou Island.

In July 1905 the steam ship *Trignac* grounded on La Soufleurese reef, off Perelle, in July 1905. Her cargo of rotting maize is said to have created an awful smell which hung over the island until the ship was refloated a week later.

In January 1974 the *Prosperity* was lost with all hands when she went aground on La Conchée reef in a Force 11 storm. Eighteen died, including a young woman. The ship's cargo was timber en route from Finland to the Mediterranean, and Guernsey's beaches were soon covered in valuable wood, piled up like matchsticks. A memorial to the *Prosperity* and the rescue services was erected on L'Eree headland. At low water on a spring tide it is possible to scramble to the wreck site. From Le Jaune Port a narrow spit leads to La Conchée, which is strewn with plating and rusting metal. A huge boiler lies among the kelp on the shoreline, testament to power of the sea. Take great care to avoid being cut off by the tide, which quickly covers the spit.

On the headland is Fort Richmond, an ugly building lacking the character of the island's other forts, and a more recent addition from the 1850s. It was garrisoned during the Occupation, and several bunkers dug into its surrounds.

Leaving Baie de la Perelle (Rocky Bay, from 'Pierrelle'), to use its proper name, we can head inland along La Route de la Maladrie, a name which reveals the presence of a Maladrie, or hospital for lepers. The site of the hospital is on the junction with La Route de la Marette, a corner with the macabre name of Le Bouillon (Death Rattle). The dead were buried near the shore by Fort Richmond. Marette is a marsh, revealing the once-swampy nature of the area. If we take the second turning on the left, La Rue Mahaut, we soon arrive back at our starting point.

LA LONGUE PIERRE

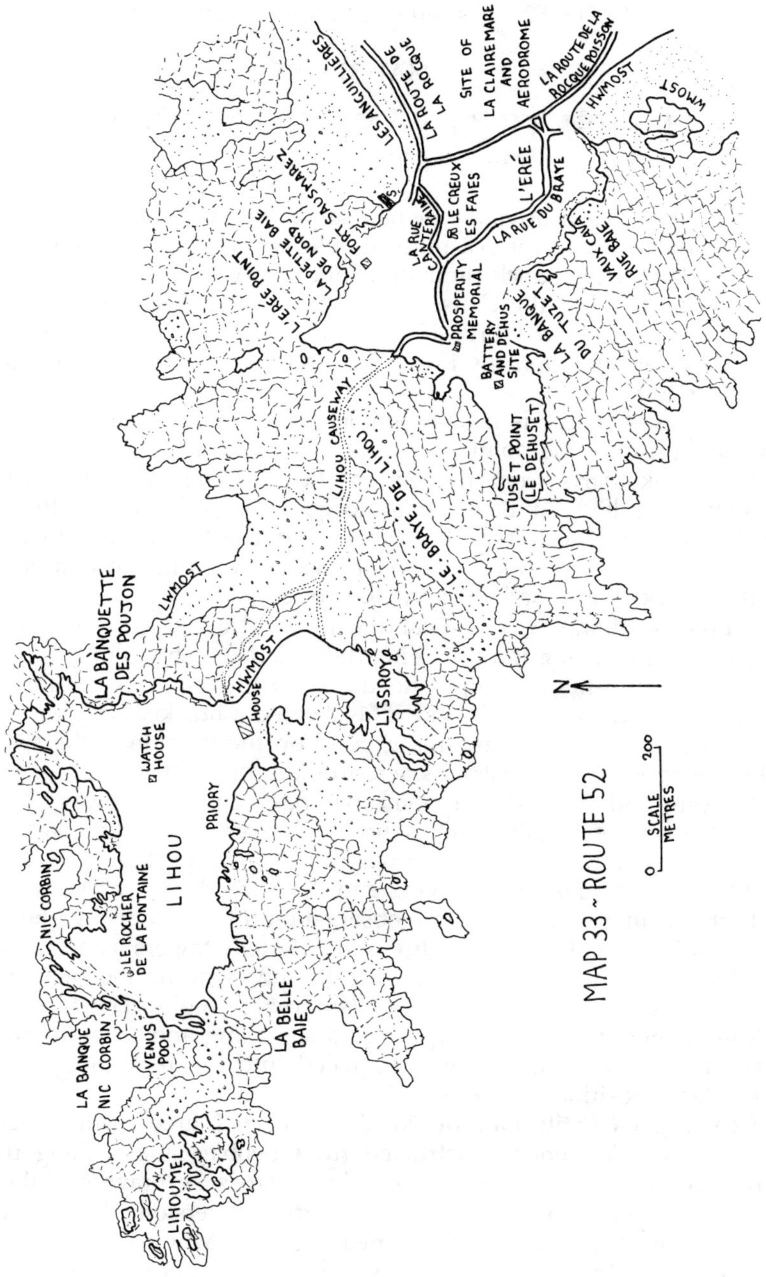

MAP 33 ~ ROUTE 52

ROUTE 52 A shoreline figure-of-eight walk

MAP 33

L'ERÉE HEADLAND AND LIHOU

DISTANCE — 2.5 miles

Lihou Island is a privately owned sanctuary, and the areas which are clearly reserved for sea birds should be avoided. This includes the cliff face, where rock climbing is not allowed.

It is safe to cross the Causeway only at certain states of the tide. There is a notice on L'Erée Head, and information is also on the back page of the Guernsey Press. Spring tides are the most suitable for visits to Lihou.

ACCESS — There is usually ample parking by the small bay on the north side of the point.

Our walk starts from the end of Les Anguillieres (The Eels), sometimes called La Baie de la Rocque, the shingly bay to the north of Fort Sausmarez. This section of coast is now a marine reserve. In the early 1900s seawater was pumped out at this point and attempts were made (briefly) to extract gold.

L'Erée headland was an island when sea levels were higher in the past. The strong tidal currents deposited the shingle bar, while wind and currents built up sand dunes to the south of the fort to join the island to the mainland. This created a brackish lake known as La Claire Mare, now the flat ground on the far side of the road. This functioned as the island's aerodrome until 1939.

Heading off around the point we pass an old slipway. This would have been built to allow horse and carts onto the beach to collect vraic (seaweed), which was once an important source of fertilizer. Vast quantities of living and dead weed were harvested.

Fort Sausmarez, with its stark observation tower, looms overhead. The fort is one of Guernsey's three true Martello towers, constructed in 1804. One of its uses was as a telegraph, sending messages up the coast using flags by day and lanterns at night. The German addition served a similar purpose as a signalling and range-finding station. Several bunkers were tunnelled into the rock to create a formidable position.

Crossing La Petite Baie de Nord we reach L'Erée Point, where there is an old bench constructed from pebbles and looking the worse for wear. From here we can look across Le Braye de Lihou to Lihou itself. "Hou" may be a shortened version "houge" or mound, and perhaps Lihou meant "The Mound". Another suggestion is that it simply means "The Island". From here Lihou

FORT SAUSMAREZ

looks barren and treeless, but in fact it has a good deal of charm, and a wide variety of plants and birds live in its numerous small habitats.

We can cross the braye using the causeway which was constructed by a tenant in the 1840s. Fine workmanship it must be to stand up to the fierce currents which rip through the strait. We arrive on the island by the farmhouse which was built in the 1970s. The original house was destroyed, along with the watch house and iodine factory, when it was used as target practice during the Occupation.

The iodine factory was sited just to the right of the house as we look at it. It was set up in 1927, and the extraction process involved drying and burning seaweed. World demand for the antiseptic was huge and the enterprise boomed. As a result the South American countries that relied on iodine for their income dramatically subsidised their producers and put Lihou out of business.

Heading around the island in a clockwise direction we pass the long promontory of Lissroy. One of the rock pools on the point is known as the Nun's Bath, though the priory was strictly males

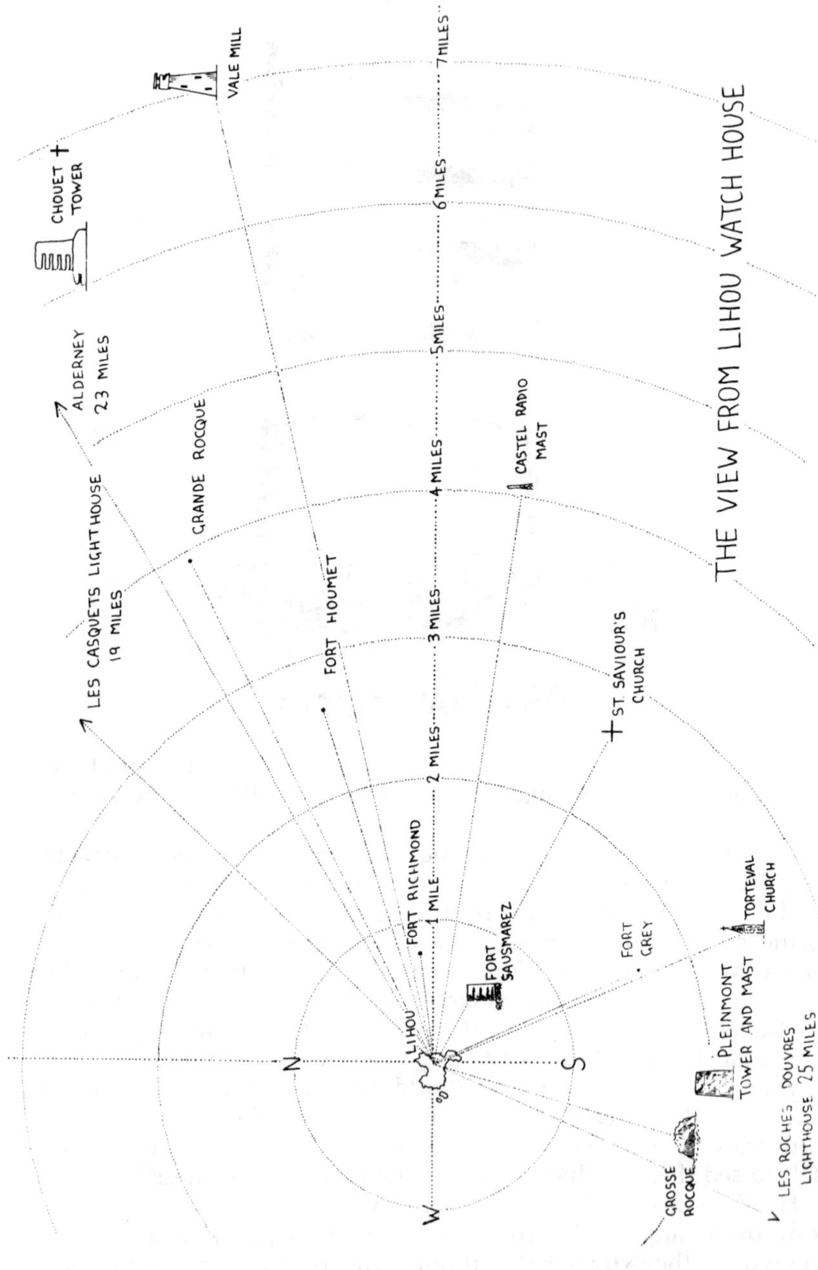
THE VIEW FROM LIHOU WATCH HOUSE
VALE MILL
CHOUET TOWER
ALDERNEY 23 MILES
GRANDE ROCQUE
LES CASQUETS LIGHTHOUSE 19 MILES
FORT HOUMET
CASTEL RADIO MAST
ST. SAVIOUR'S CHURCH
FORT RICHMOND
FORT SAUSMAREZ
FORT GREY
TORTEVAL CHURCH
PLEINMONT TOWER AND MAST
LES ROCHES DOUVRES LIGHTHOUSE 25 MILES
GROSSE ROCQUE
LIHOU
N
S
W
1 MILE
2 MILES
3 MILES
4 MILES
5 MILES
6 MILES
7 MILES

only! We soon reach the Priory of Our Lady, founded in 1114 by monks from Mont Saint Michel in Brittany. A pagan site almost certainly lies beneath the ruins. The priory demised during the Reformation and the monks left in 1568. The land became Crown property, and was leased out, initially as a rabbit warren! The priory was demolished in 1759, when there were fears that it could be occupied by an invading French army.

LIHOU HOUSE AND CAUSEWAY

Beyond the building we pass Lihoumel, a rocky islet that is now a nature reserve, and a little further on is the famous Venus Pool. This is some 100 feet long and is a favoured swimming spot, receiving fresh water twice a day as the tide floods into La Banque Nic Corbin. A little further on above the shoreline is a depression below a rocky outcrop. This is a freshwater spring and used to be called Le Rocher de la Fontaine. It is also known as La Rocque au Morts, The Rock of the Dead, and it is said that the bodies of sailors who drowned in a 19th Century shipwreck were buried here.

At the very highest point of the island is the remains of a two-storey watch house built near the end of the 18th Century when Guernsey was under threat from the French. In clear weather the views from here are extensive, and include Les Casquets lighthouse and Alderney to the north, and the French light of Les Roches Douvres over twenty miles away to the south. Descending to La Banquette des Poujon, we pass the site of the iodine factory.

Returning across the causeway to L'Erée we can either scramble around the foreshore to the right, or head up towards The Prosperity Memorial. Just beyond this are the remains of L'Erée Battery, constructed in the late 1700s on the site of Le Déhus dolmen, which was unfortunately destroyed. The small headland is known as Tuset (or Le Déhuset) Point, named after the antiquity. We can continue down to the shingle beach of La Banque du Tuzet and across Vaux Cava Rue Baie to La Route de la Rocque Poisson (Rock Fish Road, rock fish being the local name for wrasse), where there is a large bunker.

To the south is the wide expanse of Rocquaine Bay with the distinctive Chateau de Rocquaine (more commonly known as Fort Grey or the 'Cup and Saucer).' In the distance is La Pointe de Pleinmont, with its distinctive tower and mast. The view, in common with much of the west coast, is not what it used to be. Fifty years ago we would have looked across sand dunes instead of a sea wall, and L'Eree Hotel would not be the blot on the landscape which it is today.

We can avoid the main road by joining La Rue du Braye, which takes us past Le Creux es Faies, Fairies' Cave. This is a passage grave nearly 30 feet long, the third largest in Guernsey. Legend says this 5,000 year old dolmen is one of the entrances to Fairyland. For their Friday night out the fairies would emerge from the passage and dance on Le Trepied dolmen or Fairies' Hollow, above Baie de la Perelle.

La Rue Canteraine leads back to our starting point. This name is a corruption of chante reine, literally singing frog, no doubt once a breeding ground for these creatures.